Family and Gender
among American Muslims

Family and Gender among American Muslims

ISSUES FACING MIDDLE EASTERN

IMMIGRANTS AND THEIR DESCENDANTS

EDITED BY

Barbara C. Aswad

AND

Barbara Bilgé

TEMPLE UNIVERSITY PRESS

PHILADELPHIA

For permission to reprint two chapters we thank the University of Alberta
Press which published "Parents and Youth: Perceiving and Practicing Islam
in North America," by Nimet Hafez Barazangi in *Muslim Families in North
America*, edited by Earle H. Waugh, Sharon McIrvin Abu-Laban, and
Regula Burchardt Qureshi, in 1991 © 1991 by The University of Alberta
Press; and *Image* which published an earlier version of "An Assessment of
Arab American Knowledge, Attitudes, and Beliefs about AIDS by Anahid
Kulwicki and Penny S. Cass in vol. 26, no.1 (spring 1994): 13-18. And for
permission to use his wonderful photographs we are grateful to Millard Berry.

Printed in the United States of America.

The paper in this publication meets the minimum requirements of American
National Standard for Information Sciences—Permanence of Paper for
Printed Library Materials,
ANSI Z39.48-1984 ∞

TEXT DESIGNED BY Judith Martin Waterman of Martin-Waterman Associates

LIBRARY OF CONGRESS CATALOGING-IN-PUBLICATION DATA
Family and gender among American Muslims : issues facing Middle Eastern
immigrants and their descendants / edited by Barbara C. Aswad and
Barbara Bilgé

    p   cm.
    Includes bibliographical references (p.) and index.
    ISBN 1-56639-442-2 (cloth : alk. paper). —ISBN 1-56639-443-0 (pbk. :
alk paper)
    1. Muslim families—United States.   1. Aswad, Barbara C.,
1937–   II. Bilgé, Barbara, 1931– .
E184.M88F36 1996
306.85'0882971—dc20

95-54109
CIP

We would like to dedicate this volume to the many people with whom we have worked.

And to our family members,

Barbara Aswad's mother, Helen, sister, Dorothy, husband, Adnan, and son, Samir.

And to Barbara Bilgé's children, Filiz and Timur, and her friend Ümit.

Contents

vii

Illustrations

Preface

This book grew out of an interest in expanding the available scholarly information on gender and family organization among a growing religious minority in the United States, which hitherto has received limited and often negative attention: Muslims. The life-style changes and adaptations forged in North America over the years are highlighted in these essays, which cover both theoretical and practical issues. The essays treat groups from different nations, such as Bangladesh, Pakistan, Iran, Turkey, Lebanon, Palestine, and Yemen. The areas of their settlements in North America include Los Angeles; Chicago; metropolitan Detroit; and London, Ontario.

We hope that these essays will be of value to those interested in the topics of gender, family, and religious studies, as well as to Muslim migrants and their descendants in North America. The essays also should be useful to practitioners in medical, educational, and social services. The final section of this book, which offers vignettes of the lifeways of five individuals, brings the more scholarly research down to earth through representations of the everyday experiences and the words of real people.

We also hope that this volume will be of benefit to those in the various North American Muslim communities who have shared with us and other researchers diverse projects, inquiries into many issues, hospitality, and valued cultural moments over many years. These Muslim communities have made many contributions to the richness of U.S. and Canadian culture. We trust that the materials in these essays reflect some of that richness and will enhance the readers' understanding of the diversity of ethnic groups and their subcultures in both countries.

It is impossible to cover all aspects of family and gender among Muslims in North America in one book. However, this volume presents new research findings and descriptions that we hope will stimulate further scholarly exploration into related topics.

We would like to acknowledge the indefatigable efforts and invaluable assistance of Rebecca Raupp of Wayne State University in preparing our manuscript. We also extend our thanks to the photographer, Millard Berry of the *Dearborn Press and Guide* for his artistic and insightful photos. Finally, we are very grateful for the editorial recommendations of Judith Martin Waterman. They greatly improved the clarity of this book.

B.C.A. and B.B.

Family and Gender
among American Muslims

PLATE I.   *The Abdullah family at dinner. Dearborn, Michigan, 1978.*

BARBARA BILGÉ AND BARBARA C. ASWAD

Introduction

Recent scholarly interest in Muslims in America has been growing, as has the literature on their community organization, religious ideas, political activities, family organization, and adaptation to life in the United States.[1] This book has several objectives. First it will add to this growing body of information by illuminating the diversity of family life within and between Muslim communities in various parts of the United States. Second, it will help meet the need expressed by human-service professionals and educators for increased information about the cultural traditions and values of their Muslim patients, clients, students, and neighbors. Finally, we hope it will rectify some of the negative stereotypes of Middle Easterners in general and Muslims in particular that have intensified dramatically in the American media because of escalating political conflict involving the United States in this region since World War II.[2]

One example of a stereotype held by most Americans is the allegedly low position of women in Islam. According to this stereotype, Muslim women must endure arranged marriages and polygyny, be subservient to their husbands, and shroud themselves in public—as shown in countless newspaper photographs and television images of veiled Saudi and Iranian women. Similarly, sensational reports of a handful of kidnapings of children by their Middle Eastern Muslim fathers who deceive or desert their American wives depict Muslim men as domineering and authoritarian. Yet these components of the stereotype are often exaggerated, inaccurate, misinterpreted, or of infrequent occurrence. Arranged marriages are ille-gal in Turkey, although they still occur there in modified forms along with free-choice marriage; in other predominantly Muslim lands, the whole spectrum of marriages, from arranged by parents to agreed upon by mutual consent, independent of parents' wishes, can be found in varying frequencies. Although polygyny is permitted in all Muslim nations except Turkey and Tunisia, monogamy is, in fact, the predominant pattern. The interpretation of modesty for women and veiling is an issue of contention in many Muslim nations today; some Muslim women can be seen wearing bathing suits on beaches, while others prefer, or are pressured, to cover up in all public places. While it is true that a few Muslim fathers have kidnapped their children from their American ex-wives and returned to their homelands, it is also true that many American ex-husbands kidnap their children from the custodial mothers and go into hiding with their youngsters. The complex realities of gender and family relations among Muslims have many positive features, such as the kinship obligations of support through an extended family, including care of the elderly, and the right of women to own and dispose of property independently of their husbands.

Islam, based on patrilineal tradition, provides a basis for comparison of family structures because Islamic law is concerned with the regulation of many aspects of family life—of relations between husband and wife, of children to parents, of inheritance, divorce, custody of children, modest behavior of women, and proper behavior. There is a sharp differentiation between men and women, with an emphasis on premarital virginity for women, generally more controls placed on women, and a high value placed on childbearing and child rearing.

Yet, Islam also is interpreted and reinterpreted according to the specific pressures Muslims have encountered in different places at different times. Thus Islam is adapted, though rarely violated, to meet the needs of local Muslim communities. To explore Muslim communities in the United States, therefore, one must take into account the conditions both in the immigrants' homelands and in the regions of America in which they settled when they arrived. Sharon Abu-Laban provides a very useful typology of the different waves or cohorts of Arab Muslim immigration to the United States in relation to the generation concept. In her words (1989: 49): "As each cohort immigrated it carried some impress of that encounter and its reverberations through its life and to varying degrees, into the lives of its descendants." The rise of Islamic values in the Middle East as echoed in the Syrian Muslim community in Canada has been described by Yvonne Haddad (1977). Lois Keck (1989) also notes the change in the Washington Egyptian community when the Muslims defected from an Egyptian society which included Christians to join Islamic American communities.

Background factors include the immigrants' affiliation with different sects within Islam's major divisions, the Sunni and the Shi'a; political and ethnic allegiances; whether they came from villages, small towns, or cities; their socioeconomic class; educational attainments and aspirations; past occupations and future goals; and their reasons for immigrating—whether they are refugees forced out of their homelands, sojourners who intend to return eventually to their native country, or voluntary and permanent settlers in their new land. For example, peasants and farmers will adapt differently than doctors and engineers, and Lebanese mountain villagers will adapt differently than urbanites from Cairo or Istanbul. All these factors shape their cultural outlooks and behavioral strategies on arrival, and their cultural patterns must be articulated with the particular cultural values and institutional structures of the places in which they take up residence in the United States, for the American scene is also richly variegated.[3]

Political and social integration or the lack of it in the new country affect immigrant communal and family life. N. Abraham shows how American culture marginalizes Arabs both politically and culturally and simultaneously produces opposing forces for integration and isolation within the mainstream of society (1989). Political pressures and discrimination by members of the dominant group have affected the community and family lives of other minorities as well. This marginality has led to the strengthening of family and community life in most Islamic groups.[4] However, most Muslims, like European white immigrants, have worked hard and reached the middle class. The national labor laws of 1930 through 1960 benefited immigrant populations by enlarging job opportunities, controlling access to those jobs, and providing supplementary income to the unemployed. But because of racial inequality, these same benefits seldom helped the black worker until the civil-rights movements of the 1960s (Smith 1989: 151–154).

As recently as the 1960s, America was considered a nation of three major faiths: Protestant, Catholic, and Jewish (Herberg 1960; Kennedy 1952). Although Muslims have been in the United States since the early part of this century, their numbers have increased greatly since World War II. Estimates of today's Muslim population range from over five hundred thousand to nine million, but most expert estimates hover around three million Muslims, who are affiliated with over six hundred mosques (Haddad 1986: 1). They include immigrants and their descendants from many nations as well as converts whose families have lived in the United States for many generations. The essays in this book are concerned with the immigrant populations and, therefore, do not include groups such as the Nation of Islam (Black Muslims) or the orthodox Sunni Muslims of the African-American community. Although records of Arabic-speaking slaves exist from as early as the seventeenth century (Haddad 1986: 12), the vast majority were Christianized by the early decades of the nineteenth century. These essays primarily focus on Middle Eastern Muslim groups because of the paucity of published research on Muslim Americans from Indonesia, Southeast Asia, China, Central Asia, or North Africa.

In summary, in any consideration of immigration and ethnicity, several factors must be explored. First is the dynamics of ethnic relations in the home country. The complexity and locally specific character of ethnic and religious relations change from country to country. Geographical features have their effects: from the mountains of Lebanon, which support strong religious and kinship groups, to the valleys of Egypt, where state and class are pronounced. Second, the specific conditions of the historical periods that send the immigrants, and their personal characteristics, affect individual adjustments and adaptations. Does warfare drive them, so that they come as refugees? Is the motivation primarily economic? Are they peasants or doctors, single people or families with teenagers? Third is the context of interaction. A Lebanese man in Dearborn is Muslim and Arab to a Polish neighbor, whereas in south Lebanon, the distinctions of interest are whether or not he is Shi'a and the specific village from which he comes. Fourth are the conditions in the host country. Is it a time of economic expansion when immigrants may be welcome laborers, or one of economic contraction when they are seen as competitors for jobs and, therefore, a threat. The character and ethno-economic stratification of the particular region is crucial: urban or rural, Georgia or South Dakota, Boston or Detroit (Aswad 1993). For example, the stratification of the country or the local region might find a different group in the merchant niche, thereby limiting the immigrants' entrance into it.

繁 *Immigration History*

Only a few Muslims settled in the United States during the nineteenth century (see Naff 1985; Younis 1983). The first sizeable waves arrived on American shores between 1900 and 1914. They came from many countries, spoke several languages, and belonged to various Islamic sects. Nevertheless, they shared certain characteristics. The overwhelming majority were illiterate village men, primarily from the Lebanese Syrian region, who hoped to return to their homelands after amassing a fortune in America. Given their lack of education, technical skills, and capital on arrival, their prospects for financial success were slim, and most were unable to realize their dreams. Moreover, the nation from which most of them came, the Ottoman Empire, was dissolved after World War I and divided among newly constituted nations and the colonial mandates created by Britain and France. Consequently, most of these sojourners never retired to their countries of origin; instead, they ended up, sometimes unwillingly, becoming permanent residents in the United States.

EARLY EMIGRATION

Most Ottoman subjects who came to the United States between 1880 and 1923 were members of Christian minority groups. Arab Muslims, who constituted a majority in the Arab East (93%), represented only about 10 percent of the Ottoman Arab emigration (Karpat 1985; Naff 1985; Saliba 1983), and most arrived after 1900. Muslims undoubtedly were concerned about their reception in a Western Christian country. The majority of the Arabic speakers were from what is now Lebanon but was then part of the province of Syria in the Ottoman Empire and were called Syrians. Their reasons for leaving include economic stress, increased population, and stories told by returning immigrants about the wealth of the West. The growing influence of the Western Catholic Church and other Western missionaries who established schools, provided new connections with the

West. Some historians also note the lingering effect of the sectarian clashes of the 1840s and 1850s. (Issawi 1992; Nabti 1992; Batrouney 1992; Naff 1992; Khalif 1987).

Under British and French colonialism, the Middle East came under the economic control of international markets as village economies shifted from subsistence crops to cash crops, such as silk in Lebanon and cotton in Egypt and Syria. Issawi notes that this brought economic success to the area between 1880–1914, after emigration to the New World had begun (1992: 17–18), but it also brought increasing stratification, with many peasants loosing control of the means of their production and sustenance. Another factor that destabilized the Ottoman authority was the political and economic support given to minorities, especially Christian minorities, by Britain, France, and Russia. Sectarian wars and the oppression of Ottoman rule also were causes of emigration. Many Muslim and Christian intellectuals went to Egypt from Lebanon. An additional cause was the entry of the Ottoman Empire into World War I and the establishment of the draft. Many left to avoid conscription despite the Ottomans' unsuccessful efforts to stop them (Naff 1994: 144).

The vast majority of the early Muslim immigrants to the United States were traders, skilled craftsmen, and peasants (Issawi 1992). What began as a trickle about 1880 became a torrent by 1913. Many emigrants ended up in Mexico, Australia, and South America believing they had arrived in "Nay Yark" or "Amrika" (Naff 1992: 145).

Upon arriving in America some Arab Muslims associated with Christians because they worked for Christian merchants, or because of their previous political associations in the Middle East. Yet interfaith marriage between Muslims and Christians was not customary, as it was not in their home countries, and families settled in communities with village and religious ties. Population size, occupation, and political factors in the homeland and local American communities affected sectarian relations.

Many Muslim Arabs, primarily Lebanese, began working for merchants as peddlers in the coastal cities of the eastern seaboard. They then dispersed throughout the Dakotas, Montana, Alberta, and Manitoba, as well as Iowa and the Mississippi Delta. After World War I many purchased small farms, but others came to the factory cities of the east and midwest such as Pittsburgh, Gary, and Detroit. Others opened grocery stores, restaurants, and other small businesses. The Johnson Reed Immigration Act of 1924 effectively curtailed immigration by establishing quotas for emigrants from the Middle East until after World War II.

Other major Muslim groups from the Ottoman Empire include Turks, Kurds, Albanians, and Bosnians. After 1920, these groups found jobs in the steel mills and auto factories on the eastern seaboard and in the Great Lakes area. At the turn of the century Pakistanis from the northwestern part of British-controlled India began to filter into California from Canada. They worked primarily as sharecroppers, farmers, and small businessmen. Pakistani immigration also was limited by the exclusion laws of 1924 (Kahn).

Except for the Lebanese, the sex ratio was highly skewed toward men. The Lebanese often returned for their wives while many of the Turks never married and left few descendants (Bilgé 1985; Hitti 1924: 9). It was difficult for Muslim men to marry American women because of religious intolerance and the attitudes against the "new" immigrant groups (Hitti 1924: 125; Saliba 1983: 39).

In 1922 the colonial powers partitioned the Ottoman Empire, and the League of Nations awarded mandates for the control of the new Arab protectorates to Britain and France. By 1923 the Ottoman Empire was dissolved completely, and the Republic of Turkey was recognized internationally by the Treaty of Lucerne. Between World Wars I and II some Arab immigrants were able to bring wives from their homelands to the United States. During the Great Depression some returned to the old country for its duration and stayed there permanently (Aswad 1993). Pakistanis, constrained by the immigration exclusion law of 1924, remained on the west coast.

LATER MIGRATIONS

Many authors (Aswad 1974; Bozorgmehr and Sabagh 1988; Abraham and Abraham 1983; Abu-Laban 1980; Haddad 1986; and others) note that the emigration wave that left the Middle East after World War II and continued into the mid-1960s reflected changing circumstances in the newly formed Muslim countries and represented areas which had seen little previous U.S. immigration. For example, although a few Yemeni came to the United States during World War I, the vast majority arrived after World War II as did a large number of Palestinians fleeing the Israeli occupation of their lands. There were also Iraqis, (both Arabs and Kurds),

Egyptians, and Syrian Arabs who fled socialist regimes and periods of political turmoil. Peasant immigrants continued to come, often joining relatives already settled in the United States. Many of the new immigrants were educated, some had money, and many were professionals. Some already knew English and adapted well in American schools. Many had come for a university education and stayed, often marrying Americans. This was due in part to the fact that quotas established after World War II by the McCarran-Walter Immigration Act were abolished in 1965 by the Immigration Act that gave priority to professionals from all countries; and many decided to stay. With the idea of permanent settlement, Haddad (1986: 2) reports that members of the Muslim community invested time, energy, and money in the establishment of Islamic institutions, although there was also a significant number of non-mosqued Muslims. Immigrant Muslims often cooperated with the second and third generation American Muslims, who wanted their children to learn about Islam and worked to organize Islamic and Arabic classes, both in schools and mosques.

Few Iranians immigrated to the United States before World War II, but Bozorgmehr and Sabagh, through a careful census study (1988: 5–34), found that they came in two phases after the war: the first was before the 1979 revolution in Iran which toppled the Shah and brought Khomeini to power, and the second was after the revolution. The flood of Iranian students was increased by the impact of the oil boom after 1973. In 1986 the population of Iranians in the United States was estimated to be in the range of two hundred forty-five thousand to three hundred forty-one thousand and was primarily in the Los Angeles area. Because they were not only Muslims, but also Armenians, Bahais, and Jews, and their religious affiliation was not reported it is difficult to know how many of these Iranians were Muslims. Many who were of an upper-middle-class background were able to bring money with them and have been economically well established in this country.

The most recent Muslim immigrants are those who fled Lebanon's civil war from 1976–1988. They reflect a variety of occupations, ranging from professionals, the newly educated in Beirut, to both literate and illiterate villagers. Many careers have been interrupted, families separated, and finances ruined. Others brought their financial assets from the Middle East and the Lebanese Muslim communities East Africa. In areas such as Dearborn, Michigan, many new businesses are generating capital and older neighborhoods are being revitalized. The loss of family members to warfare creates emotional problems, and social service agencies, such as the Arab Community Center for Social and Economic Services in Dearborn, assist members to cope with tragedies caused by the war as well as with problems of assimilation.

In Dearborn and other cities, we find a more fervent form of Islam, reflecting the Islamic revivals in the Middle East, an increase of Islamic dress, new Islamic schools, and increased competition among mosques (Walbridge 1991; Aswad 1992). As Muslims continue to immigrate to the United States, they are rapidly becoming a significant fourth religious community that needs to be understood and accepted by other Americans.

❦ Essays

This book is divided into three sections. The first consists of essays that discuss family structures and roles; religious and social values, such as the content and importance of honor and shame; generational differences; and changing gender relations as families adapt to life in different regions of the United States. The second section specifically addresses problems encountered by social workers, health professionals, and teachers who have worked with members of various Muslim communities largely from the area around Dearborn, Michigan. Dearborn was selected in part because it has the largest community center in the United States (ACCESS) that addresses the problems of an Arab Muslim population. The third section contains descriptions of the lives of individuals in order to demonstrate the richness and diversity of their responses to the opportunities and constraints of life in the United States.

The majority of the essays are original pieces based on research by authors from several disciplines: anthropology, history, sociology, nursing, social work, and education. The book begins with a study in which Yvonne Haddad and Jane Smith concentrate on Muslims' concern with the loss of their religious values in the United States and the specific problem areas of dating, marriage, birth control and abortion, drinking of alcohol, dress, and feminism. Haddad and Smith, scholars who have written extensively on Muslims in America, have presented a concise and interesting paper reporting Muslim attitudes and values.

Louise Cainkar's paper on immigrant Palestinian women presents an excellent description of how women view their lives as women in relation to four main comparative referents: 1. women without an existing homeland as compared to those with one; 2. daughters' lives compared to those of their mothers; 3. Palestinian women's lives compared to those of Palestinian men; and 4. Palestinian women compared to western women. Interestingly, Cainkar found a similarity among Palestinian women of different socio-economic and marital statuses, places of origin, occupation, and other variables. They felt that even though American women were better off in some ways and worse off in others ways than they were, with the exception of having an existing homeland, they did not want to trade their lives for those of American women.

Barbara Bilgé's paper describes and analyzes the intermarriages of post–World War II Turkish immigrant men with American women in metropolitan Detroit and adjacent Ontario. She found that the partners' social class of origin was more important than education or religion to their, and their children's, happiness, acculturation, and assimilation. Couples fell into three groups: 1. working-class Turkish men married to American women from working-class families; 2. ex-military men who were educated in American universities, mostly from families of small shop-keepers or urban laborers who married American women of middle- and upper-middle-class background; and 3. affluent Turkish civilian professionals married to American women of working- and middle-class origins. Most couples in the first and third groups had stable, satisfactory marriages, while couples in the second group tended to have troubled relationships, many ultimately divorcing.

Arlene Dallalfar's study demonstrates how women are active participants in the Iranian ethnic economy in Los Angeles. While there are barriers such as language, age, and level of education as well as class and gender, women can make use of class, ethnicity, and gender to open small businesses. By using case studies, she demonstrates how females enjoy gender-specific opportunities for entrepreneurial activities and certain avenues of access to the resources located in their ethnic communities that are not open to men.

Nimat Barazangi analyzes the intergenerational transmission of the concepts of Islam as a religion and an Arabic heritage to the identity of the American-born generation. She studies the questions of what makes the present first generation of Arab Muslim youth associate with the two identities, and how they perceive this dual identity in North American societies.

Linda Walbridge's discussion of a special form of marriage, *mut'a*, has helped to explain a subject often questioned by Westerners, that of temporary marriage among Shi'ite Muslims. She discusses its occurrence among the Lebanese Shi'ite community and shows the ways in which it has been adapted to the American experience.

The chapter by Nilufer Ahmed, Gladis Kaufman, and Shamim Naim focuses on recent Muslim immigrant families from Pakistan and Bangladesh. Most consist of highly educated professionals—physicians, engineers, scientists, and university professors. Nuclear-family households are the norm, although ties are maintained with extended family elsewhere in the United States and in other countries. The authors found that most of the immigrant generation's marriages have been arranged, but conflicts in adjustment to American life have resulted in some divorces. They also show how families take pains to socialize their children in the Islamic faith and to find them Muslim spouses of appropriate ethnic and educational background.

Gladis Kaufman and Shamin Naim's case study of an educated Pakistani shows the many problems that separate family members spread over a wide region as they strive for better education, jobs, and economic opportunities.

The second section of the book relates to the practical problems and conditions of Muslims in America.

A registered nurse and professor of nursing, Anahid Kulwicki describes significant Arab Muslim customs and beliefs as they relate to health. Some of the areas include concepts of cleanliness, dietary restrictions, religion and mental illness, family and gender roles, knowledge and superstition, folk healers, the evil eye, and sorcery. Data were obtained through her research on several Arab-American ethnic groups in Michigan. and are extremely valuable for those medical practitioners serving an Arab population.

Also addressing health issues, Anahid Kulwicki and Penny Cass discuss the perceptions and degree of knowledge about AIDS in the Muslim Arab community in Dearborn. They find a low level of knowledge about

AIDS, many misconceptions about the transmission of HIV, and a high level of anxiety about HIV infection. Kulwicki adds an insightful discussion of the various women's attitudes.

Barbara Aswad and Nancy Adadow Gray have combined efforts to present the problems and goals of a very successful Arab Community Center (ACCESS) in Dearborn, Michigan, and the nature of the problems brought to the Center. They found that there were major problems in effectively disciplining children. Since mothers are held responsible for their children's behavior, and daughters' behavior must be guarded according to rules of honor and shame, mother-daughter problems arose in a new environment in which girls are allowed more freedom. Others reported problems such as parent-child role reversals, child custody, divorce, disruptions of roles, extended families, and even boredom. In regard to the challenges of the Center, they discuss the problems associated with a change from a grassroots, small organization to that of a large and successful one, recognized locally, nationally, and internationally, and the importance of remaining community oriented.

Jon Swanson concentrates on the dilemma of a second generation Arab-American in facing ethnicity and role conflict and the problems of marriage. Swanson has a background both in anthropology and social work.

Charlene Eisenlohr focuses on the effect of cultural conflict on adolescent Arab girls. Through the use of personal dialogues, the author shows the reader the nature of conflicts produced by the generation gap, interaction with Arab and non-Arab friends, and communication with parents in English and Arabic. She also includes the effect of the length of stay in the United States on these conflicts. The writer finds that self-esteem is related to the teenager's style of coping and to family trust, which brings a degree of personal freedom and empowerment.

Mary Sengstock's study of elderly Arab Muslims concludes that differences in family structure often block effective service to the elderly. She analyzes several factors that limit assistance and stresses that the different family structures and cultural values related to requesting assistance outside the family are basic to the inability of many non-Arab service agencies to recognize and deal with their problems sufficiently.

The third section of the book gives us a glimpse into the lives of individual immigrants. Linda Walbridge, a novelist and anthropologist, writes several interesting vignettes covering individual experiences in immigrating and adapting to the United States. Through these portraits, members of the communities come to life, and the issues brought forward in many of the previous papers become vivid.

☙ *References*

Abraham, Nabeel. 1989. "Arab-American Marginality: Myths and Praxis. *Arab Studies Quarterly* 11, nos 2 and 3.

Abraham, S. and N. Abraham. 1983. *Arabs in the New World*. Detroit. Center for Urban Studies, Wayne State University.

Abu-Laban, Baha. 1980. *An Olive Branch on the Family Tree: The Arabs in Canada*. Toronto: McClelland and Stewart.

Abu-Laban, B. and M. Suleiman, eds. 1989. "Arab Americans: Continuity and Change. *Arab Studies Quarterly*. 11, nos. 2 and 3.

Abu-Laban, B. and F. Zeady, eds. 1975. *Arabs in America: Myths and Realities*. Wilmette, Ill.: Medina University Press International.

Abu-Laban, Sharon McIrvin. 1989. "The Co-existence of Cohorts: Identity and Adaptation among Arab-American Muslims." *Arab Studies Quarterly* 11, nos. 2 and 3:45–63.

Aswad, Barbara C. 1974. *Arabic-Speaking Communities in American Cities*. Staten Island, N.Y.: Center for Migration Studies.

———. 1991. "Lebanese and Yemeni Women in Dearborn." Pp. 256–281 in *Muslim Families in North America*, ed. Earl Waugh, Sharon Abu-Laban, and Regula Qureshi. Alberta: University of Alberta Press.

———. 1992. "The Lebanese Muslim Community in Dearborn Michigan." Pp. 167–188 in *The Lebanese in the World: A Century of Migration*, ed. A. Hourani and N. Shehadi. London: Tauris Press.

———. 1993. "Arab Americans: Those Who Followed Columbus." *Middle East Studies Association Bulletin* 27, no. 1: 1–20.

Batrouney, Trevor. 1992. "The Lebanese in Australia: 1880–1989." Pp. 413–442 in *The Lebanese in the World: A Century of Migration*, ed. A. Hourani and N. Shedadi. London: Tauris Press.

Bilgé, Barbara. 1985. *Variations in Family Structure and Organization in the Turkish Community of S.E. Michigan and Adjacent Canada*. Ph.D. diss., Department of Anthropology, Wayne State University, Detroit.

———. 1989. "Islam in the Americas." *McMillan Encyclopaedia of Religion*.

Bozorgmehr, Mehdi and Georges Sabagh. 1988. "High Status Immigrants: A Statistical Profile of Iranians in the United States." *Iranian Studies,* 21, nos. 3–4: 5–36.

Elkholy, Abdo A. 1966. *The Arab Moslems in the United States: Religion and Assimilation.* New Haven: College and University Press.

Haddad, Yvonne Y., 1977. "Muslims in Canada: A Preliminary Study." Pp. 71–100 in *Religion and Ethnicity,* ed. Harold Coward and Leslie Kawamura. Waterloo: Wilfrid Laurier Univ. Press.

———. 1986. "A Century of Islam in America." *The Muslim World Today.* Occasional Paper no. 4, Middle East Institute. Washington D.C.

Haddad, Yvonne and Adair Lummis. 1987. *Islamic Values in the United States.* New York. Oxford University Press.

Hagopian, Elaine and A. Paden, eds. 1969. *The Arab Americans: Studies in Assimilation.* Wilmette, Ill.: Medina University Press International.

Herberg, Will. 1960. *Protestant-Catholic-Jew.* Garden City: N.Y., Doubleday.

Hitti, Philip K. 1924. *The Syrians in America.* New York: George H. Doran.

Hooglund, Eric, ed. 1984. *Taking Root Bearing Fruit.* Washington D.C.: The American-Arab Anti-Discrimination Committee.

———. 1985. *Taking Root: Arab American Community Studies.* Washington D.C.: The American-Arab Anti-Discrimination Committee.

———. 1987. *Crossing the Waters: Arabic-Speaking Immigrants to the United States.* Washington, D.C.: Smithsonian Institute Press.

Issawi, Charles. 1992. "The Historical Background of Lebanese Emigration: 1800–1914," Pp. 13–32 in *The Lebanese in the World: A Century of Migration,* ed. A. Hourani and N. Shehadi. London: Tauris Press.

Kahn, Salam. 1983/1984. "Pakistanis in the Western United States." *Journal Institute of Muslim Minority Affairs* 5, no. 1: 36–46.

Karpat, Kemal H. 1985. "The Ottoman Emigration to America: 1860–1914." *International Journal of Middle Eastern Studies* 17: 175–209.

Keck, Lois. 1989. "Egyptian Americans in the Washington D.C. Area." *Arab Studies Quarterly* 11, nos. 2 and 3.

Kennedy, Ruby Jo Reeves. 1952. "Single or Triple Melting Pot?: Intermarriage in New Haven 1870–1950." *American Journal of Sociology* 58: 56–59.

Khalif, Samir. 1987. "The Background and Causes of Lebanese/Syrian Immigration to the United States before World War I." Pp. 17–36 in *Crossing the Waters*, ed. Eric Hooglund. Washington D.C.: Smithsonian Institute Press.

Leighton, Neil. 1992. "Lebanese Emigration: Its Effect on the Political Economy of Sierra Leone." Pp. 579–602 in *The Lebanese in the World: A Century of Migration*, ed. A. Hourani and N. Shehadi. London: Tauris Press.

Nabti, Patricia. 1992. "Emigrants from a Lebanese Village." Pp. 41–64 in *The Lebanese in the World: A Century of Migration*, ed. A Hourani and N. Shehadi. London: Tauris Press.

Naff, Alixa. 1985. *Becoming American: The Early Arab Immigrant Experiences*. Carbondale: Southern Illinois University Press.

———. 1992. "Lebanese Immigration into the United States-1880 to the Present." Pp. 142–165 in *The Lebanese in the World: A Century of Lebanese Migration*, ed. A Hourani and N. Shehadi, London: Tauris Press.

Said, Edward. 1981. *Covering Islam: How the Media and the Experts Determine How We See the Rest of the World*. New York: Pantheon.

Saliba, N. 1983. "Emigration from Syria." Pp 30–43 in *Arabs in the New World*, ed. Abraham, N. and Abraham S. Detroit. Wayne State University Press.

Shaheen, Jack. 1984. *The T.V. Arab*. Bowling Green, Ohio: Bowling Green State University Popular Press.

Smith, J. Owens. 1987. *The Politics of Racial Inequality*. New York: Greenwood Press.

Suleiman, Michael. 1988. *The Arabs in the Mind of America*. Brattlebero, Vt.: Amana Books.

Terry, Janice. 1985. *Arab Stereotypes in Popular Writing*. Washington, D.C.: American-Arab Affairs Council.

Trix, Fransis. 1990. Telephone communication with Barbara Bilgé. Ann Arbor Mich.

Walbridge, Linda. 1991. Shi'a Islam in an American Community. Ph.D. diss., Department of Anthropology, Wayne State University, Detroit.

Waldman, Marilyn Robinson. 1991. "Reflections on Islamic Tradition, Women and Family." Pp. 309–328 in *Muslim Families in North America*, ed. Earl Waugh, Sharon Abu-Laban, and Regula Quershi, eds. Edmonton: University of Alberta Press.

Waugh, Earle H., B. Abu-Laban, and R. B. Quershi, eds. 1983. *The Muslim Community in North America*. Edmonton: University of Alberta Press.

Waugh, Earle, S. Abu-Laban and R. Quershi. eds. 1991. *Muslim Families in America*. Edmonton: University of Alberta Press.

Younis, Adele. 1983. "The First Muslims in America: Impressions and Reminiscences." *Journal Institute of Middle Eastern Studies* 1: 17–28.

PART ONE

Values, Structure, and Variation in Muslim Families

YVONNE Y. HADDAD AND JANE I. SMITH

Islamic Values among American Muslims

*I think that the one danger of interaction between my
children and non-Muslim children is loss of Muslim
identity. I think that integration into the non-Muslim
environment has to be done with the sense that we have
to preserve our Islamic identity. As long as the activity
or whatever the children are doing is not in conflict with
Islamic values or ways, it is permissible. But when we
see it is going to be something against Islamic values,
we try to teach our children that this is not correct to our
beliefs and practices. They understand it and they are
trying to cope with that.*

This testimony from a young Muslim mother in the United States expresses the dilemma in which many members of the Islamic community in the United States find themselves today. Like all immigrants to the United States, Arabs, as well as those from other areas of the Muslim world, affirm the values of their faith's tradition at the same time that they try to function as full members of American society. The majority are eager to integrate to whatever extent is possible while still maintaining their Islamic identity, but some are sharply aware of the dangers that such integration may entail. Subjected to pressures from the culture in general, from their work environments, from their often more acculturated children, and from their own personal desires to fit in their adopted environment, people are faced with the daily struggle to try to maintain the standards of Islam that are held up to them by friends and family, by other

19

members of the Muslim community, and by the many available publications and tracts delineating how to live a truly Islamic life.

Of course it is the case that not all Muslims are what is generally called "practicing." Many, perhaps the majority, do not immediately see an incompatibility between Islamic values and Western life. Like liberal Christians and Jews or those who have no relation to organized religion, they differentiate between religion and state, religion and culture, and religion and customs. They relegate customs to local Arab ethnicity and can, therefore, freely shed them. Generally, they operate successfully within the American system. For others who do struggle to maintain a specifically Islamic identity and who do not make the above kinds of differentiations, life in America can present significant challenges. The material of this essay deals primarily with the issues raised for Muslims who are involved in organized religion (the "mosqued"). It is also true, however, that the values of Islam have shaped and confirmed Arab cultural values and thus continue to influence, however indirectly, the expectations of those who do not participate directly in religious activities. This is especially true in the definition of gender roles and in setting the parameters for what constitutes proper social interaction between the sexes.

Earlier in this century Muslims immigrating to the United States from the Middle East probably were less often concerned with forming and maintaining an Islamic identity as such than they were with basic survival, making a life in this country and finding ways in which to integrate successfully into what they had come to hope was truly an American "melting pot." When they came together for community and worship it was as much for companionship with fellow speakers of Arabic and for sharing of common cultural customs as it was for the acknowledgment of a religious bond of Islam. Worship, when it happened, generally took place, not in mosques, but in private homes or in space loaned from local churches. There were no "professional" *imams* available; prayer leadership generally was assumed by people with no special training.

Over the years this situation gradually changed. In the second and third decades of the century mosques were erected in various parts of the country. A second wave of mosque building was necessitated by the dramatic growth in the Muslim community in the United States. As immigrants increased in number and became better educated and more comfortable economically, and thus more socially mobile, Islamic institutions became a necessary part of American life. By the mid-1970s local resources were enhanced by the availability of oil monies from Saudi Arabia and other Gulf states earmarked for minority Muslim communities in other parts of the world. Muslims in America have benefitted from additional funding that has helped them build mosques in many cities, provide more trained *imams* to work with Islamic communities, and enhance library and other educational resources.

The rise of Islamic consciousness in America, in the past decade, has been due to a number of factors. Recent immigrants from parts of the world in which a more conservative brand of Islam is generally observed have played the role of calling second and third generation Arab Muslims to an enhanced awareness of their Islamic identity and the necessity of observing laws and regulations that ensure that they are in line with traditional Muslim values. It is also the case that Muslims perceive a significant change in American values, and a serious lowering of ethical standards, since the hippie/sexual/feminist revolution(s). Thus, there is today a great deal of contemporary Islamic writing on Islamic values, stressing the importance of religion as the one element in the creation of a truly moral society. To be a Muslim is to belong to a kind of universal family, to share in a unity that depends on mutual cooperation. "It is basic and fundamental, it is a sacred spiritual unity that represents full awareness of fraternity and brotherhood by every individual in the community" (Hoballah, n.d.: 72). Such unity is divinely conceived and implemented, and the community is seen as the locus for a spiritual and ethical bonding not available in humanly instituted social systems. This vision of Islam is not always easy to reconcile with American society. "We indeed have high regard and great esteem for the West and its civilization," says Muhammad Abdul-Rauf, former *imam* of the Islamic Center in Washington D.C., "but there are elements in the West of which we disapprove" (1972: 136). Among these are what he calls the moral laxity of the West, including easy mixing between the sexes, the availability of pornographic materials, dating, and what he says are called euphemistically "premarital relations." Such practices, he affirms, are "unhealthy, immoral, and destructive."

Muslims in this country look with increasing alarm to what they see as the rapid decline of the ethical-moral principles of American society and find reassurance in affirming the importance of maintaining the values of Islam. They observe the increase of drug usage, rising crime rates, what appears to be a growing lack of respect for the institution of marriage, the problem of AIDS, and many other elements in American society that they deeply fear. They turn to Islam as a refuge and a guarantee that they and their families will not suffer the consequences of such deep societal problems.

Dating and Social Relations among Young People

At the heart of the concerns is the matter of male-female relationships, before and during marriage. There is obviously much in the American culture that runs counter to traditional Muslim views of the propriety of these relationships. The easy interaction between men and women in public contexts, women working alongside men, young people spending time alone together late into the evening, women dressing in ways that are considered unduly provocative—these and other issues worry Muslims as they try to define themselves and members of their families as American and at the same time as members of a community for which these practices generally are not acceptable.

The American practice of dating between young men and women has been of particular concern to Muslims. Recognizing that their young people are immersed in a context in which dating is encouraged (and in which those who do not date are even looked upon as somewhat odd), they do not wish to disaffect their youth or engender in them a lack of appreciation for Islamic ways. But neither do they want to permit the easy interaction of teens and young adults that they see all around them. A Lebanese father who has lived in America for several decades says:

> dating is not our way of life. The way it is done is ridiculous. I see some people who date one person for three days, then drop them. . . . I am not against finding yourself a partner, but I am against the way they abuse this 'dating.' I don't have as much problem with boys dating girls as I do with girls dating (Haddad and Lummus 1987: 139).

The strictest interpretation of Islamic law would say that Muslim men and women (defined as postpuberty) should not be alone together with persons with whom marriage is a legal possibility for any reason. When a man and woman sit alone together, says an often quoted *hadith* attributed to the Prophet Muhammad, the third party is Satan. A Muslim boy interested in seeing a Muslim girl is allowed to visit her at her home, provided that other members of her family are present. If he sees her in public, or takes her in his car, it must be in the company of an adult family member. His purpose for any such association should be the pursuit of marriage, not simply pleasure in female company.

Thus, for some the issue is not so much the dating as such as the necessity of a chaperon. "'Dating,' which can be defined as an arrangement for a marriageable couple to meet in order to discover each other, may be a useful thing, but this meeting should not be 'unchaperoned'" (Abdul-Rauf 1977: 103). The presence of a family member is understood to preclude the possibility of any untoward behavior such as kissing or fondling. It goes without saying that any kind of explicit sexual encounter before marriage is strictly forbidden. The now common American practice of young couples living together without benefit of marriage vows is totally unacceptable. The possibility of premarital sex for women is probably the most difficult of all American realities for Arabs to accept. While those who are Islamically committed see it as a religious issue, those for whom it is an Arab cultural value shared by many Christians, Jews, and Muslims take it no less seriously.

For many young Arab Muslims in America these restrictions on dating are extremely difficult to abide. Girls see their brothers allowed to date and resent what they see as inequity. Educated professional women find it very hard to operate with one standard of interaction in the workplace and another in their personal lives. The problem is compounded by the fact that many professional Muslim men who are eligible for marriage will not marry an Arab girl who has dated at all, but will marry an American girl who dated many men. Islamic parochial schools have sprung up in many parts of this country in hopes that such education will help in controlling the girls and shaping them to conform to the strictures of the faith. When problems do occur with girls protesting these strictures, the most common response appears to be for the family to ostracize her. She is left to fend for herself, without the support of her family ties or her inheritance. In a few extreme cases, documented in Arab communities in Dearborn, Michigan, and Milwaukee, Wisconsin, girls who have entered into sexual relationships before marriage have been killed.

Some Arab Muslim communities have found that the mosque provides a helpful context in which to encourage young men and women to meet and socialize. There, under the watchful eyes of other members of the congregation, teens and young adults can interact with each other and enjoy the pleasures of sociability without explicitly countering the wishes of their parents or crossing the boundaries of culture or the strictures of the faith. It does not solve the problem of young Muslims wanting to join their non-Muslim friends in going to the movies or to dances with a date, but it does provide a helpful intermediate solution between dating and being forced (especially in the case of girls) to stay at home. Some mosques and Islamic Centers are looking to ways in which they can provide attractive social settings for the youth of the community.

🦊 *Marriage*

In many cases the mosque also serves as the locus for the ceremony of marriage itself. This practice, not common in the Middle East, is both a reflection of some of the ways in which the mosque has taken on the functions of a local Christian church, and another way in which to ensure the feelings of community and solidarity among members of the Muslim congregation. For Arab immigrants in the first half of the century this sometimes meant enjoying the celebratory atmosphere of the wedding with traditional Middle Eastern folk dances. In recent times this has occasionally led to problems in the relations between earlier immigrants and those more recently arrived from more conservative areas of the Islamic world for whom dancing in the basement of the mosque or the Islamic center is considered a highly inappropriate activity.

A considerable literature is available to American Muslims to assist in the matter of selection of marriage partners. Traditionally, of course, such selection was done by members of the respective families. This is a difficult custom to sustain in American society where families are mobile and young people, in general, grow up expecting to make their own choices. Islamic publications offer solid suggestions for those contemplating marriage, always on the expectation that such a marriage will be for life. One may be urged to pray, to ask questions, to get to know the prospective partner and his or her family as well as possible within the above-suggested restrictions, to be clear on what each partner expects from the marriage, and to have some sense of whether the prospective mate holds firmly to the values of Islam and wants to raise children in ways consistent with those values.[1]

Some Arab-Americans have picked up the custom prevalent in the subcontinent of advertising for a partner. Several Islamic magazines carry short notices under "Matrimonials" in which eligible men and women announce that they are seeking matrimony. These announcements generally list the age, education, and profession of the candidate, and the kind of partner for which he or she is looking. The Muslim Student Association, for years, has had a matrimonial section in its publications. During the last decade they have begun to use a computerized match-making system in an effort to provide better services.

Many Arab Muslims who are new to the United States are already married and do not need to worry about the problems of mate selection in a new culture. For those who come alone, often as students who intend to return home but who find those plans changed, the issue of marriage becomes very real. Marcia Hermansen observes that while some choose to marry men from their own home cultures who share their ideology and values, others break from their background and marry non-Muslim Americans (1991: 188–201). With the increased emphasis on Islamic identity in America today, and with more Muslims present in the American context, women who marry outside the faith experience stress both in their marriages and in terms of their own sense of self-identity. Hermansen also notes the interesting and increasingly occurring phenomenon of intercultural, as opposed to interfaith, marriages. As Arab Muslim women are finding it harder to secure marriages with Arab Muslim men, they are turning increasingly to members of other Muslim cultural communities, such as Pakistanis, to find husbands. Although this is acceptable in religious terms, she remarks, it represents a startling trend in the eyes of members of the parents' generation (1991: 12).

The question of interfaith marriage has engendered a great deal of attention and commentary in the American Muslim community. According to Islamic law, Muslim men may marry Christian or Jewish as well as Muslim women. While the Qur'an does not ban the marriage of Muslim women to Christians or Jews, it is Muslim belief that such marriages should not take place. The issue, of course, is the religious identity of the children, which is based on the affiliation of the father.[2] In the Middle East, where Muslims are the vast majority, this has not imposed any particular hardship on women. In American society, however, things are different. The reality of many young Muslim men marrying outside of the Islamic faith, even though it is legally permissible, has created the obvious and very real problem of young Muslim women not having suitable marriage partners. Strongly encouraged by observant members of their families not to break Islamic tradition and marry Christians or Jews, they often face the alternatives of returning to the Middle East to find husbands or remaining single. While the latter is more tolerable in American society than in that of the Middle East, it is not an option that many Muslim women would choose. One estimate suggests that somewhere between 10 to 15 percent of Muslim women in the United States and 30 percent in Canada actually do marry outside of their faith, placing a heavy burden on parents who have to justify to the Muslim community their "failure" to raise their daughters properly.

As is true with interfaith marriage in general, various kinds of problems are likely to occur when Muslim men marry outside their faith. Carried away in the excitement of mutual attraction, interfaith couples may be quite unprepared for the realities of marriage and family life. The young Muslim man may profess himself to be "modern," released from the bonds of an inhibiting religious tradition and ready to make a new life with his non-Muslim bride. As time passes, however, it often turns out that he is more influenced by his family and the dictates of his faith than he realized, causing hardships for the new wife. He may expect her to abandon the commitment to equality in marriage that characterizes so much of current American thinking and adopt the more classically Islamic model in which the husband is in charge of the wife and responsible for the decisions of the family. He may decide that, indeed, it does matter to him that his children be raised Islamically, imposing values that are foreign to his non-Muslim wife. Some Muslim women have written poignantly about what they know about cases of severe physical abuse of non-Muslim wives, based on the husband's misinterpretation of Qur'an 4:34 in which men are permitted to beat their wives "lightly" if necessary.[3] In some rare, but not nonexistent cases, American women married to Muslim men discover that there is another wife in the home country. From the husband's perspective, he may find his wife unable to adapt to his family and their expectations, wanting more of his time and attention than he is able or ready to give. "If she is an independent sort, her behavior may appear to her husband as overly assertive or unsuitable for a Muslim woman" (Hakeem 1985: 10). She may not understand or appreciate the particular values attached, in Arab Muslim society, to hospitality and the welcoming of guests in the home.

Even the best of efforts on the part of the non-Muslim wife may not alleviate all the possible problems in the minds of more cautious Muslims. As Dawud Assad notes,

> Apart from her desire to cultivate such manifestations of Western culture as dancing and music, both of which are considered indispensable to acquire "social graces,". . . a non-Muslim wife may also be a Laodicean in matters of food and drink. Out of respect for her husband's sentiments, she may not touch wine and swine, and she may not even bring them home, but she would, very definitely, be tolerant of them. It is thus possible that she might impart unconsciously, in her children also an attitude of tolerance toward alcoholic beverages and swine's flesh" (Assad 1983: 7).

He further warns against the possibility that the wife may allow her daughters to leave the confines of the home and do such disgraceful things as wear a bikini at the beach before the eyes of thousands of men. His conclusion is, clearly, that such interfaith marriages should, if possible, be avoided. One of the real dangers of such marriages cited by concerned Muslims is the possibility that the children will grow up apart from the faith. Abdul-Rauf says:

> I was deeply shocked and appalled, when I began my duties in the United States . . . to meet grown-up children of a Muslim father who confessed that they were Protestants, Catholics, Baptists or adherents of other denominations. The more the experience was repeated, the deeper my distress became! (Abdul-Rauf 1972: 31).

It is not surprising to find that requests for marriage counseling are on the rise among Arab-American Muslims. While some feel that intervention in the personal realities of a Muslim family by someone who is not part of that family is inappropriate, many others realize that the pressures of accommodating a society with very different values makes some kind of outside counseling urgent. *Imams* find themselves forced to function as marriage counselors without benefit of any kind of professional training. A national network of Muslims has been organized with the explicit purpose of talking to young people contemplating an interfaith marriage to help them to be aware of the potential difficulties.

🐚 Birth Control and Abortion

Closely related to the concerns of marriage are issues of birth control and abortion. As non-Muslim Americans find themselves increasingly forced to take a stand in favor of or in opposition to abortion in today's society, Muslims have little such choice to make. Islam stands firmly against the taking of a life that is already considered to be in existence. Traditional Islamic literature allows abortion if it occurs before life is infused in the baby (i.e., when the baby begins to move). Recent medical opinion showing that life begins at conception has led Muslim jurists to revise their teaching and disallow abortion. There is some discussion of the possibility of abortion in cases where the life of the mother is in genuine danger.

The situation is somewhat different in relation to birth control. There is ambiguity as to whether, and when, it is permissible to practice birth control and uncertainty as to what Islamic teachings really have to say about the subject. A young Muslim woman who has emigrated from Egypt to the United States notes:

I am not sure what the Islamic position is on birth control. Some say you should control the number of births, some say you shouldn't. In Egypt, the government is trying to limit the number of births; some are trying to find the *hadiths* that say there shouldn't be too many of us. But there are also people who believe that there are passages in the Qur'an that say no to birth control" (Haddad and Lummis 1987: 142).

And a female Lebanese Muslim immigrant reports:

I did not know what the stance of my mosque was on birth control. So I asked the *imam*. He said that if the contraceptive is not long-term, like when they tie the tubes, it is not *haram*. But if you do something long term that would permanently destroy your chance to have children, that's *haram*" (Haddad and Lummis 1987: 142).

There is sufficient support for the possibility of using birth control under certain circumstances that some members of the American Muslim community do not feel it is essentially un-Islamic. The moderate view suggests that if there is a legitimate reason for needing to limit the number of children in a family, and if it can be done without unnecessary suffering on anyone's part, it should be seen as within the general purview of Islamic acceptability. This is not to deny the fact, however, that birth control without a good reason is unacceptable, and that Muslims have always put great value on the desirability of increasing the Muslim population within a given family and for the enhancement of the global community.

⚕ *Raising Children*

The issue of how to raise children in the context of Western society is one of the more serious problems facing Arab Muslims. If children are sent to public schools they quickly learn the values of the prevailing society that many Arab families disavow. Some Muslim communities are trying to set up parochial schools where students can learn Islamic values as well as become educated in the academic disciplines. There is great difference of opinion, however, as to whether or not this is advisable. Some question the possibility of providing education as thorough and good as is available in many of the public school systems in America. And some are worried about the costs of such private education. Others are concerned that the training provided in an Islamic school might be too conservative and fear that harboring children in an Islamic environment might make it more difficult for them to integrate into American society when such integration is finally necessary. As one Muslim parent said:

> We discussed [parochial education] in our mosque, and I was opposed to an Islamic school instead of public school for my children because I think that doing something like that would tend to alienate them from the rest of the community, instead of integrating them, and any lack of confidence they had about being Muslim would make it worse (Haddad and Lummis 1987: 15).

For those who are particularly concerned with establishing a home atmosphere conducive to learning and understanding the Islamic way of life there is abundant literature available. One can read how to maintain an Islamic atmosphere, what are acceptable Islamic standards of behavior, and how to set an example of sound Muslim family life in which parents show respect and consideration for each other and for their children. Parents are encouraged to regulate the activities of their children, especially during their leisure time, and are urged to bring a Muslim child into contact with other Muslims at every possible occasion. By involving themselves in activities such as working in local or national Muslim organizations, teaching in Islamic schools, or working on specifically Islamic projects parents can model for their children the importance of relating commitment to activity and can demonstrate specific ways in which the Islamic ideal of care for the community can be lived.

Muslims are concerned that because of the high incidence of broken homes in American society, and because both parents are so often working, their children will not see among their non-Muslim friends families who do things together as a unit. Members of Muslim families are expected to spend as much time with each other as possible, both in the home and doing outside activities. A girl is encouraged to be a companion to her mother going on shopping trips and other kinds of outings, planning meals and family activities and talking with her about what is going on in her life. Boys may enjoy being involved in sporting activities with their fathers or participating in some way in their professional lives. Arab children are expected to relate to members of their family as other children might relate to friends made at school or in the neighborhood. They join in family social activities more frequently than do other American children, participating, for example, in dinners or parties rather than retiring to another room to watch television. Parents are warned not to use television as a kind of babysitter and to monitor very closely the programs that their children watch. Fearing the separation from family context that they see happening in many American families, Arab Muslims hope that by keeping their children involved with them in as many ways as possible they can transmit to them the values of close family life in an Islamic environment.

An emphasis on solid family life as the nucleus of a vibrant and smoothly functioning society is, of course, not exclusive to practicing Muslims. It is shared by members of all of America's religious communities, and while many Americans appear to be adjusting to what is called the breakdown of the family there is much in American culture—structural, emotional and ideological—that continues to support the family as an ideal.

Observation of American Holidays

One of the issues with which Muslim parents must deal is the degree of involvement they allow their children, and themselves, in some of the holidays celebrated in the American context. Earlier generations of Arabs in this country tended to participate in many of the holidays observed by the rest of the culture without careful discrimination of what might or might not run counter to Islamic values. Under the guidance of more conservative *imams* and the influence of more recent immigrants, they are now raising questions about the appropriateness of celebrating some of these occasions. Some holidays are considered questionable because they tend to foster a sense of self-centeredness in children that may not be advisable. Some see that birthday celebrations, for example, lead to an exaggerated sense of personal importance. They encourage an attitude that recognizes that birth, life, and death are gifts from God and nothing deserving of special congratulation. Recognizing the pressures of living in a society in which school children are highly fussed over on their birthdays, most parents will acknowledge the importance of some recognition of this occasion.

Valentine's Day presents another kind of problem. On the one hand many Arab Muslims appreciate it as a way of stressing the importance of a loving relationship between spouses in the family context, as they do Mother's and Father's Days. On the other hand, many feel that because Valentine's Day has become so commercialized it cheapens and even vulgarizes relationships and promotes cheap romanticism in young boys and girls. Clearly the focus on "romantic" attachments between young people raises warning flags to Muslims who are not planning to allow their children to date and be involved romantically at an early age. Some have suggested that if valentine cards must be exchanged at school a child should be encouraged to give them only to good friends of the same sex. Such people feel that attendance at Valentine's Day parties should be discouraged.

For the most part Easter is simply ignored in the Islamic community, with the exception of possibly allowing children to participate in egg hunts. Parents are urged to explain to their children that this is a Christian holiday that is not related to Islam or Muslims. Memorial Day and the Fourth of July are observed by most Arab Muslims as occasions for family picnics and celebrations as well as for affirming their membership in American society. The Fourth of July serves as a reminder to many of the ideals that they expect American society to live up to, and sometimes of the disappointment that they feel with the directions in which they see the society presently going. Halloween is acceptable if children observe strict rules and go trick-or-treating with their parents; children are especially encouraged to join the UNICEF efforts at this time. Thanksgiving again provides an opportunity for affirming family solidarity and an occasion for thanking God for the blessings given to the Islamic community as well as to the American nation.

Christmas is perhaps the most problematic of the American holidays for Muslims. While some have emphasized that they share the appreciation for the birth of Jesus from the Virgin Mary, and thus can join in recognition of that event, they are increasingly pained at the extreme commercialization of Christmas in the United States. The extent to which they see Christmas intended as a celebration of the birth of "the Christian God" is also a problem for Muslims. This, of course, is anathema in the Muslim understanding. These problems have led to an increasing feeling among members of the Arab Muslim community that they should not observe Christmas. Some Muslims do celebrate Christmas in ways similar to those of secular or unchurched Christians, with a tree and exchange of presents. As one of them put it, "After all, Jesus is our Prophet."

For Christian wives of Muslim men a lack of enthusiasm for Christmas, or refusal to allow its celebration in the home, can be painful. And when Muslim children are exposed, at school and in numerous other ways, to the excitement of having a Christmas tree, receiving presents, and talking to Santa Claus, they may find it hard to understand why their own family has decided to ignore this holiday. The growth of the Muslim community in America and the immigration of many who are committed to a more culturally defined Islam have led many families who earlier used to have trees and exchange gifts to decide not to do it anymore. Children are taught that Muslims have their own holidays (*eids*) and that it is not necessary for them to try to participate in Christian celebrations. As one Muslim has commented:

> When we came to this country in 1973, one of my daughters was three years old. When she was four years old, that was the first Christmas for her. In our neighborhood there were no other Muslims. She was playing in other kids' houses and she saw Christmas lights and all sorts of things there. She asked me why our holiday doesn't have Christmas trees and lights. I tried to make her understand right there, saying, "Now look, they are Christians. They have their religion and they should celebrate it. We have our religion and we have our celebrations at that time." From then on and until today, every *eid*, even if sometimes I can't afford it, I buy each of my children a gift (Haddad and Lummis 1987: 95).

Women and Work

Muslim families are concerned that their children learn to accommodate traditional Islamic values with the values of the culture in which they must live. They recognize that what seems to work in an Arab culture in which Muslims are a majority may need to be modified in Western society. And, they recognize that, in their home countries, significant changes are taking place in ways that also serve to call into question some traditional Islamic norms. One of the areas in which there is a great deal of conversation, in virtually all Islamic communities today, is that of women and work. Should they work outside of the home? If so, what occupations are or are not appropriate for them? And what are the practical limitations on Arab immigrant women to finding jobs in many areas of this country?

The traditional Islamic view that women belong in the home finds expression in much contemporary counsel offered to Muslim families. Again Muhammad Abdul-Rauf:

> To make the gentle woman who is to be loved and adored the source of authority which exudes awe and instills fear and require her to struggle for her living and for the living of her male partner would be unjust. The dependent male would renege and be relegated from his virile nature to that of a

weak, meek creature. Yielding to an aggressive wife, he would have no legitimate outlet for his ego and innate aggressiveness or he might seek unhealthy outlets in drugs and assaults on society (1977: 61).

For many families the relegation of the wife exclusively to the domain of the home is neither desirable nor practical. Economic realities in America, as in many Arab countries, necessitate her finding some way to augment the family's income. But for many Muslims it is clear that some jobs are simply not acceptable for women. For those with limited education, for example, a natural place to look for a position might be in a restaurant. But the Muslim prohibition against the consumption of both alcohol and pork products make it difficult to work in establishments in which one or both are served. "I think being a waitress is fun," said one woman, "but then I am not serving drinks. Also, I couldn't work in a place that serves pork, it would turn me off. I can't stand to touch the stuff." Such concerns, of course, relate to both men and women as they try to avoid putting themselves in situations that might compromise what they understand to be the regulations, and the value structure, of Islam.

In some areas the reality is that a significant number of Arab immigrants, male and female, do not have the education, skills or language preparation to equip them to participate in the workforce. Barbara Aswad notes in a study of Arab immigrant women in Michigan that such factors as fewer part-time jobs, the inability of many women to see themselves in the workplace, and "increasing Islamic values operating in a host country which lacks premarital chastity values" all come to play in making it difficult for many women to secure outside employment (Aswad 1994).

In general it can be said that the more conservative the family, the less likely the idea of a woman working outside the home unless it is a real economic necessity will be accepted. These families are also the ones that place a high premium on women dressing in a modest fashion. These issues, thus, become related, and it is clear that for many Muslims the question of how women dress in the workplace is essential to the acceptance of the occupation. The other major criterion for conservative Muslims is the extent to which a woman will be put into close contact with men on the job. Occupations that are respectable and allow a woman to function in a primarily female context are most desirable, such as teaching in a girl's school or serving as a doctor to other women. There seems to be a clear correlation between the length of time an Arab immigrant has spent in America and the degree to which she, and her family, accept the idea of her being professionally employed. Implicit in the general understanding of the woman's role is the expectation that whether or not she works outside of the home she still has primary responsibility for the care of children and management of the household.

☙ *Appropriate Dress*

Perhaps few issues are of more interest in the Arab immigrant community these days than that of appropriate dress for women. It is apparent that the concern in many Arab countries that women dress "Islamically" has strongly influenced the attitude that Arab Muslims in the United States and Canada adopt toward their dress. The influence of conservative *imams* and other members of a community may be helpful in encouraging women who have not heretofore done so to adopt modes of clothing that provide a more complete covering. Yusuf al-Qaradawi, in a manual entitled *The Lawful and the Prohibited in Islam,* at the beginning of his section on appropriate dress for the Muslim woman cites this narrative from the Prophet:

> I will not be a witness for two types of people who are destined for the Fire: people with whips . . . who beat the people . . . and women who, although clothed, are yet naked, seducing and being seduced, their hair styled like the tilted humps of camels. These will not enter the Garden nor will its fragrance reach them.[4]

Al-Qaradawi continues with his assurance that the Prophet did not appreciate seeing a woman wearing a man's clothing, nor vice versa, and that women should not pluck their eyebrows, wear wigs and hairpieces, dye their hair, or otherwise interfere with their God-given attributes. (Among the suggestions of appropriate dress for females is one that advises girls going swimming in public places to wear a long-sleeved tunic and head-covering.)

In some cases Muslim women consider such interpretations to be ridiculous and inappropriate. Women who have long worn Western dress often deeply resent the criticism that they hear from others. An American born Arab woman expresses her concern this way:

Women are always encouraged in and out of the mosque to cover their hair and wear long dresses. . . . Men can wear what they please pretty much but they are fussy about clothing of the women in the mosque. Now I think women who go to the mosque to pray should be covered; I don't think any woman would go in there with a short skirt or short sleeves, or what they call these saris with so much showing or not have their head covered. But—how women dress outside of the mosque is their own private business. I don't want to go to college with my head covered, and wearing a short skirt does not make me a bad Muslim. I am a Muslim and I am proud to say it, but I want to say it in ways other than dressing in obnoxious clothing. I want to blend in as far as my clothes go. I want to look normal (Haddad and Lummis 1987: 133).

The double standard of wearing one kind of dress in the mosque and another on the street also applies, for some Arab women, to the difference in their work and their home clothing. Hermansen speaks of the sense of "schizophrenia" some women feel when they are forced to change from looking like other American women at work to clothing demanded of them when they are in contact with other Muslims (1991: 193). In general Arab Muslim women are less likely to favor wearing conservative clothing in public than those from some other ethnic groups, and thus are more likely to find themselves caught in the middle, between their desires to assimilate into American society, and the pressures to be "Islamically acceptable."

The strains on the Arab Muslim family in America today can be great as members continue to struggle with their Muslim, and Arab, identity, and various kinds of problems can surface. Children may resent the pressures to remain within the family and may finally rebel. Younger people, especially, may have difficulty understanding the fact that traditional Arab family structures leave little room for personal privacy, a right highly valued in American society. And like other members of Western society, Arab Muslims struggle with the care of the elderly. The growing trend in America to move older people out of the home into retirement and nursing-care units cuts directly against the Islamic values of honoring, respecting and caring for the senior members of one's family. As one young woman immigrant says:

> I personally could not put an elderly relative in a nursing
> home. But I can understand how Muslims do. I have seen
> women in this country going out and working eight-hour
> shifts, taking care of three kids, cooking dinner, doing the
> washing, and after a while also taking care of the person who
> is bedridden and needs constant attention. . . . But personally,
> I just feel that a person in a nursing home is doomed to die,
> there is no reason to live (Haddad and Lummis 1987: 87).

Yet the realities of American mobility and the trend towards more retirement homes in the society have led at least one Muslim community with a
substantial number of second- and third-generation members to include a
plan for construction of a home for the elderly in their community adjacent to the mosque.

﷽ *Islam and Feminism*

One of the greatest strains on the family and on Muslim society in general
in this country may indeed come when Arab Muslim women find themselves caught in some of the kinds of feminist discussions that have been
so prevalent in American society in the last few decades. Whether or not
feminism is compatible with Islamic values depends, of course, on how
one defines those elements that make up a feminist point of view. What is
clear is that much of what is valued in Islamic society is held up to
criticism and even ridicule by some in the West who cannot seem to free
themselves from unfortunate kinds of stereotyping. Nouha al-Hegelan
describes what she calls the "born yesterday assumption" of many Western women.

> Westerners begin by comparing the Arab/Moslem woman to
> her sisters in the West. Using Western women as a standard is
> only part of the insult. The injury is magnified by the added
> assumption that the Arab woman began her struggle yester-
> day—as if she was somehow born whole out a newly tapped
> oil well—a veiled, uncivilized non-entity (n.d.: 2).

What is increasingly clear to Arab women in the United States is that
whatever they may think about matters of women's rights, it is incumbent
upon them to formulate their ideas, not only in conversation with Western
women, but in clear distinction to much of what those women hold to be valid.

Azizah al-Hibri, a Lebanese lawyer/professor and spokeswoman for the maintenance of Islamic values, has cited several concerns she has had when interacting with American feminists. First, she says, the American feminist movement tends to see its own experience as applying cross-culturally to all women. Second, even educated American women, well-intentioned in trying to learn about Islam, become frustrated when they cannot translate a Muslim position into their own Judeo-Christian experience. Third, many of the concerns of Arab Muslim women are clearly political in nature, and in her experience, al-Hibri has found American feminists unwilling to risk involvement in those issues.

> Tactical considerations at home override the ideology of sisterhood; and to appease their conscience, American feminists turn with even greater vigor to denounce U.S. policy in Nicaragua, hoping to drown with their loud voices the faint moaning of dying Muslim women in the East (1988: 7).

Few Arab women have been as articulate as al-Hibri, but more and more are realizing that there are clear distinctions between the values of American feminism as it has classically been formulated and Muslim values and ideals, and that it is possible to formulate a feminism that both allows for freedom of opportunity for Muslim women and does not compromise basic Islamic values. They see that Western feminism is often politically unaware or unmotivated; that it focusses on freedom and opportunity for the individual rather than for the welfare of the larger group; that it emphasizes sexual rather than cultural identity; that consciousness-raising, for Western women, is based on the desire to avoid exploitation by males, while, for Arab women, it is to avoid exploitation by outsiders; that Western feminism is often anti-male in ways that Arab Muslims consider degrading and undesirable; that Western feminists apparently value sexual liberation and identity of sex roles in ways that are repugnant to Muslims. "I am looking for an alternative to Western feminism," says Negiba Megademeni, a young Tunisian Muslim. "Sexual behavior that may strike an American feminist as liberated may strike me as just another form of slavery, and a rather neurotic form at that."[5]

All of these concerns, then, are part of the conversations taking place on many levels throughout Arab Muslim society in the United States and Canada. The importance of the family, of the respective roles of women and men in society, of socializing children in order that they might avoid the problems of Western society, of finding appropriate ways to care for the elderly—all of these issues necessitate formulating responses to the pressures of American society that neither compromise the ideals of Islam nor take refuge in what some consider to be an unwieldy and unrealistically conservative dogmatism. Resolution and common agreement on many of these matters, at present, is less likely than the realization that a range of responses is both appropriate to the rapidly changing contemporary Western context, and possible to justify under the umbrella of an Islamic system designed for the universal application of the faith.

🕮 References

al-Hegelan, Nouha. n.d. "Women in the Arab World." In *Arab Woman, Potentials and Prospects*. New York: Arab Information Center.

al-Hibri, Azizah. 1988. "Muslim Women and the American Feminist Movement." Paper presented at the Muslims of America conference, Amherst, Mass., April 16.

al-Qaradawi, Yusuf. 1984. *The Lawful and the Prohibited in Islam*.Kuwait: IIFSO.

Abdul-Khabir. 1982. "Prevalent Problems in Muslim Marriages." *Al-Ittihad* (July–December): 19.

Abdul-Rauf, Muhammad. 1972. *Marriage in Islam*. New York: Exposition Press.

————. 1977. *The Islamic View of Women and the Family*. New York: Robert Speller and Sons.

Assad, Dawud. 1983. "Mixed Marriages." In *Christian-Muslim Marriages*, ed. Dawud Assad, Guy Harpigny, and Jorgen Nielson. Birmingham, Eng.: Centre for the Study of Islam and Christian-Muslim Relations.

Aswad, Barbara C. 1994. "Attitudes of Immigrant Women and Men in the Dearborn Area toward Women's Employment and Welfare." In *Muslim Communities in North America*, ed. Yvonne Haddad and Jane Smith. Albany: State University of New York Press.

Badawi, Gamal A. n.d. *A Muslim Woman's Dress According to Qur'an and Sunnah*. Plainfield, N.Y.: Muslim Student Association Women's Committee.

Haddad, Yvonne Y. 1991. *The Muslims of America*. New York: Oxford University Press.

Haddad, Yvonne Y. and Lummis, Adair T. 1987. *Islamic Values in the United States: A Comparative Study*. New York: Oxford University Press.

Hakeem, Rabi'ah. 1985. "Cross-cultural Marriages among Muslims: A Word of Caution." *Islamic Horizons* (October) 14: 10.

Hermansen, Marcia. 1991. "Two-Way Acculturation: Muslim Women in America between Individual Choice (Liminability) and Community Affiliation (Communitas)." In *The Muslims of America*, ed. Y. Y. Haddad. New York: Oxford University Press.

Hoballah, Mahmoud. n.d. *Islam and Modern Values*. Washington, D.C.: The Islamic Center.

Kaleem, A. U. 1981. "Emancipation of Women and Islam." *The Minaret* 8, no. 21 (November 1).

Megademeni, Negiba. 1985. "Muslim Women Developing a Theory of Islamic Feminism." *Unitarian Universalist World* 16, no. 8 (August 15).

LOUISE CAINKAR

Immigrant Palestinian Women Evaluate Their Lives

T his study describes immigrant Palestinian women's assessments of
the quality of their own lives as women, in general, and as Palestinian
women, in particular. It is based on extensive fieldwork done in Chicago's
Palestinian community, which resulted in detailed life histories of twenty-
two women. The quotes used are from these life histories.

As with all human beings, the women in this study have based the
assessment of the quality of their own lives on the values they hold, their
sense of history, what they believe to be desirable and possible achievements, and the ways in which their lives compare to the lives of those they
see around them. In making this later comparison the immigrant Palestinian women of this study compared their lives specifically to those of: 1.
people who have a country; 2. their mothers; 3. Palestinian men; and 4.
Western women, especially American women.

The result was a remarkable consensus, despite differences in socio-
economic status, marital status, place of origin, occupation, time of immigration, educational level, and subgroup membership. This is not to say
that were no differences of outlook and values. There were differences in
the way women of different backgrounds described their values as well as
individual differences not systematically related to differences in background characteristics. But, overall, there was more consensus than disparity. This consensus appears to result from a shared common social
position, one that influences their perspective and judgments—they are all

41

Palestinian *women* and, as such, they share a common national and cultural background and a common status. They judge their lives and those of other Palestinian women from a perspective grounded in these realities. A perspective that sees their being immigrants as insignificant and their being Palestinian and stateless as overwhelmingly significant.

And so the women of this study feel that, on balance, they are no worse off than are other women, except for their statelessness. In fact, they feel that, in many ways, their lives are better than those of American women; a belief that may surprise those who view the lives of Arab women as unsatisfactory lives of submission and powerlessness. This disparity in judgment is explained by the difference in outlook; one based on a cultural perspective, the other focused on individual power and self-actualization. Given this cultural perspective, it is not surprising that the women of this study attribute many of their discontents to Palestinian statelessness rather than to gender inequality. If only they were in the Middle Ease, they say, life would be better. If only their country could be liberated, they could return to the society in which their lives would be better—a society in which the level of inequality between men and women would be substantially reduced from what it is in exile in the United States. It also is not surprising that the women who most long to return to the Middle Ease are those whose lives are guided most by Palestinian cultural norms. These women describe living a Palestinian life in the United States as unrewarding and unfulfilling.

🗽 *Background Assumptions*

Almost universally, Palestinians, women and men, believe that males and females, *by nature*, are biologically and psychologically different; that they have different, although complementary, roles in life; and that gender differences in rights and duties are inevitable. This assumption, held in common by all immigrant life-history respondents, clearly influences the perspectives they have on life. The "fact" of these gender differences is perceived as limiting the possibilities of what can be. These assumptions do not inherently imply anything about superiority and inferiority, just difference. Assumptions about the natural, complementary differences between genders lie at the core of the organization of Arab hierarchical social structure and the division of labor in Arab society.

The effect of these assumptions on evaluations of the quality of life of Palestinian women is exemplified by responses to the question, "What do you think of what Western women call women's liberation?" Only one respondent said that she supported women's liberation unequivocally and only one respondent was completely against it. The remaining twenty supported the notion of women's liberation with certain reservations, the primary one being that "women are women" and should not try to be like men. This opinion is expressed in the following ways:

> I believe in equal pay for equal jobs, but some jobs are made for a man to do. Women should not be like men.

> Woman is woman. Women should have the right to work but they should leave the rough work for men.

> Women want to be like men and to be treated like men, but they are definitely different from men.

The feminist theoretical perspective, on the other hand, holds that male/female differences, in the main, have been created socially and that relations of power have sustained these differences and made them *appear* to be inevitable in the interest of one group over those of the other. This assumption, which influences this work, leads to a different analysis than that offered by holders of the *natural differences* perspective. In the end, however, the conclusions drawn from either perspective are similar: gender clearly defines certain parameters of the life experience, and women, overall, have more difficult lives than men.

🖾 *Palestinian Women Compare Their Lives to Those of Their Mothers*

When Palestinian women compare their lives with those of their mothers they feel that their own lives are significantly different from, and substantially better than, their mothers' lives.[1] The difference cited most frequently was their greater education. Indeed, the difference in many cases was quite dramatic: only a few years of formal education for the mothers, the majority of whom are illiterate, compared to at least a high-school education for the daughters. An increasing number of single immigrant Palestinian women under twenty-five in the United States have bachelors degrees and some have graduate degrees.

Palestinian women expressed the belief that their education allows them to be more in touch with their children's lives than their mothers were able to be with theirs. When these women were growing up and attending school, their mothers could not help them with schoolwork; in contrast, this generation has the educational background to allow them to work with their children. The women in this study also said that they are treated with more respect by Palestinian men because they are educated, but this respect goes only so far. Palestinian men without a college education, and even some with one, prefer to marry women who did not attend college. One woman told me:

> Some Palestinian men like educated women, but some of the guys say that they don't like educated women because they are too demanding and too much trouble.

Immigrant Palestinian women with a college education[2] feel it brings them many benefits. They say it allows them to have a different perspective on life than their mothers have. Even the way in which they make decisions is different:

> I have a lot more schooling than my mother did and I look at my life differently. She makes her decisions based on what others will say about her. I make my decisions based on what I feel is right, within the cultural limits.

A college education also makes it possible for women to find jobs. This changes their role in the family to one of potential breadwinner. One woman said, "I can look at life in a different way. If I marry and we need money, I can help my husband by working." To understand why women with a college education are more likely to get jobs than those without, we must keep in mind the cultural norm that women should not perform manual labor or "men's work." College-educated women are able to find jobs that do not do so. Finally, a college education offers women a different view of their future:

> My dream has been to get a good college degree. My mother's dream was to get a husband. All she thought about was that one day her sons would take care of her. I would never expect that from my sons. I feel I must learn to take care of myself. I would not want to put that burden on my sons.

The second most frequently mentioned difference between these women's lives and their mothers' lives is how they spend each day. These Palestinian women feel that, compared to their mothers, the way they spend their time has improved. Married women say they spend more time with their husbands than their mothers did.

> My father would go out and enjoy himself without my mother. They never did anything together. Not so for me. We do many things together.

Part of this difference comes from changes in the way married couples are viewed by younger members of Palestinian society. The concept of a romantic relationship between a man and a woman is beginning to replace the utilitarian concept of the past. Social activities, always gender-segregated in the past, are no longer necessarily so. Another difference is that while most chain immigrants grew up in the United States with their fathers while their mothers remained in Palestine—with husbands and wives sometimes seeing each other only once a year—their married children share a home with their spouses. Another difference is created by the nature of life in the United States. For instance, a significant majority of Palestinian women in the United States are dependent upon their husbands for mobility and a social life. The only other way for them to have a social life is daytime visits with other women. Further, because of long work hours and the dispersion or absence of kin in their urban neighborhoods, men are more likely to come home after work than to visit male relatives, as they would have done in a Palestinian village or town.

Palestinian women also feel they spend less time on housework and perform less manual labor than their mothers did. These difference are due mainly to modern conveniences and the fact that these women, living in the United States, do not perform the labor of village women.

> My mother never had a refrigerator or a stove. She woke up at five in the morning to clean, cook, milk the cows, and feed chickens. She made breakfast, and we went to school. All her life was only working. All their money went to feed and clothe children. I have machines to help me with laundry and cooking, whereas she did everything with her hands. Except for my children and cooking, I can finish all my housework in the afternoon, while my mother worked from the time she got up until she went to sleep. She baked bread; I buy ours. My mother had nine children; I have four.

Having fewer children than their mothers had was another commonly cited difference and improvement over their mothers lives, especially for women under age thirty-five. The life histories of my study show that immigrant women between the age of eighteen and forty-two have an average of eight siblings, whereas the largest families in Chicago, which are among the new village immigrants, average only five children. The more educated the woman, the fewer children she is likely to have. College-educated Palestinian women in Chicago say they want no more than three children. This is true despite the part of the Palestinian ethos that, to keep Palestine alive, encourages women to have as many children as possible, to make up for lost martyrs (Palestinians who have died in war, from bombing raids, and under occupation). In the Middle East, this perspective on childbearing is adopted mainly by non-college-educated peasant women and also refugees. Palestinian women in the United States, including peasant women, say it is too expensive here to have more than five children.

Immigrant Palestinian women also said that their lives are, or will be, better than their mothers' lives because of the changes in the process leading to marriage. About half (seven) of the married women and all of the single women interviewed shared this view. Among those already married, the main difference in the marital process was that they were allowed to voice their opinions as to whether they thought they could live with the man asking for their hand in marriage before they became engaged to him.

> Before, there was no question as to whether you could live with the man. It was expected that you could, and you would be whatever he wanted you to be. Now, at least, they ask us if we think we can live with the man and we have more right to say no.

A few women said they married men that they met and selected rather than men suggested by family members or outsiders. I found this to be the case only among women who finished college before marriage:

> I met my husband at the university. Many times my family wanted me to marry their choice, one of my relatives. But I refused, and my brothers were understanding. [Respondent's father is deceased.] I was frank with my family. I told them I would not marry a man I didn't know. Even if he was from a rich and good family. I always expressed my opinion on this. I told them about my husband. I told them he was a good man

and I wanted to marry him. I reached a point where either I
was going to marry him or stay unmarried [age twenty-nine].
They finally gave in, but they gave my husband many conditions. They made him write a marriage contract with many,
many conditions, especially if he divorces me. [Do you think
this path to marriage is unusual?] I don't know the statistics,
but I think it is becoming more common.

Finally, some women say that their lives are better than their mothers'
lives because they sacrifice less of themselves. This view was expressed by
one-quarter of the immigrant women interviewed. While these women
say their primary responsibility in life is to their husbands and children
and that they will sacrifice their own needs for those of their family, the
degree of their self-sacrifice will not be total, as it was for their mothers.

My mother was married at sixteen. She could not plan any of
her life. She always did what my father wanted her to do. She
did what was best for her family. I feel she never really lived
her life and I feel bad about that. But, everyone around her
was the same, so I know that she was not miserable, and she
did not question these things. She was capable of being happy
with it. In contrast, in my family, my needs also get taken into
account.

For all these reasons: more education, less time spent on household
chores, more time spent with husbands, and fewer children, Palestinian
women in the United States feel that they are better off than their mothers
and that the quality of life for Palestinian women has improved, were it
not for the fact of the occupation and their statelessness. In this regard,
both mothers and daughters have suffered from exile and family dispersion: mothers lose their daughters to exile; daughters lose their mothers'
company and support, or both go into exile.

Among women who married by arrangement, women who were given
some say about their marriage feel their marital lives are better because of
it. Women who chose their husbands also feel this way. Single Palestinian
women in the United States now expect to be given some latitude before
accepting a marriage proposal. They will not accept the traditional arranged ways of their parents—they will not marry men whom they have
not met and of whom they have not approved.

ॐ *Palestinian Women Compare Their Lives to Those of Palestinian Men*

When the immigrant Palestinian women in this study compare their lives to those of Palestinian men, they said that although men work hard to support their families, men have too many privileges. The double standard in Palestinian society became evident to these women when, even as little girls, they had to serve and clean up after their brothers.

> I had to do housework but the boys never did. The boys
> would throw their pajamas down and we had to pick them up.
> That made it wrong. We did not mind helping our mother but
> the boys did nothing but make us work. I wanted to be a boy.

Palestinian women grew up monitored and disciplined while it seemed that the boys could do whatever they wanted.

> From the time they are born, girls are looked at differently.
> Boys act superior and they grow up that way. The girls should
> be shy and obedient. Palestinian girls are always told "you
> can't do this; you can't do that." Girls have to have a good
> reason to do anything, but the boys do what they want. Girls'
> mistakes are taken very seriously, and punishment is often
> severe. The culture is too strict on girls.

As adults, Palestinian women must continue to confront male privilege. One woman said, "The culture works so that men always have the advantage." This advantage means that men are given the benefit of the doubt when there are problems between a man and a woman. If a couple gets divorced, the woman is blamed. If they can't have children, the woman is the first to be held responsible. If there are disagreements, the woman is expected to change to satisfy the wishes of the man. Men have more power than women in the culture. The male privilege that most irritated the Palestinian women in this study is that Palestinian men have far more freedom than women have, especially in the United States. As one woman put it:

> Wherever they go, Palestinian men have more freedom than
> women have. Here they are able to get away with even more.
> In the Middle East, men do not have this much freedom. I
> don't like it but there is nothing I can do about it.

The women interviewed expressed the belief that, compared to men, there are many rights that they must struggle for and that they are at a disadvantage. They feel that their mothers were not bothered by these inequalities because that was how their mothers were raised, that they didn't know any other way of life. But when the respondents were asked if they thought Arab women were oppressed, eighteen out of the twenty-two said no. They do feel that the culture is changing, bringing more equality between women and men, but that this change takes time. More importantly, these women feel the issue to be subjective. They say Arab women do not feel deprived or unhappy; they are living in accordance with the way they were raised, and most women don't expect more than they have.

Living in the United States affects responses to questions about the oppression of Arab women in two main ways. First, they said that the American media have exaggerated the level of oppression Arab women face, showing rooms full of scantily clad women serving men as if this was representative of Arab life. One woman said, "This is just propaganda to make us look like backward and ignorant people." Second, living in the United States gives them a close look at another culture and another way of life for women. American women are perceived as having more freedom than Arab women. This exposure to a different culture causes Palestinian women to reassess the good and bad points in their own culture. Yet, the result of observing the lives of American women does not seem to alter radically Palestinian women's beliefs in their Arab culture. They say that while they live in a system where there is gender inequality, American women live in a system that offers them little respect as human beings.

※ Palestinian Women Compare Their Lives to Those of American Women

When the women interviewed in this study compare their lives to those the American women they see around them, very few of them express a desire to change places with an American woman. They see American women are seen as having more social freedom than they themselves have, but, as one woman said, "the freedom has many dark sides." Palestinian women say that American women are respected less by men and the society at large than are Palestinian women. For example, they find the way women are treated when they are elderly horrifying:

> When an American woman gets old, no one cares about her.
> Her children leave her and don't care what happens to her.
> They don't visit their parents. They put them in places when
> they don't want to take care of them. We have a different way.
> Our mothers and fathers sacrifice for us when we are young,
> so, when they get old, we take care of them. We would never
> let our mothers be alone.

Palestinian women also expressed the belief that American women are not well-treated by their husbands. They say that while they know that not every American marriage is bad, the fact that American men are not criticized by the family or society for certain destructive behaviors suggests that women are placed in a very vulnerable position, far more vulnerable than that of Palestinian women. There are two aspects of American life perceived as negative by Palestinian women are: The fact that many American women are forced to work whether they want to or not.

> Arabs have more respect for women. The Arab woman has a
> better life because the man works a lot harder for the woman.
> An Arab man would never force a woman to work. If she feels
> she wants to stay home and take care of the children and not
> worry about money, he would respect her for this.

And the marital insecurity of American women.

> American women have more freedom, but I do not think they
> have a good life. Their husbands leave them and the children.
> They have girlfriends while they are married. The woman has
> to raise her family by herself. For Arab women, if the mar-
> riage is real bad they can go to their family for help. From
> what I see, American women have a hard life too.

The Palestinians in this study do not like the loose family structure seen in American society: children do not respect their parents; husbands and wives do not respect each other; there is no glue in the society, only freedom. They perceive that Americans are raised to be most concerned about themselves, while Palestinians are raised to care for one another. Palestinian woman comply with the rules of the cultural system in which they must live, whether they like all of them or not, because to defy them means to lose the support structures the culture provides. Without this structure, they feel vulnerable and empty. Loss of family, for them, is the greatest loss.

Another concern expressed by these Palestinian women is their fear for their personal safety in the United States. They see this problem as another example of the dark side of too much freedom and the lack of respect people have for each other, in general, and for women, in particular. They think that women pay for their freedom by being potential victims:

> I am not against the American people, but the customs here are not good. I think this country is like a zoo. Women get raped; fathers rape their daughters; men attack women on the street and steal from them. We do not live like this in the Middle East.

However, these Palestinian women expressed their appreciation of the fact that American women have more legal rights than Palestinian women, especially when it comes to divorce. They would like to see Palestinian women have these rights. But, overall, they would not trade their lot for that of the American woman. Although American women have more freedoms and rights than they do, these Palestinian women see the trade-off as the loss of respect, emotional support, and security provided by their traditional system. This price is seen as too high. Their conclusion is, in one woman's words, "Women everywhere have it harder than men."

The belief the women of this study expressed is that the levels of male privilege and regulation of female behavior that are part of their culture should be decreased, and they wage their struggle for these changes within the context of their families. Some are more successful than others. Women who work outside the home want their husbands to share more housework and child care; some are successful, and some are not. They want to be trusted rather than monitored, they feel they are capable of staying within the cultural limits and do not need to be controlled or watched. Yet, their symbol of a better life for women is not the life of the Western or American woman. On the contrary, they feel American women deserve some of the respect and support that Palestinian women have. "The best system," said one respondent, echoing the sentiments of her female compatriots, "is a combination of both. We should take the good things from each culture and get rid of the bad."

📖 Changing the System: Raising Daughters and Sons Differently

The women in this study hope to change the inequalities in the cultural system by raising their sons and daughters differently from the ways in which they were raised. However, they know that despite their wish to treat their children more equally, their sons will have advantages over their daughters if they raise them in the "Arab way," as all of them plan to do. These feelings are expressed as follows:

> I will give my daughters more freedom and let them have some fun in their lives. My parents raised their sons and daughters differently, but I want to raise them the same. I will try to treat them the same, not treat the boys as though they are special. But I am more afraid with my daughters. It is dangerous here for girls; there is molesting and rape. I want to give [my daughter] what I could not have, but she will not be able to do everything she wants.

It does not appear, from talking to immigrant Palestinian women who are young mothers, that the gender double standard concerning dating is going to change with this generation of Palestinian-American children. The overwhelming majority of women in this study said that they will not allow their daughters to date. They will not encourage their sons to do so either, but say what has been repeated numerous times, "You can't tell boys what to do, they just take their freedom." Sexual virginity at marriage is considered essential for girls, and these women say that they expect their daughters to remain virgins until marriage. Interestingly, these same women feel that men should have sexual experience before marriage, but they should have it with non-Arab women. Palestinian women are convinced that a man with sexual experience is more gentle and loving with his wife in bed.

The women in my study said they would let their daughters have more choice in who they married than they themselves had because the potential universe of marital partners is greater in the United States. Most of the women I spoke with said they would encourage their sons to marry Muslims but would insist on it for their daughters. A few women not from the traditional village subsector of the community said they would allow their daughters to marry non-Muslims, but under different conditions. Some said the man would have to convert to Islam. Others said that as long as the man was Palestinian, whether Christian or Moslem, they would approve the marriage; this latter from very politically active women. A very few said they would not use any force on their daughters if the daughter was determined to marry the man she loved. One woman said:

> I will not let my daughter date, but if she insisted on marrying other than an Arab Muslim, I would let her. Force is wrong when it comes to marriage, and I will try to accept what my daughter chooses.

✗ *Palestinian Women Compare Their Lives to Those of Women Who Have Countries*

It is nearly impossible to speak to a Palestinian woman about her life and not hear first about the tragedy of being a Palestinian. They say they carry the burden of statelessness on their backs and do not forget it, no matter what good fortune they may find outside of Palestine. Palestinian statelessness is a political reality that sets the normative order for the community. It also has concrete emotional effects on the daily lives of Palestinians. While Palestinian women assess the quality of their lives as compared with their mothers, Palestinian men, and American women, their primary focus is on the effects of statelessness on their daily lives. Palestinian women subsume many of the problems they face living in the United States under the problem of statelessness.

The three main attributes of their experiences of statelessness are:

1. a nagging pain—resulting from endless tales of suffering, either within their own family, among their friends, or on the part of Palestinians in general;

2. a feeling of always being unsettled, that life in any one place is temporary; and

3. the loneliness resulting from the dispersion of family members.

This nagging pain is difficult to describe in any tangible way except that it serves as a constant reminder to Palestinians, wherever they are and whatever their situation, that they should not allow themselves to be too happy or too content. Of course, there is tangible suffering that causes this pain. Every Palestinian has a story of family dispersion, land confiscation, torture, family members in prison, or harassments by military authorities. Beyond the personal, Palestinians, even those in the United States, say they suffer whenever bombs are dropped over the refugee camps in Lebanon, when massacres occur, and when youths are beaten by soldiers. The Palestinian pain is a communal pain and Palestinians feel that it is their national duty to bear it. In *After the Last Sky: Palestinian Lives*, Edward Said says that it is not possible to speak with certainty about how every Palestinian feels: "Ours has been too various and scattered a fate for that sort of correspondence. (1986: 5). However, he affirms the importance of suffering to collective and individual Palestinian lives. Said says that despite the varied and scattered fates of Palestinians, "we do in fact form a community, if at heart a community built on suffering and exile."

The mainstream American media exacerbate this communal pain. In the land of information and democracy, the Palestinians of this study feel that their suffering is discounted and their history purposely ignored. They feel that their lives and deaths are portrayed as meaningless, and that they have been reduced to a stereotype: terrorist.

> We have suffered a lot, but, when I look at the American television, I see that only Jews are people and capable of suffering. We are portrayed as madmen walking around with guns. When our people die, they don't show crying families at the funeral. Our lives mean nothing. Sometimes I feel like a knife is being turned in our bleeding wound.

The respondents described this persistent feeling of pain in various ways. For all of them, it throws a gray cover over their lives, no matter how good other aspects of their lives may be.

> I am getting a good education here, but sometimes it feels to me like I am dying day after day. Nobody cares about us. Everyone seems to want us to disappear. I want to be with my people.

As they transmit the Palestinian language and customs to their children, these women also plan to pass on the Palestinian pain, not with the intention of being sadistic, but as part of their national duty. They have varying methods of transmitting the Palestinian experience to their American-raised children. One way is to keep their children from being too spoiled:

> We don't allow ourselves to forget about what is going on
> back home. Even now I will not buy myself expensive clothes
> because I do not think it is right with what is going on there. I
> will not buy my baby toys either.

Another is to send their children to their homeland to witness life under
occupation themselves:

> Though my life is good, materially, here, I always feel the
> Palestinian problems. I dream to go back to my country some-
> day. Until then, I will raise my children as Palestinians. I want
> them to know our problems, to feel our suffering. I want them
> to live there and suffer the way we did. Our suffering has made
> us very strong.

Knowing that suffering is an integral part of the Palestinian collective
identity helps explain why Palestinian women tolerate some of the worst
aspects of their lives in the United States. They do not view them as an
outcome of gender inequalities in the culture. Rather, they see them as just
another result of having to live in exile—another pain they must suffer as
their fate as Palestinians. Consequently, women in the community who do
see the problems Palestinian women face in the United States as gender
issues and try to organize women on this basis do not receive the cooperation they might expect from other Palestinian women. Activists are further confronted with the charge that they are trying to de-Palestinianize
Palestinian women, in contradiction to the national drive to keep the
culture alive. Gender issues and political issues are ideologically en-
twined. This connection creates great obstacles when confronting gender
issues.

The Palestinian pain is augmented, as expressed by these Palestinians
living in exile, by a feeling of unsettledness and tentativeness. Wherever
they live, Palestinians live in two worlds. One is the world of survival,
which requires an orientation to the here and now. The other is the world
of returning to Palestine, which results in an ambiguous orientation to
almost any place of residence other than Palestine. In practice, responsibility for sustaining these two worlds is allocated by gender among Palestinians in the United States. The world of survival is the world that
Palestinian men in the United States sustain, while Palestinian women
sustain the world of return. The cultural division of labor is another
indication of the level to which gender and politics are integrated.

Palestinians living in many parts of the world believe that they could be uprooted and sent wandering at any time, and this feeling directs much of their day-to-day action. Palestinians in the United States are less vulnerable to fears of being expelled since most eventually are able to obtain American residency and citizenship rights through relatives or marriage to an American. Nonetheless, some of the recent United States government plans to deport and incarcerate some Palestinians for their political views struck some fear in the community. This tentative attitude towards life in the United States is expressed as follows:

No matter how much freedom we get here or how much money we make, we really do not belong here.

This tentativeness is accompanied by political alienation, which Palestinians say results from United States government policy toward them.

We are law-abiding American citizens who pay taxes, but no one wants to hear our voices. The American government does not treat us as people; it is not fair or objective about our problems. Like everyone else, the American government just wants us to go away.

Given the primacy of these sentiments on what it means to be a Palestinian and on life in exile, Palestinian women say that it is not possible to feel that they have a good life. The collective Palestinian view on exile transforms gender issues into national political issues, unresolvable among those in exile until nationhood is resolved. Gender issues in the homeland, however, can be confronted because there the culture is alive and real. It is, therefore, changeable.

Although these sentiments of exile are not unique to women, we have seen that the practical results of the statelessness of the Palestinians has created special burdens for Palestinian women in the United States. The dispersion of Palestinians that has resulted from statelessness and military occupation has physically, though not emotionally, broken up Palestinian families into pieces scattered about the globe. Family is extremely important in the Palestinian culture, but for women it is also the mainstay of their daily lives. It is their primary source of support and many times their sole devotion. Absence of family engenders a feeling of loneliness. As noted, Palestinian women have fewer alternatives than men for making a bad situation better. If they feel lonely they cannot readily jump into the car and go to a coffee shop; if they are single, they are not free to date Americans to dispel the loneliness. The end result is that even if given all the elements of what might objectively be considered a good life—health, a kind and healthy husband, nice children, a home, a solid financial base, and a meaningful daily life—Palestinian women, nonetheless, feel dissatisfied.

〰 Conclusion

The Palestinian women in this study report that their historical experience as Palestinians, and all that this entails, is the single largest detriment to the quality of their lives. Allowing for this feeling, they find that their lives have changed significantly from those of their mothers, mostly in a positive direction. They see that Palestinian men work hard and have many responsibilities, but they also have too many privileges. These women feel that American women are better off than Palestinian women in some ways, and worse off in other ways. Except for the fact that American women have a country, they would not want, for the most part, to trade their lives for those of American women. Finally, these Palestinian women believe that the fact of female hardship is universal. Were it not for their statelessness, their aggregate lives as women are no better or worse than other women's lives.

The women of this study seek changes in the traditional Palestinian cultural system, which gives them fewer rights than men. However, they are not prepared to completely abandon this system, for it provides them with community, support, security, and the promise of increasing power, status, and individual autonomy as they grow older. These advantages stand in contrast to their perceptions of American women's experiences, however limited these perceptions are by their membership in an insular ethnic community. These women found, however, that life in exile provides them with few of the traditional rewards for conformity with Palestinian values. This explains their view of their unsatisfactory situation in the United States as primarily a political problem rather than one of gender inequality, solvable only upon return to an intact Palestinian society free of foreign occupation.

※ References

Abadan-Unat, Nermin. 1977. "Implications of Migration on Emancipation and Pseudo-emancipation of Turkish Women." *International Migration Review* 6: 31–57.

Abu-Lughod, Ibrahim, ed. 1971. *The Transformation of Palestine*. Evanston, Il: Northwestern University Press.

Abu-Lughod, Janet. 1985, "The Continuing Expulsions From Palestine." In *Palestine: Continuing Dispossession*, ed. Glen Perry. Belmont, Mass.: Arab American University Graduates Press.

————. 1986. "The Demographic War for Palestine." *The Link*. New York: Americans for Middle East Understanding.

Aruri, Naseer, ed. 1983. *Occupation: Israel over Palestine*. Belmont, Mass.: Arab American University Graduates.

Alund, A. 1978. "The Immigrant Women: Emancipation via Consumption." *Ekot Fran Gardagen*. University of Umea, Sweden: Department of Sociology Research Report.

Barnard, Jessie. 1981. *The Female World*. New York: The Free Press.

Bonacich, Edna. 1973. "A Theory of Middleman Minorities." *American Sociological Review* 38, (October): 583–594.

Brouwer, L. and M. Preister. 1983. "Living in Between: Turkish Women in Their Homeland and in the Netherlands." In *One Way Ticket: Migration and Female Labour*, ed. Annie Philzacklea. London: Routledge and Kegan Paul.

Granqvist, Hilma. 1935. *Marriage Conditions in a Palestinian Village*, vol. 2. Helsingforts: Societa Scientarium Fennica. *International Migration Review*. 1984. Women In Migration (special issue) 48, no. 4.

Park, Robert. 1928. "Human Migration and the Marginal Man." *American Journal of Sociology* 33: 881–893.

Phizacklea, Annie, ed. 1983. *One Way Ticket: Migration and Female Labor*. London: Routledge and Kegan Paul.

Rosaldo, Michelle and Louis Lamphere. 1974. *Woman, Culture, and Society*. Stanford, Calif.: Stanford University Press.

Said, Edward. 1986. *After the Last Sky: Palestinian Lives*. New York: Pantheon.

Seller, Maxine Schwartz, ed. 1981. *Immigrant Women*. Philadelphia: Temple University Press.

BARBARA BILGÉ

Turkish-American Patterns of Intermarriage

Rapid expansion of global markets and increasing international migration during the nineteenth and twentieth centuries have brought once distant peoples of diverse cultural heritage into close contact. This contact has provided unprecedented opportunities for mating and intermarriage regardless of the ideological and legal barriers sometimes faced. Sociologists and anthropologists have long been fascinated by the causes, patterns, and consequences of intermarriage between members of different "racial," ethnic, religious, and national groups in complex industrial societies such as the United States. Their studies have been both theoretical and descriptive (see, for example, Barron 1946, 1972; Davis 1941; Merton 1941; Murguia 1982; Van den Berghe 1960; and Winch 1958). This chapter describes and analyzes intermarriages of American women to men born in the Republic of Turkey who settled in North America after World War II (1947–1969). Most came to earn degrees at universities in the United States and Canada to prepare for professions such as engineering and medicine and intended to return to their homeland to practice these professions, thereby helping their nation to modernize. However, whether already married to Turkish women or not, the majority chose to live in the United States or Canada after completing their educations. They and their

I am very grateful to Barbara C. Aswad for taking the time to read over my first draft of this chapter, and for her insightful comments and constructive suggestions.

59

families are now dispersed in the suburbs of both countries. This study focuses on the intermarried couples living in Michigan and adjacent Ontario. The Turkish families in this area constitute a small community characterized by friendship and frequent visits, despite the international border separating their residences and workplaces.

Three major concerns have informed sociological and anthropological research into intermarriage in the United States and Canada:

1. rates of intermarriage in relation to boundary maintenance/permeability between participating groups;

2. conflicts heterogamous couples often experience as a result of dissonance between their culturally structured values and behavioral styles, and the problems they and their children may encounter as a result of prejudice and discrimination from the larger society in which they live; and, only recently; and

3. the impact of gender hierarchies on rates and patterns of intermarriage between groups and the degree of marital satisfaction the couples achieve.

All of these topics are complex and will be discussed briefly below.

Assessments and explanations of rates of "interracial," interethnic, and interfaith marriages in the United States usually have dealt with heterogamy between members of a specific minority group and Euroamericans of the dominant "white" majority, compared the rates among groups, or reported statistics from a particular city, county, or state, or the entire nation (see Alba and Golden 1986; Barnett 1963; Blau, Blum, and Schwartz 1982; Bogelski 1961; Burma 1963; Heer 1974; Kikumura and Kitano 1973; Kitano et al. 1984; Lazerwitz 1987; Rosenthal 1963; Sanjek 1994; Sickles 1972; Tinker 1973; Williamson 1980; and Wong 1989). Marriages between people in different minority groups have been largely neglected by researchers (for an exception, see Labrack and Leonard 1984) as has marriage between whites of different European ancestries (however, see Alba and Golden 1986; and Kennedy 1944, 1952). The probable reason is that researchers often view minority-majority intermarriage rates as indices of the degree of structural assimilation of the minorities into the white American mainstream (see, for instance, Simpson and Yinger 1985: 296). Keeping in mind that the concept of "race" is a cultural construction, not a biological reality, periodic increases in rates of mating and marriage between African-Americans and Euroamericans scarcely have weakened the demarcation between the two groups see Sanjek 1994). Gender figures as importantly as "race" in the group affiliation of each conjugal partner and their offspring. Except perhaps among highly educated, professional elites today, a white wife of a black man is thought to have married "out" of her group, but her black husband remains in his group, which may not accept his wife. Both black wife and her white husband may be viewed as having married "out" of their communities of birth. Offspring of such unions, no matter how they may define themselves, are viewed by most whites as black and often are rejected by African-Americans, especially by their youthful peers. Except perhaps in states of the Deep South such as Louisiana, their continuing efforts to gain recognition as Creoles or mulattos have met with little success (Atkins 1991; *Detroit Free Press* 1982; and Wilkerson 1991). In contemporary marriages between Americans of East Asian ancestry and Euroamericans, both marital partners often enjoy affiliation with their own and one another's ethnic communities, as do their children. This phenomenon was not seen until the mid-1970s; indeed, such marriages were illegal in many states before the 1950s. The low rate of intermarriage between Americans of East Asian and African ancestry, however, has received little comment in the scholarly literature. In summary, historical transformations in "race" and gender hierarchies and conceptualizations are useful predictors of changes in rates and patterns of "interracial" mating and marriage. Nowhere are such transformations so well articulated as in the law.

Miscegenation laws prohibiting "interracial" sex, but much more stringently, mixed "race" marriages, first were enacted in the colonial South and then, after the Revolutionary War, in many territories and states as they joined the nation. In the South such laws specifically forbade whites from marrying "Negroes" or "mulattos." As the West was settled by Euroamericans in the nineteenth century, legislators in Western territories and states elaborated and expanded miscegenation laws to prohibit marriages between whites and Chinese, Japanese, Filipinos, Hawaiians, Hindus, and Native Americans. Many of these laws were not rescinded until 1967, when the U.S. Supreme Court ruled all such laws unconstitutional (see Pascoe 1991: 7, who notes that miscegenation laws, though mostly phrased generically, were designed to control white women's sexuality even as white men were permitted informal access to women of color). In no state, however, were whites forbidden to marry Turks,

Kurds, Iranians, Arabs, or Muslims, whose presence in this country was minuscule until the 1950s. The physiognomy of most Turks is similar enough to that of Euroamericans. Thus, even the twenty-five thousand Turkish and Kurdish men who immigrated to the United States before World War I and formed small communities in northern industrial cities were not singled out as a separate "race," despite the vicious anti-Turkish, anti-Muslim propaganda in the U.S. press attending the collapse of the Ottoman Empire (1923). By the time the second wave of Turks arrived on American shores, Turkey was a respected republic in the world's community of nations and anti-Turkish and anti-Muslim sentiments in the United States had subsided.

The social, cultural, and psychological dimensions of "racial," ethnic, and religious intermarriage require meticulous, humanistic analyses of the motivations, expectations, values, and material and social resources of heterogamous individuals within the cultural and subcultural contexts of the groups with which they are affiliated before and after marriage. A small body of social-psychological, psychological, clinical, and social-work literature addresses these issues. Most of it is group-specific; comparative studies are rare. Moreover, some heterogamous combinations are covered more fully than others: African-Americans, Japanese-Americans, and Korean-Americans with Euroamerican partners, or Jews wed to Gentiles, and Catholics to non-Catholics. Some of this literature is therapeutic in orientation, offering practical advice for a successful marriage and family life (see Aldridge 1978; Barron 1969; Berman 1968; Kiev 1973; Kim 1972; Lazerwitz 1981; Mayer 1980; Murguia 1982; Porterfield 1978; Poussaint 1983; Tseng et al. 1977; and Wagatsuma 1973). Research into other intermarriage combinations has been skimpy. Interesting data on marital satisfaction and family life of Arab Muslims wed to non-Muslim Euroamericans are reported by Elkholy (1966, 1971, 1988). The research findings on Turkish and American intermarried couples and their families presented below add to the budding literature on Muslim—non-Muslim intermarriages in North America.

This study of intermarried Turkish-American couples is derived from my research on variations in family structure and organization within the older and more recent Turkish communities in Michigan and nearby Ontario (Bilgé 1984). I identified thirty-three heterogamous couples in the post–World War II community; of these, I was able to gather comprehensive data on twenty-six and less complete data on the remaining seven. My association with this ethnic community began as a married-in, foreign insider and lasted twenty-one years, after which I divorced. However, I remain enmeshed in its webs of friendship and retain membership in the Turkish-American Cultural Association of Michigan (TACAM).

My primary method of gathering data was by participant observation, involving hundreds of informative contacts with the intermarried couples whose lives are here described. These contacts ranged from impromptu, casual intimate visits with one or more American women—with or without our Turkish husbands' presence, over coffee in someone's kitchen—to lavish, formal dinner parties. If someone fell ill, we visited that person at home or in the hospital. Some of the American wives, including myself, have been active in the Turkish-American Cultural Association of Michigan, both as officers and committee members, and we attend the Turkish and American national holiday celebrations, religious festivities (*bayramlar*), balls, dinners, picnics, and cultural events the association organizes. I wrote extensive field notes after participating in these events which I supplemented by analyses of photos taken on these occasions. Pictorial evidence freezes moments in time and gives clues to the cultural frames guiding demeanor and spatial interaction of family members with one another and with outsiders.

Information on the quality of a marriage, decision-making processes within the family, child-rearing dogmas and practices, and attitudes and behavior toward elders becomes comprehensible only through long-term, repeated observations of people interacting in a variety of settings—their homes, other people's homes, and diverse public places; by exchanging information; giving and accepting advice; and listening to what people say about one another and about the researcher. Reliable data on such topics simply cannot be gleaned just by asking questions of strangers during a formal interview. Even the most truthful respondent has blind spots. My long-term association with the Turkish community's intermarried couples has given me many opportunities to deepen my knowledge of their outlooks, concerns, aspirations, and behavioral strategies for achieving valued goals, as well as my own.

Information on educational attainment, occupational and residential histories, visits to relatives in Turkey, visits to purely Turkish and to mixed families, and memberships in various organizations was most efficiently gathered by questionnaire. These and other questions were answered during ethnographic interviews conducted from 1978 to 1984 with twenty-five of the thirty-three couples. They were told about my research objectives, that their confidentiality would be protected in the final article, that they could refuse to answer any question they felt invaded their privacy, and that they could terminate the interview at any time. Respondents included all the wives and some of their husbands.

The interviews were launched by charting genealogies and taking family histories, after which questions on the questionnaire were answered. This sequence worked well, engaging the Turkish husbands in discussion, for most Turks thoroughly enjoy talking about their ancestors, collateral relatives, who married whom, and when children were born. By the time we got to the questionnaire, our discourse was relaxed and cordial. The whole process took three to six hours, with occasional follow-up visits or telephone conversations. Interviews were not taped, but extensive notes were taken. Interaction between spouses during joint interviews was carefully noted. In some cases, husbands and wives were interviewed separately. They sometimes offered discrepant information and divergent perspectives on their relationship. Children often breezed in, and their interactions with parents, and with me, also were noted.

My data on the community are continually updated as I go to the showers, marriage ceremonies, and funerals of its members and converse with them in many other social situations. Research results are quantified below whenever possible for descriptive clarity and meaningful comparisons. The complex, virtually unmeasurable, qualitative dimensions of social phenomena yielded by participant observation are characterized as precisely and lucidly as possible.

🕸 Community Formation and Structure

The post–World War II Turkish community of metropolitan Detroit and adjacent Ontario was formed during the late 1940s through the 1960s, when students from Turkey came to North America to earn degrees at U.S. and Canadian universities. The overwhelming majority were males aged twenty to thirty-five. Many already were married to Turkish women. They either were accompanied by their wives or were able to bring them over within a year of their own arrival. Among the institutions of higher learning receiving Turkish students was the University of Michigan, graduates of which form the core of suburban Detroit's present Turkish-American population. Nevertheless, many Turks who attended universities elsewhere in Michigan, in other states, or in Canada settled in Michigan after completing their degrees. They constitute a typical post–World War II "brain drain" immigrant community. Peripherally associated with the core community are twenty-three Turkish families and a few individual Turks who came to Michigan from the 1950s through the 1970s in quest of work rather than a higher education. About 8 percent of all the couples are heterogamous. Children of the community founders are now young adults, and many of them are married and have children of their own.

Most members of Michigan's post–World War II Turkish community never cultivated friendships with their pre–World War II predecessors. In the 1960s when the newer community was crystallizing and the older community still boasted a few hundred people, members of the two groups rarely socialized together. Two factors account for the disjunction between the two communities. The first is demographic. The new community consists primarily of families, while the older one was composed predominantly of never-married men. The few couples in the older community were mostly mixed, and their U.S.–born children were largely assimilated into the white American mainstream, taking little interest in their Turkish heritage. When the more recent immigrants were just establishing their first households, often in the same or adjoining neighborhoods where many of the old timers lived, the older group was approaching or had reached retirement. Newcomers with growing family obligations did not seek out the company of the aging bachelors who convened in local Turkish coffeehouses. In fact, only a few new community members even knew of the existence of the earlier community until a 1976 Turkish-American exhibit at Detroit's International Institute. By the mid-1970s, less than a dozen of the elderly Turks survived (Bilgé 1984, 1994).

The second factor is sociocultural. Disparities in educational attainment, occupation, and income level further separated old and new community members. Nothing really fostered empathy and cooperation across community boundaries except pride in the achievements of the Turkish Republic and religious affiliation. While on limited incomes during their years as students or interns, few newly arrived Turkish couples celebrated their national and religious holidays with their senior compatriots at the South Dearborn Turkish Crescent coffeehouse, which was closed in 1968. As the incomes of the young couples rose and they moved into Detroit's affluent suburbs, they preferred to observe these holidays in more luxurious settings, such as expensive hotel ballrooms, where they could dance after a catered dinner. The new community did not continue the older community's charitable societies. Instead, a few doctors and engineers and their Turkish wives founded a new ethnic organization, TACAM, in 1972.

Focusing on the intermarried couples, differences in socioeconomic background within the cohort of post–World War II Turkish immigrant men here described, their diverse paths to North America, and their American wives' ethnicities and social class origins have produced significant variations in their family relations. Nevertheless, they can be categorized into three major groups: working-class families; middle-class, ex-military Turks and their non-Turkish spouses; and families of affluent doctors and engineers who were civilians when they were students in the United States or Canada. Couples within each category show similar family dynamics but differ significantly in this respect from couples of the other categories.

🕰 *Working-Class Families*

Eight of the thirty-three mixed couples are working class. I interviewed one couple in depth, had frequent contacts with them and three more couples until 1984, and have enjoyed sporadic contacts with them ever since. With two more couples, I have had ongoing, but infrequent, encounters. The two other couples are known to me only through what others have told me about them and through announcements in ethnic newsletters.

The Turkish men were born in villages, of peasant families, or in provincial towns, of small shopkeeper or artisan families. All of them completed elementary school in Turkey. One received no further education. Two graduated from technical institutes in Turkey. Another became a pilot in the Turkish air force and was sent to Canada for further training. There he met and married a Canadian woman and stayed. He secured a job on the assembly line at the 3M plant in London, Ontario, joined the union, was elected to represent workers in his unit, and eventually rose to a leading position in the union administration. One technical-institute graduate met his American wife while she was vacationing in Istanbul in the late 1970s. They married in Turkey, and he returned to the United

States with her. She, alone among the wives of this group, is a college graduate, certified in elementary education. Her husband obtained a job as an auto mechanic in Dearborn, Michigan, where they settled. A few men came illegally to the United States or Canada, but their marriages to citizens of these countries and sponsorship by employers paved the way for them to gain legal immigrant status. The American wives were mostly from working-class families, had completed high school, and worked as clerks, secretaries, or waitresses until their marriages. They are of mixed or pure Sicilian, French, Polish, and Hungarian Catholic ancestry, or of Anglo-Canadian ethnicity.

Of the four couples I know best, two are happy in their marriages, but the other two experience difficulties, according to the wives. All working-class marital partners shared similar conjugal role expectations, but problems arose when both spouses became dissatisfied with one another's role performances. Both spouses expected husbands to be good providers and wives to keep house and raise children. Cooperation between spouses was oriented toward these goals. Neither spouse expected to discuss their deepest feelings or philosophy of life with the other but did expect sexual fidelity, common courtesy, and consideration of their reasonable needs in their relationship. Husbands and wives sought close friendship and recreation in same-sex social networks. Wives had no objections to their husbands' weekly "night out with the boys," usually non-Turkish co-workers, of bowling or playing cards. Wives assumed husbands would not meddle in their activities with female kin and chums from their high-school days. The women would meet for luncheon in someone's home or in a mall, and then play cards, shop, or go to a matinée, always getting home when the children came home from school. The wives' female friends often were married to their husbands' male friends, and these couples hosted one another for dinner on weekends or went on picnics together. Though husbands and wives sat next to each other at the dinner table, they usually broke into same-sex activity and conversation groups afterwards.

None of the working-class couples are divorced. All of them have children, ranging from two to six per couple. In some families all the children have undergraduate degrees, and a few have masters degrees. The young men work as chemical engineers, computer-software engineers, or manage electronic firms. The young women are social workers, medical technicians, or real-estate brokers. Thus, they have become middle-to upper-middle-class. Most now are married and have children. None so far has wed anyone of Turkish ancestry or a Muslim. Like their parents before them, they do not go to local mosques. Though sometimes intrigued with their Turkish heritage, they are well assimilated into the white, Catholic-American and Anglo-Canadian mainstreams.

To convey a sense of the quality of family life among these couples, we should look at two cases. The first is a vignette of a troubled marriage; the second, a lengthier portrayal of a satisfactory marriage.

ORHAN AND GINA

Married in 1965, Orphan and Gina have a daughter, born in 1967, and a son, born in 1969. A stocky, but attractive woman, Gina is a Detroiter of Sicilian and French ancestry. She graduated from high school in 1953 and then worked as a secretary until her wedding in a Roman Catholic church. In 1978 Orphan was a laborer on the Chrysler assembly line and toiled long hours. The family lived in a modest, single-family home in a working- to middle-class suburb north of Detroit. By phone, Gina informed me that she had been elected vice-president of her children's school's PTA. Her husband, eavesdropping on another line, had not known this before, and he angrily expressed his displeasure.

On other occasions, when Orphan was not present, Gina told me he bossed her around and had an explosive temper. He did not, however, abuse her physically. He curtailed her social activities by giving her little extra money when she requested any for entertaining friends at home or giving her father a lavish birthday party. So she earned pin money by holding garage sales or selling various product lines for a while at parties she scheduled at other peoples' homes. She was contemplating returning to work part time as a secretary.

SOPHIA AND HASAN

Sophia and Hasan married in 1964. He was born in a mountain village near the Black Sea, where his family owned land. His father sold, in the local town, the walnuts, tea, and green corn he grew on the farm. In 1940, at age seven, Hasan went to Istanbul to work for an older cousin in the latter's bakeries and grocery stores. He shared a tiny cubicle with his cousin, who cheated him out of his wages, so in 1953 at age twenty he quit. In 1955 Hasan was hired as a steward on a Turkish cargo ship headed for Belgium, then Caribbean and Gulf of Mexico ports. He jumped ship in November in Mobile, Alabama. Speaking no English but determined to stay in the United States, he hopped on a bus with a Turkish friend and ended up in Dearborn at the Salinas Street Turkish Crescent coffeehouse. There his compatriots found him work at the Lockjoint Pipe Company. Perhaps tipped off by a Turkish Crescent member, immigration authorities eventually caught up with him at work, and he was deported. He went voluntarily to Windsor, Ontario, and worked illegally at odd jobs—washing dishes in a barbecue joint, setting tables at a fancy hotel.

In Windsor, a go-between arranged a contractual marriage for Hasan with an American woman. In 1958, he got his green card and was rehired by Lockjoint. He moonlighted for his pal, "George the Greek," a co-worker who taught him welding and who owned a restaurant and travel agency in Detroit's Greektown. Hasan met his future bride, Sophia, at her grandfather's house on Easter Sunday, 1962. Hasan and her uncle lifted weights at the local YMCA and had become friends; her uncle had invited Hasan to Easter dinner. Sophia is of Polish and Hungarian ancestry and always has been a devout Catholic. Hasan was attracted to her immediately. She was greeting relatives with kisses when he arrived, and he asked, "How about me?" She quipped, "Wait until I know you better!" He liked that.

Hasan did not ask Sophia out until December. After three months of dating, he proposed marriage, and she accepted. Besides, his friend, George the Greek approved of her. The only impediment to their marriage was Hasan's still existing contractual marriage, about which he confided to Sophia's uncle. She found out and became very depressed. As she put it, "I didn't stick around." She had dreamed of being married in the Catholic church. How could she marry Hasan, after he divorced his first wife, in the church? He sought her out and swore he had "never kissed his first wife or gone to bed with her." Sophia and Hasan decided to consult a priest in Windsor who had befriended and helped Hasan there in years past. The priest was able to have Hasan's first marriage annulled, as it had not been sanctioned by the church and thus was invalid in the eyes of the church. Hasan legally divorced his first wife in 1963. Sophia and Hasan finally were married by the Windsor priest in her metropolitan Detroit Catholic church. Sophia had met Hasan before she graduated from high school. While she took classes at night in business school after graduating, she also worked as a payroll supervisor during her engagement to save money to pay for her wedding and reception. Her wedding was splendid! Hasan became a naturalized U.S. citizen in 1965.

When first married, Sophia and Hasan moved into the house in Dearborn's South end where he had been renting a room. His landlord moved out and rented them the whole house. The next year they took out a mortgage on a two-story home near Detroit's Tiger baseball stadium and rented the upstairs flat to an ex-military Turk and his Turkish wife. The rent received covered their mortgage payments. This home was just across the street from where Sophia's grandfather and mother lived. In 1972 Hasan and his family moved to a tri-level home on a large lot in a rural township south and west of Detroit.

Sophia continued working until 1966, when Hasan found a job as welder at Ford's new Woodhaven plant, and the first of their two daughters was born. The second girl was born in 1970. Hasan worked the four-to-midnight shift, often worked overtime, and retired in 1994. Sophia always has managed their joint checking account, into which Hasan deposited his entire paycheck, minus a little "gas money." They shop together, using many credit cards, which they pay in full at the end of each month. Hasan deplores paying interest on extended credit.

Hasan is handy at repairing appliances. He built and finished custom-fitted, corner shelves in the girls' bedrooms, and he helped Sophia wallpaper the girls' bedrooms. He mows the lawn, Sophia gardens and cleans the outdoor pool. She does most of the indoor cleaning, laundry, and cooking, but Hasan barbecues meat outside in summertime and often dries the dishes. As the girls reached their teen years, they did chores and worked part-time baby-sitting or as clerks in retail stores. The older girl earned money to purchase curtains and a comforter for her bedroom.

Though Sophia mainly disciplined their daughters, Hasan always backed her up. In 1978 the teenage girls sometimes boldly contradicted their parents, who barked at or swatted them if they got out of hand. The girls generally observed the limits their parents set on their behavior. Hasan and Sophia often hugged and joked freely with their daughters, who reciprocated affectionately. In 1978 the older girl became engaged to an American youth, whom both Sophia and Hasan liked and made comfortable in their presence. But they warned the two, "no sex before marriage!" The wedding was held six months later.

Hasan and Sophia moved to Florida in 1994. Both daughters remained in Michigan. The older one was completing a B.S. in math at a local university. The younger had graduated from a nearby university and now works as a dietician at the University of Michigan hospital complex. Sophia and Hasan have an eight-year-old granddaughter. Sophia and Hasan went to Turkey and traveled through Europe in the summer of 1994. They had not been to Turkey since 1969.

Hasan never brought relatives from Turkey to the United States. Very few Turkish objects could be seen in their house in 1978; the decor was American colonial. Though Hasan still identifies as a Muslim, he does not observe daily prayers or fast during *Ramadan*; he has no particular desire to make the pilgrimage to Mecca. In the summer of 1978 his wife and teenaged daughters wore shorts, tank tops, and bathing suits in mixed company. The girls dated and went to their high-school proms. Furthermore, Hasan often accompanied Sophia and their daughters to mass on Sundays, for he had agreed to rear them as Catholics. The family celebrates Christmas and Easter with all the trappings.

Hasan is amiable, accommodating, energetic, and intelligent. But Sophia rules the roost, albeit most pleasantly. The daughters are neither ashamed of nor particularly interested in their Turkish heritage. They seem thoroughly Americanized.

⚜ *Middle-Class, Ex-military Families*

My association with the twelve heterogamous couples in this group, compared with the couples in the other two groups, is of longest duration, for I became one of them with my own marriage in 1959. Intensive participant observation has been ongoing, even when couples moved away from Michigan; visiting, telephone conversations, and letters have served to keep us in touch over the years. I interviewed nine couples, mapped their genealogies, and wrote up their life histories. Two of the couples not interviewed had moved out of the state by the time I began intensive research in the community. The third declined my interview request.

In the mid-1970s, I also located three older ex-military officers who married American women in the late 1940s. They studied in Germany and the United States in the 1930s and early 1940s, went home to Turkey in 1941 when the United States entered World War II, and returned to this country when the war ended in 1945. They experienced the military constraint described below and worked as engineers with middle-class incomes in the United States. However, their marital and family life resembled that of the affluent group more than that of others in the ex-military group for reasons suggested below.

Military Constraint

Under the stimulus of the U.S.-Turkish North Atlantic Treaty Organization (NATO) Agreement in 1952, Turkey endeavored to upgrade the technical training of its high-ranking military personnel. Groups of officers were dispatched by the Turkish army, navy, and air force each year from about 1955 through 1965 to study different fields of engineering at several American universities. The Turkish government paid their tuition and for their text books and gave each student a monthly living allotment ($250.00 in the early 1960s) during his college years. In addition the salary he would have earned, as determined by his current rank, was deposited in a bank account in his name, or that of a designee, in Turkey.

Officers selected for the privilege of studying abroad qualified by means of their scores on a day-long, written examination administered annually by each branch of the Turkish armed forces. Of the hundreds who took the test each year, only the top twenty in each branch were sent to America. Every Turkish university student sponsored by the military was required to earn a B.S. degree within five years of matriculation. Two-year extensions were granted to applicants who wished to acquire the M.S. Very few of these students dropped out of college before completing the B.S., and about 60 percent earned the M.S. degree as well.

Turkish officers came to the University of Michigan in units of twenty. Each unit had a leader who periodically reported on the status of its members by letter to the appropriate military attache in Washington, D.C. Students were all males, seventeen to thirty-five years of age; approximately 50 percent were not married on arrival. All the officers entered the United States with student visas but were issued diplomatic passports within a year.

Every career officer chosen to attend an American university had to sign a contract with the Turkish government pledging to return to Turkey after acquiring his degree and to serve his remaining years of military duty, as calculated from his date of enlistment. Breach of contract brought discharge and incurred an enormous debt. Nevertheless, within six years of departure from the United States, two officers already married to Turkish women and two more who wed Turkish women after returning home managed to resign from the armed forces and immigrate to the United States with their families, and 50 percent of the men who were unwed on arrival married American women and settled in the United States. The purely Turkish and mixed couples became friends and formed a closely knit visiting network within the larger Turkish community. Another ex-pilot who was sent to Canada for training and wed an Anglo-Catholic Canadian woman joined this network. The aforementioned three senior officers and their wives, however, were not a part of it.

Turkish military men who married American women broke the military code that governed them, as no Turk could be wed to a foreigner while in military service. In 1980 the Turkish Parliament finally declared this archaic military rule unconstitutional.

The Turkish military regulations of the 1960s and 1970s forced the mixed couples to remain in North America; most of the debts they thereby incurred were around twenty thousand U.S. dollars in 1965. To pay them off in Turkish liras would have been well nigh impossible. Rates of exchange then were unfavorable and have become increasingly more so over the years. Although a discharged, indebted ex-officer living in Turkey could not be jailed, his government could garnishee a portion of his earnings until his debt plus interest was paid in full. The two American families who eventually offered their sons-in-law money for debt repayment in the mid-1970s did so only after they felt certain that their daughter and son-in-law would not leave the United States to settle in Turkey. Thus, Turkey lost the skills of several well educated military officers whose American wives, at least at first, were willing to live with their husbands in Turkey. Most Turkish officers who wed Americans remained loyal to their homeland and initially did not want to reside in North America.

Husbands' Backgrounds

The three senior ex-military officers who married American women in the late 1940s were born into genteel Istanbul families. One was headed by a medical colonel in the Ottoman army, another, by a rear admiral in the Ottoman navy. I lack information on the third. The two men's fathers were university graduates and described as "progressive." Often away from home for long periods, the fathers were not involved in the sons' daily upbringing. Both men were reared primarily by domestic servants supervised by their mother or step-mother. More or less left to their own devices in their youth, they were lonely youngsters. Neither recalls ever having been beaten or verbally abused. They were disciplined by being deprived of privileges and were praised for good behavior. All three men entered a military academy at the junior high–school level. Their outstanding academic achievement qualified them for further training at the prestigious Roberts College in Istanbul, where they became proficient in English. Then they were sent to universities abroad.

Most post-1955 Turkish military cadets were of different social origin. They tended to come from working- and lower-middle-class families of major cities and provincial towns and were ethnically diversified— Turkmen, Circassians, Georgians, Laz, and Kurds as well as Turks. Fathers of the junior ex-military officers in this study included an urban policeman, an electrician, copper and brass workers, a baker with a grocery store, an owner of a small retail dry-goods store, and a public-health aide in a remote district. Many of these families were one generation removed from small land-holding peasants. Fathers typically struggled to provide a decent living for their wives and children. There were no servants in these households. Mothers were full-time homemakers. Many fathers felt they could not continue to feed and house their sons beyond the mandatory years of public schooling. A military career was virtually the only legitimate route of upward social mobility for ambitious sons of such families during the late 1940s and 1950s. One man's father died when he was just a child, so he enlisted in the air force to support his widowed mother and siblings when he reached the appropriate age. None of these ex-military Turks went to Robert College; they were very fortunate to have been selected to study at North American universities.

Two fathers were loyal supporters of Ataturk's secular government and echoed his atheism, prohibiting their wives and children from praying at neighborhood mosques. Fathers of the others ranged from devout to nominal Muslims. All the men's mothers were devout Muslims. A few could read and write Turkish in the old Arabic script, but none became literate in Turkish as written in the new Latin alphabet.

In big cities such as Istanbul, where the men's families lived among strangers rather than kin, their fathers expended much energy guarding family honor, which is culturally vested in the purity of their women. They, therefore, curtailed their wives' ventures outside the home and tried to isolate them from neighbors. Most teenage daughters were removed from school as soon as the law allowed and were secluded, but not veiled, until marriages could be arranged for them. A few urban fathers expressed frustration and anger by shouting at and striking their wives and also beat their children, particularly sons who displeased them.

Parents of the ex-military Turks whose families had been established in towns for a few generations usually were enmeshed in a web of kin. Unrelated families had been neighbors for years, and their children played together in the streets in age-graded, sex-segregated peer groups. Both men and women had access to a pool of related and unrelated same-sex companions who could provide practical aid and emotional support in times of duress or intervene if a wife or child was being maltreated.

Thus, contrasts in social milieu created distinctive family atmospheres despite the unitary cultural definition of honor and pervasive social segregation of the sexes. Patriarchy was harshest among isolated, working-class, urban families; ameliorated by kin and neighbor support in small towns; and rarely expressed in genteel families with fathers whose jobs required long absences from home.

WIVES' BACKGROUNDS

Of the twelve American and one English-born women who wed Turkish military men, three had working-class parents and, as children, had lived in modest, but adequate urban dwellings. Nine women were daughters of middle- to upper-middle– class families with varying amounts of wealth. Their childhood homes ranged from a pleasant row house in an East Coast metropolis to stately residences in Detroit's suburbs, small cities in southern Michigan, and London, Ontario. (See Table 1.)

The women all grew up in nuclear-family households. Seven families were geographically distant from other relatives and saw them rarely or not at all. Five maintained frequent contacts with grandparents, aunts and uncles, and cousins. One woman was an only child. The others had from one to seven siblings. Parents of six of the women were described as happy in marriage; parents of three, as having satisfactory marriages; and parents of the remaining three, as experiencing problem-ridden marriages.

TABLE I
SOCIAL BACKGROUNDS OF WOMEN MARRIED TO
EX-MILITARY TURKS

WIVES' PARENTS'		WIVES' FATHERS'	
CITIZENSHIP	ETHNICITY	RELIGION	OCCUPATION
1 American	Polish-American	Roman Catholic	Tool and die maker
2 Naturalized American	English-American	Episcopalian	Accountant
3 American	Jewish-American	None	Dry cleaning equipment salesman, owns own business
4 Canadian	Irish-Canadian	Roman Catholic	Insurance Agent
5 American	Anglo-American	Episcopalian	Owner and manager of shoe factory
6 American	French-Canadian	None	Machine parts salesman, owns own business
7 American	German-American	Lutheran	Guidance counselor
8 American	Anglo-American	Presbyterian	Owner of landscaping business
9 American	Anglo-American	None	Tool and die maker
10 American	Anglo-American	Protestant	Upper manager in corporation
11 American	Scotch; Irish-American; Native Indian	Baptist	Middle manager in corporation
12 British	English	None	Tool and die maker

Control of the family income by a domineering, stingy husband who withheld financial information from his wife characterized all three unhappy parent teams. One woman's father was chronically unemployed and alcoholic; he physically and verbally abused his wife.

All women, nonetheless, described their childhoods as basically pleasant and carefree, although four suffered verbal abuse, which eroded their self esteem. Some women, attractive by objective standards, worried about their physical imperfections. No matter what skills they possessed, they

TABLE I CONTINUED

SOCIAL BACKGROUNDS OF WOMEN MARRIED TO
EX-MILITARY TURKS

ETHNICITY	WIVES' MOTHERS' RELIGION	OCCUPATION AFTER MARRIAGE
1 Polish-American	Roman Catholic	Homemaker
2 English-American	Episcopalian	Homemaker
3 French-Canadian American	Roman Catholic	Homemaker
4 English-Canadian	Episcopalian	Homemaker
5 Anglo-American	Episcopalian	Homemaker
6 Polish-American	Roman Catholic	Homemaker
7 Anglo-American	Protestant	Homemaker
8 Anglo-American	Presbyterian	Public-school teacher
9 Anglo-American	Lutheran	Social worker; public-school teacher
10 Anglo-American	Protestant	Homemaker
11 Scotch-Irish American	Protestant	Homemaker; secretary; practical nurse
12 English	Protestant	Homemaker

were convinced their value on the marriage market lay in their beauty and charming personalities.

The highest educational diploma or degree and the occupations of the twelve couples at marriage are listed in Table 2. Seven women said both parents encouraged them to get a college education, chiefly to acquire occupational credentials in case they never married or their marriages failed. However, their parents thought that active pursuit of a career was inappropriate for a married woman. Only three women thought otherwise

TABLE 2

EDUCATION AND OCCUPATION OF MIXED EX-MILLITARY
COUPLES AT MARRIAGE

	HIGHEST DEGREE EARNED		OCCUPATION	
	HUSBAND	WIFE	HUSBAND	WIFE
1	M.S.	High school	Engineer	Beautician
2	M.S.	M.A.	Captain, Turkish army	With Red Cross
3	M.S.	B.A.	Engineer	Public-school teacher
4	Military academy	High school	Sales personnel	Retail clerk
5	B.S.	B.A.	Engineer	Public-school teacher
6	Military academy	B.F.A.	University student	Museum exhibit designer
7	M.S.	M.A.	Engineer	Librarian
8	B.S.	B.A.	Engineer	Editorial assistant
9	M.S.	B.A.	Engineer	Public-school teacher
10	M.S.	B.A.	University lecturer	None
11	M.S.	B.A.	Engineer	Real-estate agent
12	M.S.	High School	Engineer	Nanny-governess

when they reached the threshold of matrimony. The parents of one woman worried that a college education might deter their daughter's chances of landing a husband, because men shun "girls" who are too intellectual. Thus, for most of these women, pressures to marry overrode full commitment to a career. Yet, on the eve of their weddings, many were well educated and held interesting jobs.

COURTSHIP AND WEDDINGS

Several factors promoted a 50 percent out-marriage rate among the unwed Turkish military students in North America at mid-twentieth century. First, no single Turkish females of comparable background were enrolled at their American universities, although a handful of young women from elite Turkish families were then studying at prestigious American institutions of higher learning. Second, the men were in their youthful prime, at an age when they probably would have married had they remained in

Turkey. Third, they were unaccustomed to the American-style casual dating and romance. Most latched on to the first woman they dated more than twice, fell deeply in love with her, and proposed marriage.

The Turks were persistent and ardent suitors, often jealous of their sweethearts' other friends. They wanted to spend the bulk of every evening with their girl friends. In retrospect, many of the women feel that their suitors were possessive. Yet these same women valued their Turkish suitors' honorable intentions. So many American university men they had dated once or twice and then rejected had just wanted sex without commitment to marriage. Moreover, upon proposing, the Turks explained their contractual dilemma with the Turkish government should they wed a foreigner. None of them tried to deceive their future wives.

Couples first met at parties—a dance after a soccer game, a sorority mixer for foreign students, a "wild bash" thrown by a roommate at her parents' home, or a sedate university-sponsored tea for international students. One couple met at a fast-food restaurant they both regularly patronized, another at the home of a mutual friend on Christmas Eve. The Turk sent to Canada spotted his future bride strolling on the street and, entranced by the shimmer of the sun upon her hair, struck up a conversation on the pretext that he was lost.

All couples began dating within three weeks of their first encounter. They went to parties, college sports events, or an occasional movie, but rarely to concerts, plays, or special lectures. The Turks purchased serviceable, used cars as soon as they could afford them. Many dates culminated in love-making, either in their cars or in their rented rooms. Eight women had dated Americans before meeting their Turkish husbands-to-be. Of these, three said they had had sexual intercourse with a few previously. Five said they had not, but confessed to having indulged in light petting. Five mixed couples enjoyed sexual intercourse before marriage. One couple went to bed together on their first date. Another couple first slept together in the week-long interval between their engagement and wedding. Seven women were virgins on marriage, although they had "done everything but" with their Turkish fiances beforehand. The marital relations of virgins on marriage who once dated American men, and of women who never had gone out with anyone but their Turkish husbands but slept with them before their weddings, were troubled. Their Turkish husbands came to doubt their purity and fidelity. Ironically, some of these doubting Turks had a few sexual encounters with prostitutes and/or gullible young women in their homeland before coming to North America.

Courtships varied considerably in duration. Length of time between first meeting and marriage proposal ranged from a month to five years, and between proposal and wedding, from one week to five years. One Turk wed an American women before he completed his undergraduate program, but was not "discovered" until he received his B.S. The others waited until they had a B.S. or M.S. in hand. Unit leaders ordinarily learned of these unions shortly after the weddings but postponed filing official reports as long as possible.

Brides were from twenty to twenty-seven years old, and grooms, twenty-two to thirty-five at the time of their marriage. Three wives were three to four years older than their husbands. Seven husbands were two to ten years older than their wives. In two cases, the spouses were the same age.

All the men married without telling their parents. When they did tell them it was by letter, from one month to five years after the fact. Three of the couples eloped, informing the women's parents of their weddings two days to six months afterwards. Parents or siblings of the bride attended only five of the weddings. Marriage ceremonies included perfunctory pronouncements of wedlock by busy justices-of-the-peace, simple rites in a chapel, and two lavish church weddings. Three Turks took instructions in Catholicism, promising to bring their children up as Catholics, in compliance with their brides' wish that their marriage be sanctified by the church. Couples who were married in quick, civil ceremonies lack memories of their weddings as special occasions. One couple drove to Lansing, Michigan, were united by a "repulsively sanctimonious" justice-of-the-peace with a few friends as witnesses, and then dined out at a "greasy little restaurant." Returning to their new flat in Detroit, the bride ironed the groom's shirts.

RELATIONS WITH KIN

THE BRIDE'S SIDE. Interaction between mixed ex-military couples and the bride's relatives have depended upon the number of her living kin, her closeness to them, and how they and her Turkish husband have reacted to one another. Some parents of the wives died before their daughters' marriages or shortly afterwards.

Surviving parents of four women emphatically did not welcome their Turkish sons-in-law into the family. In one case, the wife's father rejected his son-in-law for three years, then softened; thereafter, he and his daughter and her family enjoyed warm, weekly contacts. He sometimes gave them money. In another case, a resentful husband stirred up trouble, to his wife's grief. The wife tried to cover her husband's dislike of her relatives and to nurture ties with them in spite of his frequently unpleasant opposition. In the most extreme case, the husband ordered his mother-in-law out of his home and told her never to come back. A few years later, the rift was bridged when the mother apologized to him, but hostilities between the two flared anew ten years later. In the other two cases of ill feeling between a Turkish husband and his in-laws, the Turk eventually adopted the strategy of avoiding them, but not meddling in his wife's relationship with them.

Parents of six women discouraged their daughter's prospective marriage before her engagement, but made an effort to welcome their Turkish sons-in-law when the wedding was imminent or an accomplished fact. These parents do not interfere in the marriages, but are willing to give their daughters refuge if needed. Transactions between the six couples and the brides' parents and grandparents include visiting, gift exchanges, and occasional financial assistance from the brides' families. Some brides' mothers helped their daughters with newborn babies but rarely baby-sat with their grandchildren.

THE GROOM'S SIDE. Five couples lived in Turkey for a year or two after their marriage. They did not disclose their marital status to Turkish military officials, and husbands continued to serve in their respective branches of the Turkish armed forces. Eventually the men grew disenchanted with their situations, resigned their commissions, were formally discharged, and quickly left the country before they were billed for their debt.

Two foreign wives, while living in Turkey, had difficulties with domineering mothers-in-law who rejected them. The other three were befriended by kindly mothers-in-law, hard-working women whom they came to love and admire. The two surviving fathers-in-law of brides who lived briefly in Turkey received them warmly into their homes, as did all the grooms' siblings.

Of the seven couples who never lived in Turkey, three never visited there, while four did. Three of the four traveled there after resolution of their military debts, some twelve to fourteen years after they were married. One of the four did not visit Turkey until thirty-nine years after he settled in the United States and seventeen years after his first wife's death. His second wife, a Turkish psychiatrist from Michigan, helped him pay off his debt to the Turkish government. They toured their homeland and visited her kin, but the relatives he had known in childhood were long since dead.

Another Turk who did not return to Turkey until the late 1980s, and then with his second American wife, brought his relatives to America for three-month visits while still married to his first American wife. He brought his parents in the summer of 1965, his widowed mother and married sister in the summer of 1976, and his mother and sister's older daughter in 1979. His first wife liked his kin more than she liked him, yet she never visited them in Turkey, though she wished to do so. Two Turkish husbands brought many siblings to North America for visits. In all cases, the Turkish American couple paid all the traveling expenses.

Three ex-military Turks helped a relative immigrate to North America. Two immigrants are brothers of their sponsors. Both pairs of brothers have drifted apart because of differences in life style. Instead of two expanded kindreds in North America, the brothers make up four separated family units. One childless ex-military couple adopted the husband's young second cousin with the permission of the boy's natural parents, giving the boy educational advantages he lacked in Turkey.

FACTORS AFFECTING MARITAL RELATIONS

Most ex-military Turks and their foreign brides entered matrimony with radically different expectations about conjugal roles and family life. They also held contrasting ground rules for negotiation of decisions and for conflict resolution within marriage. With two notable exceptions, ex-military Turks envisioned a husband as a primary provider for the family, its leader, major decision-maker, and guardian of its honor. As noted above, family honor among Turks depends upon the purity of its women and is demonstrated in their modesty and circumspect behavior. These men expected their wives never to contradict them openly, especially in front of other people. A wife was expected to be loyal to her husband against his adversaries, heed his wishes, and dedicate herself to the care of home and children. The wives, on the other hand, wanted a "partnership marriage," in which problems are solved by democratic consensus after everyone has a say. "Talking it over" is essential for gaining a sense of participation in decisions. This is a mainstream ideal cherished by educated, middle- and upper-middle-class men and women. Ex-military Turks tend to define conflict in terms of winners and losers, and they play an all-or-nothing, confrontational game. Communication in marriage is the educated American woman's goal; wifely obedience, the mainstream Turkish man's wish. One point of agreement between couples of the ex-military group is that home and children are primarily the wife's responsibilities. As long as wives fulfilled these obligations, seven of the twelve husbands had no objections to their wives' working outside the home. However, the Turks did not plan to increase their share of household or child-rearing tasks, although three eventually did, occasionally cooking or drying dishes. Five men opposed their wives' working; only one of these wives did secure outside employment. Another point of agreement is that a wife should adjust to her husband's ways within reason and share his destiny.

The American wives acknowledged their husbands' Turkish origins and did not pressure them to become Westernized or to become naturalized U.S. or Canadian citizens. Though psychologically difficult for some, all the ex-military Turks did acquire U.S. or Canadian citizenship within nine to twelve years of their marriage date. Thus, accommodation to conditions of life in North America occurred at the husband's own pace. Acculturation of wives to Turkish norms and values has varied considerably. The manifest results of the intercultural exchanges have been influenced by the personalities of the spouses, the power contests within their marriage, and the attitudes of close relatives and friends. Intercultural differences in cuisine and religion have presented few problems, and subtle differences in styles of sexual intimacy usually were overcome.

Examples of the ex-military couples' voluntary intercultural exchanges include a blend of cuisines, with most North American wives proficiently preparing many Turkish dishes; in families with children, the use of some Turkish kinship terms, such as *baba* for father; and Turkish hospitality, involving welcoming unannounced visitors and formally invited guests into one's home and plying them with generous heaps of food.

Religion never became a focus of marital conflict, even among troubled couples. On marriage, four ex-military Turks were and still are atheists, secularized in the spirit of Ataturk. Three of their wives are nominal Christians, and one, of mixed Jewish and gentile ancestry, leans toward Unitarianism. Four Turks were nominal Muslims on marriage, but were not and have not become well versed in Islam. One is married to a Canadian Catholic who soon dissociated herself from the church because of the bigotry of a local priest who fulminated against Protestants. She and her husband then attended a Sunni mosque in London, Ontario, but both were repelled by the Lebanese *imam*'s seeming hatred of Turks and by his highly political sermons. Another couple took their children to Sunday school at the Albanian Islamic mosque in a Detroit suburb for a few years and went to the Dearborn Sunni mosque to celebrate Islamic holidays. Though none of the eight wives became Muslims, all learned about and came to respect Islam. Two of the older Turks of genteel background held intellectually sophisticated versions of Islam. One wife, who earned a PH.D. in archeology and worked at the University of Michigan, was a Secular Humanist. The other was a devout Catholic as long as she lived. She did not prevail upon her husband to convert to Christianity, and they never belittled one another's religions. Her husband kept his promise to bring their children up as Catholics and even escorted them to Catechism lessons and Sunday school when his wife became too ill to take them herself. None of the Turks described above fast during *Ramadan*, (spelled *Ramaẕan* in Turkish) entertain hopes of making the *haj*, or pray five times a day. Some circumvent the Qur'anic prohibition against wine by drinking beer and hard liquor. One of the atheists developed a drinking problem, which disrupted his marriage. The others either do not drink or are moderate social drinkers.

Two ex-military Turks became devout Muslims only after living in the United States for two or three years and try to observe strictly the rules of Islam.

One man's wife formally embraced Islam; another, in her own words, is "Muslim-oriented." The former, who once wore bikinis and chic, Western apparel, now covers herself completely, except that she does not veil her face. She manages the money she inherited and the earnings she brings home from a series of part-time jobs, which accords with the precepts of Islam. She successfully deals with problems arising in her marriage by appealing to her husband's piety and goodness. A third woman converted to Islam to please her moderately devout husband. Nevertheless, in 1978, when I last saw them, both confessed that they were unhappy in their marriage.

It is very difficult in North America for couples with children to ignore Christmas, and so all engage in gift-giving, but the three Muslim families described above buy presents for New Year rather than for Christmas, do not take their children to see Santa Claus, and have no Christmas tree. Three other wives, all now divorced, experienced escalating marital tension during the Christmas holidays, when their nominally Muslim husbands became especially obdurate and cranky. Three Turks, all with happy or satisfying marriages, celebrate Christmas with their families without feeling they have betrayed their own religious beliefs.

Only one American wife has been active in the TACAM, serving on many committees, arranging exhibits, and giving public lectures on Ottoman and Turkish culture in museums and institutes. The Canadian wife has been similarly involved in the Turkish Canadian Cultural Association.

All the men and working wives of the ex-military group are well educated and occupationally successful. Seven of the Turks have a B.S.; three, an M.S.; and two, a PH.D. One wife took two years of university courses before her marriage, but never earned a degree. Four wives have a B.A.; two, an M.A.; one is on the brink of completing her PH.D.; and two have a PH.D. The men's occupations range from senior research engineers in metropolitan Detroit's major auto firms to independent engineering consultants to these firms, salesmen, and real estate speculators. Some have retired, and the others are close to retirement. One man who settled in the United States in the late 1940s is now deceased. The wives, two of whom are deceased, have been university professors and research associates, administrative librarians, an author of a popular book as well as a newspaper reporter, editorial assistants, public school teachers, and retail clerks. The men's incomes in the 1990s are in the $60,000 per year range; the assets of some are considerable. One man, in the words of one of his compatriots, "must be worth over $2,000,000," as he owns several rental properties.

Depending upon each marital partner's degree of personal flexibility and commitment with their respective sets of values and guidelines for family interaction (described above), satisfaction in marriage has varied enormously. Only two couples report very happy marriages. Four have worked out a mutually agreeable conjugal life, three of them after troubled early years. Half of the couples have endured great unhappiness in their marital lives. Four of the couples eventually divorced.

Occasional systematic physical abuse by husbands occurred in five of the disturbed marriages, and explosive outbursts of temper and verbal abuse were reported in all of them. The problems sprang from attempts by oppressive husbands to control their wives in four areas: the division of labor at home; access to and allocation of family income; the husband's infidelity, and, in one case, the wife's as well; and the husband's jealousy and attempts to restrict his wife's outside friendships and activities—her working outside the home, their attending her work-related social events together, her returning to a university to obtain a graduate degree. Two of the three divorced couples with children also disagreed on parenting methods, especially discipline techniques and the amount of freedom to be given to a teenage daughter.

DIVORCE AND AFTER

The marriages of divorced couples lasted from five to twenty-three years. In all four cases, the wife initiated the divorce. Only one divorce went smoothly. Three husbands put up protracted battles, first against the suit itself, then over the property settlement. Children figured in three of the four divorces. Two fathers contested the judge's decision to award custody of the children to their mothers. No father, however, ever defaulted on child support payments.

The ex-parte period was tumultuous for three couples. Two of the three husbands threatened to harm their wives. One, fearing for her life, went into hiding until her divorce was finalized. Two of the three wives with children said they deferred divorce until their children were in their mid-teens or older because they worried that their husbands would kidnap the children and flee with them to Turkey. In fact, one took his young son on a trip to Turkey, with his anxious ex-wife's permission, but brought him back on schedule.

Before divorce two women held stable, full-time jobs and consequently did not suffer a marked reduction in their living standards afterwards. Two women remarried within a year after their first marriages ended. One woman, who did not remarry, experienced fluctuations in her income for about four years after her divorce was finalized and barely could meet her basic living expenses. All four women received emotional support, practical help, and some financial assistance from parents, siblings, and close friends.

The post-divorce experiences of the four ex-husbands vary. One, divorced in 1970, advertised for a bride in Turkish newspapers and, in 1971, wed a Turkish nurse with a masters degree in nursing from an American university. She immigrated to the United States and was hired as a nursing supervisor in a suburban hospital. But the pair were incompatible, pursued separate social lives, and divorced in 1976, upon which she returned to Turkey. Again this man placed ads in Turkish newspapers for a wife, and a law student responded. They married, and she came to the United States. Now they have two children and are well integrated into the community's visiting networks. Another man initiated a relationship with a Filipina-American nurse before his divorce was finalized. He wed her three years later, but they divorced after seven years of marriage as a result of problems concerning her adopted son from her previous marriage. He currently dates three American women.

Contacts between two sets of ex-spouses have increased over time. After eight years of avoidance, one pair of ex-spouses made peace when their daughter became pregnant with their first grandchild. Now friends, they nevertheless have no intention of remarrying each other. They do help one another on occasion, exchange gifts, and visit their grandchildren together.

CHILDREN AND GRANDCHILDREN

Three couples had no children by choice. Two women arrived at this decision within two months of marriage after evaluating their goals and their husbands as potential fathers. The third couple wanted no children because they both "just wanted to get ahead," as they put it. However, when they were middle-aged, they adopted the husband's second cousin from Turkey.

Five couples have offspring, one to five per couple. Boys and girls were welcomed with equal joy by both parents in all families. Yet the wives with only sons said they were happy to have no girls. One wife who converted to Islam worried about fighting a losing battle for preservation of a daughter's virtue against powerful hedonistic trends in the contemporary United States. Another woman feared her husband would not bend to America's dating customs, would harm a daughter psychologically and disrupt family life violently in his zeal to bring a girl up in seclusion.

Turkish parenting has been characterized as restrictive, yet warmly affectionate. Infants and toddlers are fed when they express hunger rather than according to schedule. Toilet training is accomplished casually, without putting undue pressure on the child; little accidents usually are cleaned up without fuss. Preschoolers who throw temper tantrums, grab toys from playmates, or are disrespectful to adults are corrected and shamed, sometimes slapped, but not made to internalize guilt, "because they don't know any better." However, by the age of six, children are expected to express their natural drives appropriately, to be considerate of others, to help at home, to study diligently at school, and to comply with the instructions of parents and other authority figures. Corporal punishment administered by fathers is most intense for recalcitrant boys between six and twelve years of age. It does not necessarily signify personal rejection, but rather conveys a sharp message to "shape up."

A daughter's activities with boys are curtailed as she approaches adolescence, for her virginity, and, thus, family honor, are at stake. A mother grows protective toward her sons and watchful over her daughters, sheltering them both from the potential wrath of their father. Nuclear families enmeshed in large kindreds have safety nets for children with tyrannical fathers or nervous, nagging mothers, as sympathetic aunts, uncles, grandparents, and neighbors can offer harshly treated youngsters solace and persuade punitive parents to let up on their children. However, as in America, urban children in isolated nuclear or matrifocal families have no cushion against the outbursts of over-stressed, enraged parents (Kâğıtçıbaşı 1970, 1973; Olson 1981; and Stirling 1965). As noted above, some Turks in the ex-military group grew up in just such households. One man described in elaborate detail the physical abuse inflicted on him by his father, who nonetheless loved him deeply.

In the 1960s most middle-class white American mothers fed their infants on schedule as soon after birth as possible. Toilet training, then, as now, viewed as a difficult process, was a major focus of much emotion. Children, depending upon their performance, either receive exaggerated praise or become targets of their mother's (or other care-givers') vented frustration. Mainstream American psychiatrists, psychologists, and social workers recommended a firmly united parental front against a disobedient child. Corporal punishment was deplored. Instead, a system of rewards and deprivations was thought by some experts to promote good behavior; motivating children to do the right thing because it is morally good or practical was recommended by others (Flacks 1979; Zuckerman 1975). Most of the college-educated American wives in this group had taken a course or two in child development, and all the mothers were advised by pediatricians and further guided by popular child-care handbooks, such as Dr. Spock's.

Such opposing approaches to child-rearing precipitated occasional to frequent clashes between husbands and wives in most families. Ironically, some American wives whose husbands behaved as angry Turkish fathers found themselves shielding and indulging their children more than they otherwise would have, had the fathers not been so restrictive and severe. All ex-military couples with children generally agreed upon what constituted misbehavior—disrespectful behavior, not doing chores on request, telling lies, staying outside too late, and harassing younger siblings. Except for one of the senior couples and the happy Muslim couple, conflicts between spouses often flared over proper disciplinary measures. Disagreements also arose between them over whether or not a school-age child should receive an allowance. Most of the wives felt that a regular, weekly allowance teaches a child how to budget and save money. Turkish fathers preferred that a child ask them for what they needed and wanted, a policy which makes children dependent on their fathers to satisfy even their most trivial wants and strengthens his authority over them.

Paternal harshness and parental conflict shaped the children's view of their dual cultural heritage. The more lenient the father, the more positive their attitude toward their Turkish heritage, including Islam. As most fathers became less restrictive toward teenage sons than daughters, these sons acquired a mild to strong interest in their Turkish heritage. Teenage daughters, on the other hand, rejected both their Turkish heritage (except the cuisine) and Islam, and some rebelled dramatically. One got pregnant while a senior in high school; one ran away from home for a few weeks while her sympathetic paternal grandmother and cousin were visiting; and two moved in with their boy friends, one while a senior in high school, the other in her freshman year of college. The first two daughters and their fathers soon reconciled, as eventually did one of the last two. The remaining daughter still will not speak to her father, nor he to her. Five other daughters, while adolescents, had disputes with their fathers, who, however, "mellowed," as one woman explained, as the girls grew older.

All children of ex-military couples earned high-school diplomas. Five couples sent their children only to public schools. Those of one senior couple went only to parochial schools. One of the Muslim couples enrolled their children in a parochial elementary school, hoping that the strict discipline and restrained sexual expression prevalent in Catholic schools would have a beneficial effect on their children's behavior. However, the children suffered discrimination because of their father's nationality and parents' religion, and their parents transferred them to a public school. The son of the contented Muslim couple was educated in public schools in the United States, and in a private British school when the family lived overseas in North Africa for two years.

Except for one son with a mild developmental disability, all children in this group have studied in community colleges and/or universities. According to information available to me in 1995, six of the daughters earned a B.A. or B.S.; two still are completing their undergraduate programs. One son has a B.S. and two an M.S. in engineering. Another is a practicing physician. Other sons are computer engineers, a manager of his own consulting firm in Turkey, an oriental-rug dealer on the West Coast, and an actor who has played in British TV dramas. Daughters' current jobs include computer engineer with a major U.S. corporation, stock broker, microbiologist, veterinarian's assistant, and off-Broadway stage actress. The second generation is geographically dispersed, residing far from their siblings, from where they grew up, and from where their parents live.

Seven children are as yet unmarried . None of the married children has wed a Turk or Muslim. Their spouses are Americans of Christian background; one husband was born and grew up in France; one daughter has been married and divorced three times; three divorced their first husband. Of these three divorcées, one lives with her paramour; one has a steady boy friend; and one has remarried.

The third generation, in 1995, ranges in age from one to twenty-seven years old. The oldest is a college graduate. It remains to be seen if any of them will retain aspects of their Turkish or Islamic heritage.

Affluent Families

My contacts with purely Turkish and mixed, wealthy couples occurred during large parties at their homes and at TACAM events. However, my close friendships with affluent Turks have been with three purely Turkish families rather than with those of the mixed couples. Gaps in information about the latter were filled by in-depth, ethnographic interviews, genealogies, and life histories of six couples. The section below describes the family life of these six couples. My information about the other seven mixed, affluent couples in the community, though not as complete, shows similar patterns.

Husbands' Backgrounds

Though the nationality and self-stated identity of all the men is Turk, their ancestors include Georgian Turks, Crimean Tatars, Circassians, and Laz. All interview respondents could trace ancestors in their paternal lines back at least three generations and often more, unlike most men in the other two groups, many of whom knew little about their grandparents. Lineages of some affluent men contained nomads who were settled in central and eastern Anatolia in the nineteenth century by the Ottoman government. Their descendants became landowners and government officials. Many were known locally for their piety and charity. Fathers of the Turks in this group included a local administrator in the Turkish republic's postal service, a career military officer, a newspaper editor jailed for leading the liberal opposition against Ataturk in the 1930s, and a Muslim lawyer who also managed a lucrative flour mill. Some of the men's mothers were literate in both Turkish and Arabic in the old Arabic script. All were homemakers. Some, according to their American daughters-in-law, were "liberated women."

The fathers of the intermarried, affluent men were able to support them and some of their siblings, even a few of their sisters, during their completion of professional degrees in Turkey's finest institutions of higher learning, a strategy pursued for family advancement by forward-looking, eastern Anatolian elites in smaller cities and towns as Turkey began to modernize after World War II (Aswad 1971, 1978; and Eberhard 1970). Five of the six male respondents were physicians who came to the United

States for advanced training in medical specialties such as plastic surgery or radiology. The sixth earned a B.S., then an M.S. in engineering at the University of Michigan. All were Turkish civilians with student or special visas on arrival.

WIVES' BACKGROUNDS

The American wives were born into middle- to working-class families, so the Turks married women of lower socioeconomic class origin than their own. Five women are, ethnically, WASP Americans. One of them was born in Scotland of a mother whose ancestors included sea captains and makers of fine footwear. Her father was in the RAF during World War II, earned a degree in engineering at Oxford afterwards, and migrated with his family to Canada, where he served on provincial transportation commissions. Her first marriage to a Scotsman produced two children but ended in divorce. She migrated to the United States, becoming a naturalized citizen in 1958. Another woman's English-born parents migrated to Canada, then to the United States. Her father, a commercial artist, died soon after her birth in Detroit. Her mother worked as an accountant to support her, an only child. The third woman's ancestors left England to settle in Mississippi in the 1730s. She showed me her thick, family history books with genealogical tables and vignettes of her now widely dispersed, numerous kin. Her father had a small, commercially-oriented farm, and her mother was a homemaker. Another woman of English ancestry was born in Missouri, where her father had a tiny farm, which he sold; then he was employed as a truck driver. Her mother worked part time as a motel clerk. The fifth wife had Irish and German ancestors. Her father, a policeman in Massachusetts, left the Catholic church, switching to a Presbyterian congregation; her mother kept house and raised the six children. The only Catholic among the six wives I interviewed is of Polish ancestry. Both her father and mother were born in America of immigrant parents and were bilingual. Both also worked in factories in northern Ohio.

The women were educated primarily in public U.S. or in British schools. Two took a few art courses after graduating from high school, where they majored in the commercial curriculum. Neither pursued a university education. Both were skilled medical secretaries when they met their husbands. A third earned certification in X-ray technology at a junior college. Two women graduated as registered nurses after training

in university hospitals. One woman completed her B.A. and M.A. in education at two southern universities and also took classes at a Methodist
seminary. While in college, she directed church-sponsored summer programs for children and taught high school social studies at an Appalachian
boarding school. In 1951 she was hired as an administrator by the University of Michigan.

COURTSHIP AND WEDDINGS

Five spouse pairs met in hospitals where the Turkish doctors were interns
and their future wives were nurses, medical technicians, or secretaries.
The engineer and his wife met at a weekend social for Turkish students
hosted by the University of Michigan, where she worked. In some cases,
the women initiated dating. One asked her husband-to-be and his Turkish
roommates to dinner in her apartment. In other cases, the men asked the
women out. One asked the medical secretary with whom he had interacted
at work to a Turkish ball. The time span between first date and marriage
proposal ranged from eight to eighteen months. One couple dated, broke
off and dated others for about a month, then decided to marry.

Three weddings were conducted by a justice-of-the peace, with a few
friends present. In two, no kin from either side attended. In the third,
parents on both sides had vehemently opposed the couple's marriage on
religious grounds. However, the wife's family came to the modest American wedding, and her parents gave them a small reception afterwards in
their home. When the couple went to Turkey to introduce the bride to the
husband's family, his parents accepted her completely. To please her
husband, she had converted to Islam. His father then held a Muslim
wedding ceremony (*nikâh*) for the couple in his home. Two couples were
wed in Protestant churches by ministers who did not require the husbands
to convert or pledge any children they might have to the church. The
Polish Catholic woman and her husband were married in a Catholic
church after he completed a course of instructions and promised to bring
up their children as Catholics. This couple saved their money to pay for an
elaborate church wedding and lavish reception. Her family attended.

RELATIONS WITH KIN

None of the couples reported any significant tensions between themselves
and the wife's relatives. Before their marriages, four men already had

completed their mandatory two-year term of military service required of all Turkish male citizens. One of these couples lived in Turkey the first four years after their marriage. The husband taught medicine at a Turkish university in Izmir while his wife worked as an intensive care nurse at the U.S. air force base there. Their eldest child was born in Turkey during these years. The other three couples lived in the United States. They could freely visit Turkey at any time, but did not make their first trip overseas until four to eleven years after their weddings. The two remaining Turks still had to fulfill their military service. One did so by working as a physician at an American air force base, his wife, meanwhile, was a medical secretary at its commissary. The engineer and his wife, however, actually divorced so he could serve his term. Nevertheless, she lived with his kin, working first as a secretary, than as assistant personnel manager for Mobil Oil Corporation in Turkey. She and her husband remarried in Turkey after he completed his military service, had their marriage registered in the U.S. embassy, and then returned to the United States.

Thereafter, the five doctors' families have visited Turkey every three to six years, in summer, when their children have been on vacation from school. The doctors stay two to five weeks, but leave their wives and children with relatives for two or three months. American wives praised the generous hospitality of their in-laws and spoke of gatherings of many of their husbands' kin at meals in their homes or at restaurants, gift exchanges, shopping excursions, and visits with his relatives to points of interest. One woman explained, "Life there is different (i.e., more gregarious). Here we lead singular lives, cut off even from neighbors. In, Turkey, women go out every day to stroll, visit, shop. They see neighbors and friends all the time." These overseas visits also have given the children frequent, prolonged, largely positive experiences in their fathers' homeland and contribute greatly to their pride in their Turkish heritage. Moreover, every three to six years, the doctors have funded, at least in part, trips to America from Turkey by their parents, siblings, cousins, and even nieces and nephews. Only the engineer and his wife did not return to Turkey for a visit until twenty-five years after they left his homeland to settle in the United States. Their vacations, over the years, were confined to the United States. However, after their children left home to attend universities, this couple took in unrelated, college exchange students from Turkey.

FACTORS AFFECTING MARITAL RELATIONS

When interviewed in the early 1980s, both spouses of four couples reported happy marriages, despite occasional disagreements. These couples are solicitous of one another and relaxed wherever I encounter them. Wives of the other two couples reported troubles in their marriages. One of these couples divorced in 1994.

After moving to successively larger homes and more upscale neighborhoods, all couples occupied spacious homes by the late 1970s. Interior decor ranges from American colonial, to eighteenth century French to modern. Turkish heritage is expressed strongly in four houses, hardly at all in the other two. Ornamental Turkish items seen in these homes include fine carpets, brass braziers, etched copper plaques, traditional pottery vases, dishes, and tiles crafted in Kutahya, cut glass tea sets, and dolls wearing regional folk or historical Ottoman costumes.

All six couples, even the two with troubled marriages, do not fight over money. The five doctors were earning between $60,000 and $150,000 annually by the early 1980s; in addition, they and their wives had large savings accounts, stocks, and bonds. Four couples owned lots, apartments, condominia, or homes in Turkey, and one had a condominium in Florida as well. One physician and the engineer have no Turkish properties but have other assets.

All couples have joint checking accounts. Three wives write most checks and balance the family budget. Even where the husbands do the family bookkeeping, their wives said they buy what they please, either charging or writing checks for their purchases. They receive ample household allowances, and their requests for extra money are granted generously. Three spouse pairs shop together and make joint decisions on major purchases such as cars and appliances. Two husbands make financial decisions for the family after consulting their wives. One wife said she makes all major purchases after obtaining her husband's opinion. None of the women were working in the early 1980s, and they had not worked for fifteen to twenty years. Two employ a maid to clean their homes once a week. The others do all their housework themselves.

Each wife learned how to cook Turkish food, which she prepares once a week on average and serves when entertaining both Turkish and American friends. Turkish customs adopted by wives and transmitted to children include respectful behavior toward elders and removing shoes before entering the home. One doctor's wife especially enjoys Turkish hospitality. She commented that none of her relatives ever drop in on kin or friends unannounced, as Turks do. Four of the wives were active in TACAM.

English is spoken predominantly in all households. One couple said they speak Turkish in the presence of their children if they want to keep something secret from them. One doctor periodically ruled that only Turkish be spoken at home, which never lasted more than twenty-four hours before everyone lapsed into English. All the wives know some Turkish. Those who lived in Turkey a year or more can understand most Turkish conversations. Two speak fluent Turkish and read Turkish language magazines and newspapers. All the Turkish husbands speak idiomatic English, two with no trace of an accent.

The men's desire to preserve Turkish identity is reflected most sharply in their attitudes toward becoming U.S. citizens. During the swearing-in naturalization ceremony, immigrant must repudiate citizenship in any other nation. The United States does not recognize dual citizenship. Two doctors and the engineer were glad to become American citizens. One doctor said he especially values the political freedom Americans enjoy by law. These three men retain pride in their Turkish ancestry and cultural heritage, but are committed to making a good life for themselves and their children in the United States. The three remaining doctors acquired U.S. citizenship reluctantly, to remain in the United States for the sake of their wives and children. Until 1971 no foreign doctors in America could renew their medical licenses after practicing here for seven years unless they became U.S. citizens. Their seven-year terms expired in the late 1960s and in 1970, so they became U.S. citizens.

The loyalty conflicts the Turkish doctors experienced disappeared in 1982, when Turkey recognized dual citizenship. People born of a Turkish parent, in Turkey or elsewhere, are always Turkish citizens, even if they become citizens of another country. Children with only one Turkish parent, if living outside Turkey, must decide at age eighteen whether or not to become Turkish citizens.

Islam never became an issue among these couples. Four of the men are secularized agnostics. One is a nominal Muslim, and one is best described as a Unitarian-like Muslim. Only these last two expressed a mild interest in making the *haj*, and both of their wives converted to Islam. One is more pious than her husband in most aspects of Islam, but she occasionally accepts an alcoholic beverage at a party. Her husband is the only abstainer from alcohol among the six affluent Turks. Neither the Muslim husbands nor their converted wives pray five times a day. All six families occasionally eat pork. They usually attend TACAM sponsored *bayram* festivities, but do not fast during *Ramadan*.

The secularized doctor who married the Polish-American Catholic woman saw that their children were reared in the Church, as he had promised. Five families celebrated Christian holidays when their children lived at home. Christmas trees, gifts, and Easter baskets were annual highlights. One Muslim physician whose wife converted to Islam enjoyed celebrating Christmas and Easter with his wife and children, noting that Muslims honor Jesus as a Prophet second only to Muhammad. Only the nominally Muslim doctor forbade Christmas trees and Easter baskets in his house. Despite his wife's conversion to Islam, she wanted to have them for their children's enjoyment. Heated arguments over this issue would erupt between them so she finally kept quiet and yielded to his wishes.

One couple's marriage has been marred by the husband's attempt to dominate his wife, who, according to some Turkish women, never stood up to him. His frequent temper tantrums and occasional physical abuse of her and their children are found in countless purely American marriages and have nothing to do with Islam or Turkish heritage. Turkish men are apt to be more verbally assertive than most American men, quickly ignited but just as quickly cooling off. As one contented wife put it, "We (i.e., Americans) must learn how to cope with the Turkish male disposition, which is difficult to adjust to, but in the end, you learn."

As noted above, one couple divorced in 1994 after some thirty years of marriage. The husband's adultery and belittling of his wife's capabilities finally drove her from him.

CHILDREN AND GRANDCHILDREN

All the affluent couples have children, ranging from one to six per couple. Styles of child rearing and areas of cultural conflict among these couples echo those described previously for the ex-military couples. Four of the Turks were "too strict" with their children and "tended to yell" at them, according to their American wives, three of whom admitted that they too shouted at their naughty offspring sometimes. Only in one family, however, did the children fear and avoid their father who rarely showed them affection. The three other fathers were loving and jovial toward their children when pleased with their behavior. The engineer and his wife did not tolerate disrespect or disobedience from their children, but rarely shouted at them and always backed one another's disciplinary measures, usually deprivation of something valued, or grounding. These are the ideal middle- and upper-middle class American patterns described above. One woman said her husband was so indulgent, both to his adopted daughter from her first marriage and to their son, that she became the children's primary disciplinarian.

All the Turkish fathers suffered as their daughters began to express interest in boys. The men felt pressured to concede their girls' "reasonable" requests in order to keep their own and their beloved daughters' sanity intact. Mixed gender group activities, known and approved boy friends, curfews, and going to high-school proms, were norms in these families, all well within the mainstream American range of variation. Virginity before marriage was mandatory for daughters, but not as important for sons. Teenage sons were free to date whom they pleased and stay out as late as they wished, as long as they did not get into trouble. The recent divorcée declared, during our interview in the early 1980s that when her son turned sixteen, her husband would take him out and "teach him the ropes," which she opposed and hoped to prevent.

Today all the children are young adults. All have bachelor's degrees, and some have master's degrees. The young men's occupations include architect, microbiologist, chemist, optometrist, and owner of a small consulting business. The young women include a psychological counselor, school administrator, nurses, an executive secretary, an office worker with her own art studio on the side, a business consultant, and married, full-time homemakers. Many of the children are geographically scattered, living in states other than Michigan, where their parents still reside.

Of the twenty natural children of these couples, five daughters and two sons have married. One girl wed an Italian-American, Roman Catholic law student; another, a Puerto Rican medical student; and a third, an American whom she met at the university they both attended. Two young women wed Turks; both now are divorced. One of them married a first cousin, with whom she fell in love during a visit to Turkey. The other eloped with a nephew of one of the community's affluent Turkish couples. Her father had opposed the marriage, but allowed them to live in his house after it while he and his wife took a prolonged trip to Turkey. Her brother married an American of Eastern European ancestry in a Roman Catholic church. The father did not attend the nuptials, nor did his wife, who wished to, but did not for fear her husband would "blow up" and ruin the ceremony. Turks were not invited to the church wedding, which hurt the groom deeply, but his parents and their Turkish friends came to the reception afterwards.

Nine offspring of three doctors have a strong sense of their Turkish as well as American identity. One son, for example, became active on TACAM's Youth Committee while a university student in the 1980s, and he joined a Turkish Student Association. Today he remains active in the TACAM. He and another young man have taken Turkish citizenship, which requires all males to do a term of military service. They both fulfilled this requirement by paying a fee to the Turkish courts, which then reduced their term of service to two months. The failed marriages of the two women who married Turks were not forced upon them, and they remain proud of their Turkish ancestry and heritage. Their many visits to relatives in Turkey over the years and their American mothers' love of and respect for Turkish culture have helped build these women's love of their fathers' homeland.

The first grandchild was born in 1983, and more have arrived since. All are young, but some already have been to Turkey.

Changing Trends

The conjugal relations of American wives and Turkish husbands described in this paper do not constitute the eternal pattern found in such marriages, but are situated in a mid- to late-twentieth-century historical context in specific geographical areas. The Turkish husbands grew up and were enculturated in a Turkey in which secularism and strong national pride prevailed in its media and educational system, and in which Islamic currents were suppressed. The North American wives reached adulthood before the second wave of feminism rose in the United States, experiencing its impact differentially in the early to middle years of their marriages. Sociocultural environments in both nations have undergone many transformations since the mid-1960s. The feminist movement and sexual revolution have produced unprecedented variations and contradictions in gender relations and attitudes toward sexuality in North America. Turkish military regulations concerning marriages to foreigners have been rescinded, and rights to Turkish citizenship, expanded. Since the early 1980s in Turkey, secularism has come under increasing attack from all segments of society, and Islamic voices are asserting their views ever more forcefully.

From the mid-1970s on, numbers of single Turkish women studying at North American universities have grown, providing opportunities for them to meet and marry American men. Some U.S. soldiers stationed temporarily at American military bases in Turkey have brought home Turkish brides. Today's Turkish male students at North American universities have learned how to date casually. A few, like their American counterparts, take advantage of local women's readiness to enter into intimate, premarital relationships.

🎴 *Conclusions*

Both the affluent and the smaller number of working-class couples were most compatible in their expectations of conjugal roles upon their marriages, despite the different social origins of members of each group. Both expected the husband to be the primary breadwinner and public spokesman for the family. Problems that arose in both groups centered around disappointments in one or more aspects of role performance. Islam has not played a significant role in the marital life of the working-class couples and is not a source of conflict among the affluent couples, whose interpretation of Islam is flexible and broadly tolerant rather than literal.

Affluent doctors married intelligent women whose social class origins and educational attainment were, nonetheless, well below theirs. American wives in the affluent group had less interest in building careers of their own than did the wives in the ex-military group. Doctors' wives were happy to be full-time homemakers and mothers. Their creative energies were poured into these roles, at which they excelled, in an upper- middle-class milieu of material abundance and security. The engineer and his wife were more similar to one another in their social origins and educational attainment and created a solid marriage because of their commitment to and respect for each other. As the American wives adjusted to their husbands' style of interaction at home and enriched themselves by adopting selected Turkish customs, their husbands adapted to the American ways prevailing outside the home in their professional microcosms.

The most incompatible couples were in the ex-military group. Husbands' and wives' ideals of marriage as well as definitions of conjugal roles contrasted sharply. These disparities can be traced to their social class backgrounds in the two countries in which they grew up during the years before and after World War II. The men's families were from the more conservative, strongly patriarchal sectors of Turkish society, the working and lower-middle classes of Turkey's towns and cities. The military offered them a possible route of upward social mobility via educational channels culminating in study at a university abroad. The American women were born into skilled working- and middle-class families of varying wealth. Most went to college to train for a career. The educational attainment (PH.D.) of two wives exceeded that of their husbands (M.S.), but this caused problems only between one couple. Most wives in this group found many aspects of Turkish culture exciting, but some resented their husbands' attempts to control their movements and behavior. The highest rate of divorce (four out of twelve couples) was in this group, and three of the eight couples who have not separated have had problem-ridden marriages.

Transmission of Turkish heritage and identity to offspring has been most successful among the affluent families, who have the money to visit Turkey often and show their children its most pleasant aspects. A positive attitude toward Turkish culture on the part of some American wives in this group is an added factor in the children's internalization of a Turkish component in their overall identity. This is not found in any of the working-class couples' offspring and is weakly developed in a few of the ex-military group's children.

The most literal interpretations of Islam are by two of the ex-military Turks, whose American wives either converted completely or in large part. Yet only one of these marriages has been happy, while the other has been troubled, as is that of a third couple in which the wife embraced Islam without actually converting. Clearly Islam has not had a unitary positive or negative effect on marital relations of the couples in any of the three groups described in this study. Islam takes multifaceted forms, depending on the social backgrounds and personalities of the believers and those with whom they are affiliated.

Each couple forged its own "patriarchal bargain" (see Kandiyoti 1988) in terms of the material and social resources, skills, and hopes and dreams each spouse brought into their marriage. Cases of marital dissatisfaction and turbulence in all groups can be attributed to aspects of patriarchy filtered through the harsh end of the spectrum of Turkish male behavior. The three elements of patriarchy expressed were: occasional to cyclical physical abuse, found in all groups; attempts to dominate the wife through control of resources, working-class and ex-military groups only; and philandering, ex-military and affluent groups only. Satisfactory-to-happy marriages can be attributed to low levels of patriarchal values and behavior in one case and paternalistic kindness in the others. In these cases, both spouses agreed that the husband should provide for, lead, and exercise ultimate control over his family, but paternalistic husbands treated their wives with consideration and respect, valued their wives' contributions to family well being, and allowed them great latitude in domestic matters.

Finally, a basic factor contributing to dissonance between troubled couples was the strain these Turkish men felt living as foreigners in an alien American cultural environment. This was experienced most keenly by many men of the ex-military group, whose backgrounds had not prepared them for the total continuum of North American gender relations, especially the independent and individualistic outlooks of their particular wives. Furthermore, mostly employed as engineers in Detroit's auto companies, their occupational milieu was often hostile. Engineers with whom they worked were largely white, ethnocentric, fairly conservative men who were insensitive to differences in the cultural styles of foreign co-workers.

Most of the affluent Turks, on the other hand, were preadapted to life in America. Secularized to varying degrees, they admired aspects of Western culture and wished to be "modern" wherever they lived. The doctors reached the pinnacle of success by American standards, becoming wealthy and generally admired by hospital staff and American neighbors alike. They were better equipped to make necessary behavioral adjustments and slight value shifts to accommodate American norms and mores without sacrificing their integrity as Turks.

ᵂ *References*

Alba, Richard D. and Reid M. Golden. 1986. "Patterns of Ethnic Marriage in the United States." *Social Forces* 65: 202–223.

Aldridge, Delores P. 1978. "Interracial Marriages" *Journal of Black Studies* (March): 355–368.

Aswad, Barbara C. 1971. *Property Control and Social Strategies: Settlers on a Middle Eastern Plain.* Anthropological Papers, no. 44. Museum of Anthropology, University of Michigan.

————. 1978. "Women, Class, and Power: Examples from the Hatay, Turkey." Pp. 473–481 in *Women in the Muslim World*, ed. Lois Beck and Nikki Keddie. Cambridge: Harvard University Press.

Atkins, Elizabeth. 1991. "The Colors of Love." *Detroit News*, November 18, pp. lc, 5c.

Barnett, Larry D. 1963. "Interracial Marriage in California." *Marriage and Family Living* 25, no. 4: 425–427.

Barron, Milton L. 1946. *People Who Intermarry.* Syracuse, N.Y.: Syracuse University Press.

————. 1969. "Jewish Husbands and Gentile Wives" *Congress Biweekly* 36: 11–15.

————, ed., 1972. *The Blending American.* Chicago: Quadrangle Books.

Berman, Louis. 1968. *Jews and Intermarriage: A Study in Personality and Culture.* New York: Thomas Yoseloff.

Bilgé, Barbara J. 1984. "Variations in Family Structure and Organization in the Turkish Community of Southeast Michigan and Adjacent Canada." Ph.D. diss., Department of anthropology, Wayne State University, Detroit.

————. 1994. "Voluntary Associations in the Old Turkish Community of Metropolitan Detroit." Pp. 381–405 in *Muslim Communities in North America*, ed. Yvonne Yazbeck Haddad and Jane Idleman Smith. Albany, N.Y.: State University of New York Press.

Blau, Peter M.; Terry C. Blum; and Joseph E. Schwartz. 1982. "Heterogeneity and Intermarriage." *American Sociological Review* (February): 45–62.

Bogelski, B. R. 1961. "Assimilation through Intermarriage." *Social Forces* 40 (December): 156–165.

Burma, John H. 1963. "Interethnic Marriages in Los Angeles, 1948–1959" *Social Forces* 42 (December): 156–165.

Davis, Kingsley, 1941. "Intermarriage in Caste Societies." *American Anthropologist* 43: 376–395.

Detroit Free Press. 1982. "Who Is Black? And When Does It Matter? Louisiana Clings to a Racist Past." October 2, p. 6H.

Eberhard, Wolfram. 1970. "Changes in Leading Families in Southern Turkey." Pp. 242–256 in *Peoples and Cultures of the Middle East*, ed. Louise E. Sweet. Garden City, N.Y.: Natural History Press.

Elkholy, Abdo A. 1966. *The Arab Moslems in the United States: Religion and Assimilation.* New Haven: College and University Press.

———. 1971. "The Moslems and Inter-religious Marriage in the New World." *International Journal of Sociology of the Family*: special issue (May): 69–84.

———. 1988. "The Arab American Family." Pp. 438–455 in *Ethnic Families in America: Patterns and Variations*, 3rd ed., ed. Charles H. Mindel, Robert W. Habenstein, and Roosevelt Wright, Jr., eds. New York: Elsevier.

Flacks, Richard. 1979. "Growing up Confused." Pp. 21–32 in *Socialization and the Life Cycle*, ed. Peter I. Rose. New York: St. Martin's Press.

Heer, David M. 1974. "The Prevalence of Black-White Marriages in the United States: 1960 and 1970." *Journal of Marriage and the Family* 36: 246–258.

Kâğıtçıbaşı, Çiğdem, 1970. "Social Norms and Authoritarianism: A Comparison of Turkish and American Adolescents." *Journal of Personality and Social Psychology* 16: 444–451.

———, 1973. "Psychological Aspects of Modernization in Turkey." *Journal of Cross-Cultural Psychology* 14, no. 2: 157–174.

Kandiyoti, Deniz. 1988. "Bargaining with Patriarchy" *Gender and Society* 2, no. 3: 274–290.

Kennedy, Ruby Jo Reeves, 1944. "Single or Triple Melting Pot? Intermarriage Trends in New Haven, 1870–1940." *American Journal of Sociology* 49: 331–339.

———. 1952. "Single or Triple Melting Pot? Intermarriage in New Haven, 1870–1950." *American Journal of Sociology* 58: 56–59.

Kiev, Ari. 1973. "The Psychiatric Implications of Interracial Marriage."

In *Interracial Marriage*, ed. Irving R. Stuart and L.E. Abi. New York: Grossman.

Kikumura, Akemi and Harry H. L. Kitano. 1973. "Interracial Marriage: A Picture of the Japanese Americans." *Journal of Social Issues* 25, no. 2: 67–81.

Kim, Bok-Lim. 1972. "Casework with Japanese and Korean Wives of Americans." *Social Casework* 53: 273–279.

Kitano, Harry; Wai-Tsang Yeung; Lynn Chai; and Herbert Hatanaka. 1984. "Asian American Interracial Marriage." *Journal of Marriage and the Family* 46: 179–190.

Labrack, Bruce and Karen Leonard. 1984. "Conflict and Compatibility in Punjabi-Mexican Immigrant Families in Rural California, 1915–1965." *Journal of Marriage and the Family* 46: 527–537.

Lazerwitz, Bernard. 1981. "Jewish-Christian Marriages and Conversions." *Jewish Social Studies* 43: 31–46.

———. 1987. "Trends in National Jewish Identification Indicators: 1971–1985." *Contemporary Jewry* 9: 87–103.

Mayer, Egon. 1980. "Processes and Outcomes in Marriages between Jews and Non-Jews." *Journal of Behavioral Scientist* 23: 487–518.

Merton, Robert K. 1941. "Intermarriage and Social Structure: Fact and Theory." *Psychiatry* 4: 361–374.

Murguia, E. 1982. *Chicano Intermarriage: A Theoretical and Empirical Study*. San Antonio, Texas: Trinity University Press.

Olson, Emilie A. 1981. "Socioeconomic and Psychocultural Contexts of Child Abuse and Neglect in Turkey." Pp. 96–119 in *Child Abuse and Neglect: Cross-Cultural Perspectives*, ed. Jill E. Korbin. Berkeley and Los Angeles: University of California Press.

Pascoe, Peggy. 1991. "Race, Gender, and Intercultural Relations: The Case of Interracial Marriage." *Frontiers* 12, no. 1: 5–18.

Porterfield, Ernest. 1978. *Black and White Mixed Marriages*. Chicago: Nelson Hall.

Poussaint, Alvin. 1983. "Black Men-White Women: An Update." *Ebony* 38 (August): 124–131.

Rosenthal, Erich. 1963. "Studies of Jewish Intermarriage in the United States." *American Jewish Year Book* 64: 3–53.

Sanjek, Roger. 1994. "Intermarriage and the Future of Races in the United

States." Pp. 103–150 in *Race*, ed. Steven Gregory and Roger Sanjek. New Brunswick, N.J. Rutgers University Press.

Sickles, R. J. 1972. *Race, Marriage, and the Law*. Albuquerque: University of New Mexico Press.

Simpson, George Eaton and J. Milton Yinger. 1985. *Racial and Cultural Minorities: An Analysis of Prejudice and Discrimination*, 5th ed. New York: Plenum Press.

Stirling, Paul. 1965. *Turkish Village*. London: Weidenfeld & Nicholson.

Tinker, John N. 1973. "Intermarriage and Ethnic Boundaries: The Japanese Case." *Journal of Social Issues* 29, no. 2: 49–66.

Tseng, Weng-Shing; John F. McDermott, Jr.' and Thomas W. Maretzki, eds. 1977. *Adjustment in Intercultural Marriage*. Honolulu: University of Hawaii Press.

Van den Berghe, Pierre. 1960. "Hypergamy, Hypergenation, and Miscegenation." *Human Relations* 13: 83–91.

Wagatsuma, Hiroshi. 1973. "Some Problems of Interracial Marriage for the Japanese." Pp. 247–264 in *Interracial Marriage: Expectations and Realities*, ed. Irving R. Stuart and L.E. Abi. New York: Grossman.

Wilkerson, Isabel. 1991. "Interracial Marriage Rises, Acceptance Lags." *New York Times*, December 2, p. A1, A10.

Williamson, Joel. 1980. *New People: Miscegenation and Mulattos in the United States*. New York: Free Press.

Winch, Robert F. 1958. *Mate Selection: A Study of Complementary Needs*. New York: Harper.

Wong, Morrison G. 1989. "A Look at Intermarriage Among the Chinese in the United States in 1980." *Sociological Perspectives* 32: 87–107.

Zuckerman, Michael. 1975. "Dr. Spock: The Confidence Man." Pp. 179–207 in *The Family in History*, ed. Charles E. Rosenberg. Philadelphia: University of Pennsylvania Press.

ARLENE DALLALFAR

᠊᠊᠊

The Iranian Ethnic Economy in Los Angeles
Gender and Entrepreneurship

The impact of migration on the social and economic status of women has been the subject of much interest and debate in recent scholarly literature (Pedraza 1991; Abadan-Unat 1977; Pessar 1984; Gold 1994; Glenn 1986; Kibria 1990; Brettell and Simon 1986; Hondagneu-Sotelo 1992). Until recently, most approaches to the study of migration were distinctly male-centric, and gender differentiation was not an important methodological concern. Despite the increasing numbers of female sojourners and immigrants over the past two decades, a lack of gender specificity has continued to persist in the models addressing economic activity and daily experiences of immigrants in the host society.

Data on legal immigration to the United States indicate that female immigrants have outnumbered their male counterparts since the 1930s, yet this demographic fact and its implications in relation to women and social-policy consequences in the host society has been neglected in the immigration literature (Pedraza 1991; Houstoun, Kramer, and Barrett 1984; Tienda, Jenson, and Bach 1984; Westwood and Bhachu 1988; Morokvasic 1985). Often in instances where gender issues were addressed, they were done so in a traditional manner whereby migrant women were seen as dependents in their capacity as sisters, daughters, wives, or mothers.

I would like to thank Ivan Light and Fereydoun Safizadeh for their comments and suggestions while reading various drafts of this paper.

These women were viewed as unproductive and passive partners in the immigration process who were to carry out their previously established roles in the family or in particular work settings.

Recent immigrants, refugees, and exiles face a dramatically different labor market than did their predecessors, one dominated by service rather than factory and manufacturing jobs. Immigrant women are not only working in sweatshops, the garment industry, in the informal sectors of the economy, and in agricultural work; they are also visible as entrepreneurs and businesswomen in emerging ethnic economies in the urban landscape across cities in the United States.

Research on Middle Eastern immigrants in the United States has also challenged previous conceptualizations of women's involvement in the various stages of immigrant adjustment, accommodation, and restructuring of family and cultural life that occurs in the host society. Research by Barbara Aswad (1994) on Yemeni and Lebanese women in Dearborn, Michigan; Louise Cainkar on Palestinian Muslim women in Chicago (1985), Yvonne Haddad and Adair Lummis's research on Muslims in the United States (1987), Afaf Melies, J. Lipson and S. Paul's on ethnicity and health among Middle Eastern immigrants in the United States (1992), and Arlene Avakian's biographic book on growing up Armenian in the United States (1992) all illustrate the importance of addressing women's experiences in the immigrant community. Other issues that merit further attention are women's socio-economic status; premigration characteristics, such as urban or rural origins or minority/majority status in the home society; the importance of maintaining, accommodating, and negotiating with the patrilineal extended family and changes in gender status; the geographic locations that these immigrant women and their families move into; as well as the availability of social networks, primarily family and kin as well as an ethnic community and economy in the host society. In addition, issues related to legal status and experiences of discrimination in the host society are important considerations in how women and men mediate and interact within their own communities and households as well as in their daily contact with institutions, the economy, and North American society. The role of patriarchy in family dynamics and employment patterns and the effects of patrilocal postmarital residency on female and male accommodation and adjustment patterns among Middle Eastern and North African immigrants merit further scholarly attention.

Given that self-employment appears to be the most remunerative occupation in the ethnic economy, in this paper I explore the development of small businesses among Iranian immigrant women in Los Angeles. More specifically, I address women's active participation in two arenas of the Iranian ethnic economy: in small businesses that are located in the home, and in family operated businesses in the ethnic economy. Types of ethnic resources, such as family and social networks that these immigrant women are adeptly incorporating in their work experiences, are demonstrated, indicating that males and females have differential access to ethnic resources within the immigrant community. In addition, avenues for entrepreneurial activity that are gender specific, in particular businesses that are home operated, which still are female dominated among Iranian immigrants, are demonstrated through case studies to illustrate differential access to gender resources in the ethnic economy as well.

🦝 *Ethnic Economies*

Sociological literature on immigrant entrepreneurs focuses on employers and employees working in an immigrant sector of the economy that coexists with primary and secondary sectors of the general labor market. The ethnic-economy paradigm investigates the entrepreneurial capacity of immigrant groups, particularly those individuals who are self-employed in small businesses in which ethnic and class resources are used to increase opportunities for higher earnings and employment. The direction of research on ethnic-group business activity has focused on issues related to how certain immigrant/ethnic groups create business activity and the availability of capital and class as well as ethnic resources for business in the ethnic economy and community. The work site in the ethnic economy is culturally and symbolically tied to the customs, traditions, aptitudes, and values of the home society, and recent developments in this scholarly literature address the need to observe the intersection of capital and ethnic resources in the ethnic economy. Within this paradigm two general perspectives, the disadvantage theory and the cultural theory of entrepreneurship, are the dominant frameworks used to analyze how immigrant entrepreneurs utilize ethnic resources in their businesses. In both these frameworks, ethnic resources and cultural attributes are analyzed in order to better understand the various types, as well as the success or failure of immigrant entrepreneurial activities (Light 1972, 1984; Waldinger 1986; Wong 1987; Portes and Bach 1985).

Disadvantage theory provides a theoretical perspective that regards immigrants as disadvantaged both economically and culturally in the host society, due to factors such as language problems, lack of credentials, under-employment, loss of socio-economic status, as well as having to confront legal and social forms of discrimination and racism (Bonacich 1973; Bonacich, Light, and Wong 1980). Due to a combination of the above factors, immigrant groups often turn to self-employment in business endeavors in the host country. Bonacich's middle-man minority model is a part of this paradigm, which states that when jobs available to the immigrants in the host country are not commensurate with their pre-immigration economic and social status, many will resort to self-employment in small businesses in order to combat external barriers in the labor market. Long hours of work by family members and kin are common in these small businesses. Having access to family labor is a definitive factor in determining the economic success and ability of the small family business to accumulate capital. In many documented cases, family laborers are often women in such enterprises. The continued use of the terms family labor and migrant labor veils and distorts the gender-specific component of workers in the ethnic economy, especially women's participation in these labor processes. Thus, female labor is neither peripheral nor minimal in most work environments in the ethnic economy (Morokvasic 1985; Safa 1981; Phizacklea 1983).

The cultural theory of immigrant entrepreneurs is a perspective that argues that the over representation of certain ethnic groups in small businesses can be analyzed on the basis of particular cultural attributes of the group in question (Light 1984). Here the accumulation of capital is seen as occurring through the utilization of traditional value systems embedded in cultural practices of the immigrant group in the host society. Immigrant entrepreneurs also make use of other cultural and social institutions, such as family, marriage, and rotating credit associations for capital formation and growth of small businesses. In documenting ethnic-resources utilization in small businesses in the ethnic economy there is an increased usage of a historically specific contextual framework in addressing the fluidity of ethnic resources as they intersect with capital and class resources used by entrepreneurs in the ethnic economy (Tenenbaum 1993;

Light 1984; Bozorgmehr forthcoming; Waldinger, Morokvasic, and Phizacklea 1990). This approach, which is both historical and relational, allows for a more dynamic analysis of how immigrant businesswomen and -men have adjusted and adapted to the specific social and economic circumstances facing them as they enter and develop businesses in ethnic economies in the United States.

🗃 *Methodology*

Data for this paper were collected between 1986–1988, using participant observation methods, oral histories, and open-ended interviews with sixty Iranian women between the ages of twenty and seventy-five. The large influx of Iranian immigrants to the United States in the decade since 1979 has been the direct consequence of the Iranian revolution. In the last fifteen years, the profile of Iranians has changed dramatically from those coming abroad to study, to visit, or to work to include a larger proportion of religious, political, and economic exiles, refugees, and asylees fleeing Iran for fear of persecution (Dallalfar 1989; Bozorgmehr, Sabagh, and Der-Martirosian 1993; Sabagh and Bozorgmehr 1987, 1994). According to census data, the decade of the 1980s witnessed a doubling of the population of Iranians in the United States from 121,500 to 285,000. Iranians in the United States are a heterogeneous population, comprised of diverse ethnic, cultural, and religious minorities. In Los Angeles as well, the Iranian immigrant community is heterogeneous, with both religious and ethnic diversity. It is comprised of Shi'ite and Sunni Muslims, Bahais, Armenians, Christian Assyrians, Zoroastrians, and Jews as well as Azerbaijani Turks and Kurds.

Given the religio-ethnic, geographic, and class diversity of Iranians in Los Angeles, I interviewed thirty Muslim and thirty Jewish working Iranian women of different ages and socio-economic and marital backgrounds. These women were active in diverse occupations in the ethnic economy, such as in the professions, home operated businesses, and family-run businesses as well as in the service and informal economic sectors. These categories allowed me to investigate the variety of women's work experiences, in the market, as paid or underpaid labor, and in the home, as nonincome producing workers maintaining family ties and social networks as well as carrying out the domestic and child-care needs of the household. It has been documented that the Iranian ethnic economy in Los Angeles is large, and over 60 percent of Iranians who were interviewed in a survey sample in Los Angeles in 1988 indicated they were self-employed in the Iranian ethnic economy (Light et al. 1993). My particular interest was to observe and document the status of women entrepreneurs and workers in the Iranian ethnic economy.

My observations of the rapid changes occurring within the Iranian immigrant community are located within a framework of an eight-years residence in the Westwood area of Los Angeles. In the early stages of data collection, I spent one day a week driving around specific neighborhoods in Los Angeles, (Westwood, Bentwood, Santa Monica, Beverly Hills, Fairfax, Pico, and downtown Los Angeles), jotting down types of stores and small business in which Iranian women were working. I then began to gather more detailed information about Iranian women hired in service, retail, and wholesale stores, as well as distinguishing between those businesses run solely by Iranian women and those that were family run businesses.

I chose the above geographic locations because of the predominance of Iranians living in these Los Angeles neighborhoods. It is beyond the scope of this study to address Iranians living in other areas of Los Angeles, such as primarily Armenian Iranian neighborhoods in Glendale. Certain localities in particular, such as Westwood and Santa Monica in Los Angeles, have, over the past decade, become identified with an Iranian population and clientele.

In the service industry in Los Angeles, Iranian women are visible both as owners and operators, such as in the case of family-run businesses and businesses run from the home, and as employees in diverse small businesses such as travel agencies, accounting firms, legal and real estate agencies, in laundromats and dry cleaning, and as cashiers in restaurants. In the retail business, one can locate women working in grocery stores, fruit and vegetable stores, liquor stores, other types of food-related stores, as well as in businesses that sell cosmetic and beauty products, clothing and night apparel, jewelry, and also stores that sell Iranian music, tapes, and videos. I was not able to locate any Iranian women working in gas stations or as taxi drivers, and I only saw three Iranian women working as waitresses in Iranian restaurants in Los Angeles during the time of collection of data. The absence of Iranian women in the aforementioned work environments can be explained socio-culturally and can be traced back to sex segregated job and role models established in Iran; particular professions are male oriented, with distinct social taboos restricting female participation in these types of work. A trend had developed in Tehran and other major urban centers during the early 1970s, whereby a stratum of middle- and upper-middle-class women were providing a wide range of items for sale from their home by converting some of their home space into a semibusiness space. Interestingly enough, it is this very pattern of making use of one's home, and using the social relationships and networks of friends and kin to create opportunities for career sponsorship and economic activity that are currently being used by this stratum of Iranian women in Los Angeles.

Having made lists of the various types of business activity in which Iranian women were working in various capacities, I then began to visit shopkeepers, stores where Iranian women worked, and family-run businesses, asking about other business locations that I may have missed. It was through these individuals, as well as family and friends, that I learned of a large network of women engaged in entrepreneurial activity from their homes, discovering a dimension of female entrepreneurial work that is not visible to a passerby on the street. I then began to visit these women as well, noting their businesses and the types of services they were offering. Numerous women entrepreneurs engaged in the service industry in Los Angeles have begun small businesses from their homes, working as seamstresses and dressmakers, as wholesalers to evening- and day-apparel outlets, cooks and caterers, manicurists, hair removal specialists, hair stylists and beauticians, florists, nannies and baby sitters, interior decorators, teachers of Persian, and, in one case, as a tutor of private etiquette classes for young marriageable girls.

🖎 *Small Businesses Run from the Home*

I interviewed ten Iranian women who worked as small business entrepreneurs from their home. Despite the diversity of their businesses, whether service or retail, I found the following similarities: the work was labor intensive; the operating space was small (not more than two rooms in their

home); transactions were by cash; start-up costs were relatively low (often not more than $10,000); both ethnic and class resources were available
to start a business; and the business was dependant on finding and maintaining clients within the ethnic economy. In most cases, the women who
operate businesses from their homes relied predominantly on their existing Iranian clientele for additional publicity, through word of mouth, also
using their own social networks to attract clients. Thus, there is not much
diversity in their clientele. The ten businesses that I covered in this
category of work, that of women entrepreneurs using the home as a
business site, are: a florist, a seamstress, two clothing retailers, a cook and
pastry maker, a fortune teller, a hair removal specialist with an epilation
parlor, a beautician and make-up specialist, a Persian language teacher
and typist, and a woman offering etiquette classes for unmarried girls.

Iranian women of various age groups can be located in these diverse
small businesses. I found that out of the ten women whom I interviewed,
five were over the age of fifty, two were in their forties, and three were in
their late twenties. All ten of these women came from upper-middle-class
or upper-class backgrounds before they immigrated and, thus, have faced
a change in their socio-economic status within the span of the past four to
six years at the most, during which time it has become necessary, for the
first time, for these women to earn a living.

As for their marital status: three were never married, six were married
and had grown children, and one woman was divorced and had immigrated with her child to Los Angeles. Two of these women's husbands
have not been able to find employment since immigration, they had been
working in government or in the military prior to the revolution and have
not been able to transfer their skills to the available jobs in Los Angeles.
One woman indicated that her husband was still working and living in
Iran. She has chosen to live in Los Angeles with her children, starting up
this small business to support them. One woman, stated that her husband
does not have a full-time job, but has begun a partnership with an Iranian
businessman with whom he is trying to start a small businesses. All of
these immigrant women had been in the United States for at least four
years at the time of my interviews. Members of six households had left
Iran by 1981, those of the remaining four by 1983. Families are still not
completely united, and households are still separated because of immigra-

tion restrictions or the fact that some husbands have chosen (for economic or other reasons) to stay in Iran, visiting their wives and children every few years.

For six of these women this endeavor was their first business experience since immigration. Three women in their late twenties were fluent in English; their secondary education in Iran included English along with Persian. The remaining seven women, in their forties and above, had little fluency in English and could not converse as easily in this language. Of these women, six had high-school diplomas from Iran, two had university degrees, and two were married before they finished high school and had not continued with their educations.

The above profile of women engaging in businesses run from the home is not surprising, given the types of work activity available to them with their particular class and ethnic resources as well as their immigration history, education, age, and place in their own lifecycles. Class resources, of course, lay the foundation for having sufficient capital to begin a small business. These entrepreneurial women have also utilized existing ethnic resources and social capital, such as resorting to family members, kin, and friends for capital formation as well as in their work setting both as suppliers and employees and also as customers. Noncontractual forms of interaction in immigrant businesses embody what is generally referred to as ethnic resources in the more recent literature on ethnic economies, and is of primary importance to female entrepreneurial activity operated from the home. Many of the Iranian women who have opened stores in Los Angeles first started out selling merchandise from their homes. Only after they had an established clientele and felt they could afford to pay rent and utilities did they move out of their homes and lease store space in which to sell their goods. This pattern was followed in the cases of a florist, a beautician, a dressmaker, and a woman who opened a clothing store. In fact, one finds that the transferability of the skills that cross the public and private domains allow for more flexibility in starting businesses slowly, and not having to invest a large sum of money at the very beginning of their business endeavor. The following case of female entrepreneurial activity illustrates the necessity and complementarity of ethnic resources, where issues other than material and contractual relations become determining factors for the success of the business.

SIMIN

Simin[1] is a divorced Muslim woman in her mid-forties who lives near Westwood with her adolescent son. Her English is not very good, and she speaks with an accent. When she arrived in Los Angeles in 1981, she met many Iranian women who complained about the high cost of having to go to beauty salons for epilation (hair removal through waxing). Although she had no previous professional experience in this area, Simin knew that she could provide this service at a relatively low price. For Simin, immigrant status as a divorced woman, lack of language skills, and the urgency of finding employment made it rather appealing to start her own business, in which she knew she could earn more in the long run than she could working for someone else. The initial cost of setting up her business was close to $8,000 in 1983, and a woman friend of hers lent her the money to buy the items necessary to set up a salon in a room in her apartment and begin working. Most important at the time was to get out the word that she was providing a much needed service for Iranian women in the community at a very reasonable price. An added advantage that Simin had is that she knew how to style and shape eyebrows using a traditional Iranian technique of thread for hair removal. Through this skill she gained quite a good reputation and many new clients, since once women received compliments on their appearance, they would mention her as the one who performed the service.

When Simin first started she worked alone and made appointments seven days a week and evenings. She always had tea brewing in an electric samovar in the kitchen and would schedule her appointments so that she had at least half an hour between clients. This offered her an opportunity to socialize and form a relationship with her customers, especially if they were not part of her immediate circle of kin, family, or friends. After a few months she learned how to make the wax that she used for hair removal, which further cut costs. She also began to buy the material in bulk from a florist friend who worked in downtown Los Angeles. In the first year of operating her business she kept her prices at least 30 percent below those of others providing the same kind of services. Mostly through word of mouth about her cleanliness and speed, her clientele increased monthly. To further publicize her business, Simin made a flyer, had it photocopied, and left it outside some of the night language classes that Iranian women attended. By 1985 she had saved enough to be able to move into a larger home, separating the lower section of her house for the business.

Simin had arranged her new business setting such that one first enters a waiting room, with a television, comfortable chairs, and a couch, in which she socializes and has tea with customers. Off of this main room is another room, divided into two compartments, one for epilation and one for manicures and pedicures. She hired an Iranian woman to help her, paying her a monthly salary in cash, which is off the record. Simin, when making an appointment, mentions that she does not take checks and only accepts cash. She herself works less intensely now than before and has set hours for appointments six days a week, taking Mondays off. When calling to make an appointment, Simin leaves more time than is needed for those clients with whom she wants to have tea. Since her business is rather busy, she only has social visits with friends and acquaintances on certain days when she knows that there is less need for her to work. She plans on eventually being available to only a select clientele, and styling eyebrows more than waxing, hoping to hire another woman to do the waxing. At present, she has a successful business. By now non-Iranian women, who then further publicize her services and create a more diversified clientele, are using her services.

⬚ The Family-Run Business

Both disadvantage theory and the cultural theory of entrepreneurship can be limited by the use of gender neutral terms, such as family labor or migrant labor, in describing small family-run businesses in the ethnic economy. The work performed by immigrant women in family-run businesses is highly labor intensive. There is much pressure to increase profitability by working longer hours at the business, given limited amounts of available capital that can be invested in it. Consequently, the survival, expansion, and profitability of the business are contingent on having an available pool of labor to run and operate for longer hours and during times when other stores and businesses are closed. Mirjana Morokvasic (1985) has documented cases in which labor in family-run businesses among Pakistanis in France was predominantly female labor, yet women's participation in the business was not seen as a determining factor in the business endeavor; instead, their work was viewed as a natural expectation and extension of their gender roles in the family. Here, I will discuss women's participation in family-run businesses in Los Angeles, demonstrating how gender neutral terms in this area of social inquiry have served to render invisible women's work in the ethnic economy in Los Angeles.

The ten women I interviewed in family-run businesses had the following occupations: one worked with her husband in an owner-operated dry cleaning facility; one worked with her husband and son in a travel agency; one worked with her two daughters in a shoe and leather repair shop; one worked with her husband in a retail clothing store; one worked with her husband and her son in a retail clothing store; one worked with her husband in a small coffee and pastry shop in a commercial building; two worked with their husbands, with partial participation of their children, in mom-and-pop grocery and delicatessen stores; one worked with her husband and hired help in a restaurant; and one worked with her husband in a pastry shop and delicatessen.

In addition to capital formation, entry into a business requires: learning and obtaining information regarding market opportunities, deciding the type of business one is going to enter, deciding the location of the business, legally registering the business with the state, contracting with suppliers of the necessary goods and services, designing the layout of the store, and learning management and customer service skills. All of ten women I interviewed mentioned the necessity of somehow surviving economically in Los Angeles as the main reason for starting their businesses. Their choice of business had more to do with their skills and perceptions about the demand for the services they would be offering than with any other variables, but other factors were discussed. These included the geographic location of the business, the amount of capital resources available in the family for investment as well as sources for borrowing, money from family and friends in the community, the types of activities demanded by each business they were considering and their ability to handle the work environment. Information about starting a business was often obtained from friends and kin who either had personal experiences starting their own business or knew of someone who had this experience and could help them get started as well. All of these skills are being mastered by Iranian women, who are getting hands on experience in their daily encounters in their newly acquired roles as business women.

Seven of these women were in their fifties or over, and the remaining three were in their forties. All ten of these women are married and have grown children who help, either directly or indirectly, with the business. Sometimes this help takes the form of taking care of forms and legal matters associated with running a small business. In one case, a Muslim woman, whose husband is in Iran, operates and works at the family-run business with her daughters, and in the remaining nine cases, the husbands were the primary partners in the family-run business. None of the women I interviewed had worked with their husbands before, but two had previous work experiences prior to immigration. Of the ten women I interviewed, seven had a high-school education, and three did not finish high school because they became engaged and married before finishing the twelfth grade. Two women spoke relatively good English, and the remaining eight spoke English with difficulty, but they were improving daily because of their interaction with clients and their attending language classes when time permitted. The following case illustrates the active and necessary work of Iranian women in family-run businesses. The profitability of these businesses is directly contingent on the long hours of work of women as well as men. By not adequately addressing gender issues when discussing small businesses in the ethnic economy, women's work contributions are rendered invisible and are devalued, in that women's contributions to the business are regarded as being less important and having less value than the tasks that their husbands perform in the family-run business.

EFFAT

Effat is a Muslim woman in her mid-fifties, a little overweight with a friendly disposition as she stands behind the counter of the family operated dry-cleaning business in Santa Monica. There are two other laundromat/dry-cleaning businesses within walking distance of their store. Among the strategies her family have used to attract clients to their store have been to keep the store open for longer hours, to charge a little less, to have the articles of clothing ready faster than their immediate competitors, to do alterations in one day, and to advertize in Farsi in order to draw Iranian customers who are driving by.

Effat, her husband Kerim, and their son, who is in his early twenties, arrive at the store around seven in the morning and leave close to seven in the evening every day except Sunday. Some weeks Effat ends up working more than eighty hours, especially when she has alterations to do.

Effat's husband worked for an international airline in Iran, and is fluent in French and German, his English being the weakest of his foreign languages. When they first arrived in 1985, they did not have much money saved and were in need of a source of income. Effat studied Persian up to the sixth grade; when she got married at fourteen, she did not continue her education, saying, "In those days, once a girl was married, she did not go to school anymore. Now it's different, and even my own daughter continued studying after she got married." She said that her husband would prefer that she not work, but given the conditions of their life here, she has no choice.

> Life here is so hard, I think that our men made money more easily in Iran, . . . here we have so many additional expenses that we never had there, like taxes, utilities, rental and even food is so much more expensive here, but I shouldn't be unthankful *na shokri nakonam*, at least we have work and a roof over our heads at night.

Effat, given all her responsibilities, decided that the best arrangement for an interview would be at the store, early on a Saturday morning. She mentioned that this was a time when there would be fewer clients, and she really did not have time to see me outside of her work environment. I arrived promptly at eight, and I could see Effat already at work behind the sewing machine located in one the corner of the store. I observed her throughout the day, carrying out various tasks at the laundromat. It became strikingly clear that the operation and survival of this family business is directly contingent on her labor. She spent the longest hours at the store, her husband also works long hours, but his involvement in trying to start another business made him less frequently available at this particular site.

During the first year of operation her son, Ahmad, helped in the back of the store. He was responsible for all the technical aspects of putting the chemicals in the machines and running them, as well as making sure that the rest of the equipment, such as the ironing presses, were functioning properly. Ahmad would also help up front, writing up orders and taking special requests when he had a free moment. The family had also hired an

African-American man to help them three days a week with the ironing in order to spend more time learning how to run and maintain the business.

After their first year of successfully operating this business, the family became increasingly concerned about the strong odor of the chemicals they used for dry cleaning, especially in the back of the store. They had heard that prolonged exposure to these chemical fumes could cause sterility. This posed a major dilemma for them, in that they did not want Ahmad, who is not even married, to continue working there.

About a month before Ahmad stopped working at the laundromat full-time, the family rented the liquor store next door to them and converted it into a mini-market and liquor store. Since Effat's husband and Ahmad spend most of their time working there now, she, in turn, manages most of the work at the laundromat. Of course, sometimes when she is unable to understand what the customer wants, she apologetically asks them to wait and rushes next door to fetch her son or husband, who then translates for her. She laughingly told me, "We are like sparrows, we hop between these two stores, especially when I can't understand what the customer wants."

Having these two stores located next to each other has been quite beneficial for the family, in that between the three of them, they can keep both stores open longer hours, and the men can go back and forth depending on where the service is most needed. Effat told me that she tries not to think about being in the store alone, and when she gets nervous about a particular person in the store, she reminds herself that her husband and son are within reach. She said that she will never forget the day they were burglarized at gun point, when her husband and son were also in the store. Because of this incident the back door has been closed, and now the only entry is through the front. This, of course, gives her more control over who is coming and going from the store, but also makes the environment more toxic, since there is little air circulation in the back of the store.

Presently, Effat bears the primary responsibility for dealing with clients, registering and returning clothes to customers, and doing any sewing and alteration work that is required. She described alterations as easy money, in that she can charge up to five dollars for fixing a hem or shortening a pair of trousers, and she is still charging below her immediate competitors. She mentioned that some people don't even sew their own buttons anymore and bring her jobs like that too. They are willing to pay because they lack the time (*hoseleh*) or patience to make these repairs themselves. She said that labor is so expensive here, whereas in Iran it was so cheap.

When she first started to come to the store, she was at a loss when standing behind the counter. She said:

> I didn't understand a word of English, and spoke with my hands; it was hard then. I didn't know how to fill out the form or even just understand what the customer wanted to be done, I didn't even know the names of colors in English. . . . In Iran, most of the women like me were housewives (*khanehdar*), but here, having to work is not a question of choice. My husband does not like the fact that I work, but he has no choice, and he needs my help here.

Effat is extremely cordial and friendly with all her customers, always making a little special offer for Iranian customers with whom she easily communicates and socializes. Sometimes she doesn't charge for an item, or prepares an article of clothing within a day and does not charge extra for the service. Even non-Iranian customers are not treated formally and anonymously. I witnessed a look of surprise on some faces as she rounded off the price, waved her hand and said, "no pennies." Through her actions, one notices a distinguishing component of the family-run business in the ethnic economy, the mannerisms used to establish a non-material relationship and bond with clients. There is a concerted effort to lessen the anonymity of the customer and create an amiable environment that will motivate the customer to return for future services. Effat worked throughout the day, taking only a few short breaks to sit on a wooden chair and rest her feet. She complained about how tired she was by the end of the day, when she still must go home and prepare a meal for her husband. She said that despite her work at the dry-cleaning store, she is the one responsible for cooking and keeping a clean home. Her husband, she said:

> does not cook anything so that even though I am not home in the day to prepare a good meal and keep a clean home, his expectations are that I do that work as well. When I was leaving my parents' home, I remember that they told me whatever your husband tells you, you must accept and follow; first is the word of God and then your husband. Out of respect to them (*be ehteram-eh-ounha*), I have lived my life as my husband has wanted.

Effat mentioned numerous times that she believed her primary responsibility and role in the family was as a wife and mother, and her work, responsibilities, and contributions to the family-operated business are second.

For Effat her labor in the household and in the workplace are interdependent spheres, between which she is constantly negotiating. Her involvement in the family business has not changed dramatically her status and domestic responsibilities within the household. The increased tensions of working in the family-operated business and daily discovering that she did not have enough time to handle all the work necessary for family maintenance was an issue of concern and frustration for her.

☙ Conclusion

Women are active participants in the Iranian ethnic economy in Los Angeles. The barriers to employment for these women are different from those they faced in Iran. Here they comprise a distinct ethnic and immigrant population, where issues such as language, age, and the level of education interact with their class and gender to sometimes create barriers and discrimination in finding employment in the labor market. In turn, women have made use of class, ethnic and gender resources to open small businesses in a setting where work and social activity converge, such as in jobs in the service industry that can be run from the home, or in family-run businesses in the ethnic economy.

This glimpse at women's active roles in the ethnic economy is already indicative of how gender is an important factor in determining one's access to ethnic resource utilization for economic activity. As seen in both the case of Simin and Effat, their participation in the ethnic economy is a full-time activity. By addressing the gender of those working in the family business, distortions of degree to which the role of the spouse or female kin is significant to the survival and profitability of the business becomes very visible. Effat has multiple roles in this family-run business: as a cashier, as the primary seamstress, and as the one who engages in public relations during business hours. Her involvement in this family-run business is not secondary to her husband's, and her labor and involvement are central to the survival of the small ethnic entrepreneurial business. Both these case studies demonstrate how women's ethnic resource utilization in an ethnic business is vital to its material success. It also appears that

Iranian women are more able than their male counterparts to utilize social and family networks in some business environments, given their overlap with the home environment. Many women who are engaged in entrepreneurial activities that are home-based make use of the skills they learned to carry out their domestic, maternal and family responsibilities, and transfer the appropriate skills with much energy and enthusiasm to their recently acquired status as businesswomen. These entrepreneurial women are involved daily in noncontractual relations, one of the distinguishing features of Iranian and other minority-owned small businesses in the United States.

This transferability of skills, the ability to socialize and simultaneously engage in business through use of their home environment, is an arena to which Iranian men do not have access, particularly since their work environment in Iran was separate from their home environment, and, similarly, in work settings in Los Angeles. These Iranian women have been better able than their male counterparts to make use of their class resources as well as their ethnic resources in these small entrepreneurial endeavors. Iranian men who desperately want a job, such as starting a business for themselves that has a low start-up cost, do not have this alternative available to them. Thus, gender in work settings that are located in the homes, either facilitates the possibility of business entry or deters it.

🖾 *References*

Abadan-Unat, Nermin. 1977. "Implications of Migration on Emancipation and Pseudo-Emancipation of Turkish Women." *International Migration Review* 11: 31–57.

Aswad, Barbara. 1994. "Attitudes of Immigrant Women and Men in the Dearborn Area toward Women's Employment and Welfare." In *Muslim Communities in North America*, ed. Yvonne Yazbeck Haddad and J. Smith. Albany: State University of New York Press.

Avakian, Arlene. 1992. *Lion Woman's Legacy: An Armenian-American Memoir*. New York: Feminist Press at the City University of New York.

Bonacich, Edna. 1972. "A Theory of Ethnic Antagonism: The Split Labor Market." *American Sociological Review* 37: 547–559.

————. 1973. "A Theory of Middlemen Minorities." *American Sociological Review* 38: 583–594.

Bonacich, Edna; I. Light; and Charles Wong. 1980. "Small Business among Koreans in Los Angeles." In *The New Immigration*, ed. Roy S. Bryce Laporte. New Brunswick, N.J.: Transaction.

Bonacich, Edna and J. Modell. 1980. *The Economic Basis of Ethnic Solidarity*. Los Angeles: University of California Press.

Bozorgmehr, Mehdi. Forthcoming. "Diaspora in Postrevolutionary Period. *Encyclopedia Iranica*.

Bozorgmehr, Mehdi; G. Sabagh; and C. Der-Martirosian. 1993. "Beyond Nationality: Religio-ethnic Diversity." In *Irangeles: Iranians in Los Angeles*, ed. Ron Kelly and Jonathan Friedlander. Berkeley and Los Angeles: University of California Press.

Brettell, Caroline and R. J. Simon. 1986. "Immigrant Women: An Introduction." In *International Migration: The Female Experience*, ed. by Rita Simon and C. Brettell. Totowa, N.J.: Rowman & Allanheld.

Cainkar, Louise, 1985. "Life Experiences of Palestinian Women in the United States." Paper presented at the nineteenth annual meeting of Middle East Studies of North America, Chicago.

Chiswick, Barry. 1980. "Immigrant Earnings Patterns by Sex, Race, and Ethnic Groupings." *Monthly Labor Review* 103: 22–25.

Dallalfar, Arlene. 1989. *Iranian Immigrant Women in Los Angeles: The Reconstruction of Work, Ethnicity and Community*. Ph.D. diss., Department of Sociology, University of California, Los Angeles.

————. 1994. "Iranian Women as Immigrant Entrepreneurs." *Gender and Society* 8: 541–561.

England, Paula; B. S. Kilbourne; G. Farkas; and T. Dou. 1988. "Explaining Occupational Sex Segregation and Wages: Findings from a Model with Fixed Effects." *American Sociological Review* 53: 544–558.

Feldberg, Roslyn and Evelyn N. Glenn. 1979. "Male and Female: Job versus Gender Models in the Sociology of Work." *Social Problems* 26: 524–538.

Glenn, Evelyn Nakano. 1986. *Issei, Nisei, War Bride: Three Generations of Japanese American Women in Domestic Service*. Philadelphia: Temple University Press.

Gold, Steve. 1994. "Israeli Immigrants in the United States: The Question of Community." *Qualitative Sociology* 17: 325–363.

Haddad Yvonne and Adair Lummis. 1987. *Islamic Values in the United States*, New York: Oxford University Press.

Haddad, Yvonne and Jane Smith, eds. 1994. *Muslim Communities in North America*. Albany: State University of New York Press.

Hondagneu-Sotelo, Pierrette. 1992. "Overcoming Patriarchal Constraints: The Reconstruction of Gender Relations among Mexican Immigrant Women and Men." *Gender and Society* 6: 393–415.

Houstoun, Marion; Roger G. Kramer; and Joan M. Barrett. 1984. "Female Predominance in Immigration to the United States since 1930: A First Look." *International Migration Review* 18: 908–963.

Juteau-Lee, Danielle and Barbara Roberts. 1981. "Ethnicity and Femininity: Aprés Nos Experience." *Canadian Ethnic Studies* 13: 1–23.

Kessler-Harris, Alice. 1981. *Women Have always Worked*. Old Westbury, Conn.: Feminist Press.

Kibria, Nazli. 1990. "Power, Patriarchy, and Gender Conflict in the Vietnamese Immigrant Community." *Gender and Society* 4: 9–24.

Kim, Kwang Chung and Won Moo Hurh. 1985. "Ethnic Resource Utilization of Korean Immigrant Entrepreneurs in the Chicago Minority Area." *International Migration Review* 19: 82–111.

Light, Ivan. 1972. *Ethnic Enterprise in America*. Berkeley: University of California Press.

———. 1979. "Disadvantaged Minorities in Self-Employment." *International Journal of Comparative Sociology* 20: 31–45.

———. 1984. "Immigrant and Ethnic Enterprise in North America." *Ethnic and Racial Studies* 7: 195–216.

Light, Ivan; G. Sabagh; M. Bozorgmehr; and C. Der-Martirosian. 1993. "International Ethnicity in the Ethnic Economy." *Ethnic and Racial Studies*. 16: 581–597.

Massay, Douglas S. 1981. "Dimensions of the New Immigration to the United States and the Prospects of Assimilation." *Annual Review of Sociology* 7: 57–85.

Melies, Afaf; J. Lipson; and S. Paul. 1992. "Ethnicity and Health among Five Middle Eastern Immigrant Groups." *Nursing Research* 41: 98–103.

Mies, Maria. 1982. *The Lace Makers of Narsapur: Indian Housewives Produce for the World Market*. London: Zed.

Moallem, Minoo. 1991. "Ethnic Entrepreneurship and Gender Relations among Iranians in Montreal, Quebec, Canada." In *Iranian Refugees and Exiles Since Khomeini* ed. A. Fathi. Costa Mesa, Calif.: Mazda.

Morokvasic, Mirjana, 1984. "Birds of Passage are also Women." *International Migration Review* 18: 886–907.

————. 1985. "The Visible and the Hidden Side of the Parisian Garment Industry." Paper presented at the Conference on Economic Restructuring and Urban Decline. University of Warick.

Pedraza, Silvia, 1991. "Women and Migration: The Social Consequences of Gender." *Annual Review of Sociology* 17: 303–325.

Pessar, Patricia. 1984. "The Linkage between the Household and Workplace of Dominican Women in the U.S." *International Migration Review* 18: 1188–1211.

Phizacklea, Annie. 1983. "In the Frontline." In *One Way Ticket, Migration, and Female Labor*, ed. A. Phizacklea. London: Routledge, Kegan Paul.

Portes, Alejandro. 1984. "The Rise of Ethnicity: Determinants of Ethnic Perception among Cuban Exiles in Miami." *American Sociological Review* 49: 383–397.

Portes, Alejandro and R. Bach. 1985. *Latin Journey, Cuban and Mexican Immigrants in the United States*. Berkeley and Los Angeles: University of California Press.

Portes, Alejandro and J. Walton. 1981. *Labor, Class, and the International System*. New York: Academic Press.

Sabagh, Georges and Mehdi Bozorgmehr. 1987. "Are the Characteristics of Exiles Different from Immigrants: The Case of Iranians in Los Angeles." *Sociology and Social Research* 71: 77–83.

————. 1994. "Secular Immigrants: Religiosity and Ethnicity among Iranian Muslims in Los Angeles." In *Muslim Communities in North America*, ed. Yvonne Haddad and Jane Smith. Albany: State University of New York Press.

Safa, Helen. 1981. "Runaway Shops and Female Employment: The Search for Cheap Labor." *Signs* 7: 418–433.

Sassen-Koob, Saski., 1984. "Notes on the Incorporation of Third World Women into Wage-Labor through Immigration and Off-Shore Production." *International Migration Review* 18: 1144–1167.

Tenenbaum, Shelly. 1993. *A Credit to Their Community*. Detroit: Wayne State University Press.

Tienda, Marta. 1980. "Familism and Structural Assimilation of Mexican Immigrants in the United States." *International Migration Review* 14: 383–408.

Tienda, Marta; Leif Jenson; and Robert Bach. 1984. "Immigration, Gender, and the Process of Occupational Change in the United States: 1970–80." *International Migration Review* 18:1021–1044.

Waldinger, Roger. 1986. *Through the Eye of the Needle.* New York: New York University Press.

Waldinger, Roger; M. Morokvasic; and A. Phizacklea. 1990. "Business on the Ragged Edge: Immigrant and Minority Businesses in the Garment Industries of Paris, London, and New York." In *Ethnic Entrepreneurs: Immigrant and Ethnic Businesses in Western Industrial Societies,* ed. Roger Waldinger, H. Aldrich, and R. Ward. Beverly Hills: Sage.

Westwood, Sallie and Paraminder Bhachu. 1988. *Enterprising Women: Ethnicity, Economy and Gender Relations.* New York: Routledge.

Wong, Bernard. 1987. "The Role of Ethnicity in Enclave Enterprises: A Study of Chinese Garment Factories in New York City." *Human Organization* 46: 120–130.

Woo, Deborah. 1985. "The Socio-economic Status of Asian Women in the Labor Force: An Alternative View." *Sociological Perspectives* 28: 307–339.

NIMAT HAFEZ BARAZANGI

Parents and Youth

Perceiving and Practicing Islam in North America

This chapter examines how some Arab Muslim youth and families in North America perceive themselves both as Arabs and as Muslims in the context of Canadian and United States societies. Parents are concerned with how best to transmit the Islamic ideological and Arab cultural heritage to their children. One of their problems derives from differences among Arab Muslims, who come from varied national origins and hold several interpretations of the Islamic view, not all of which are based on the Qur'an; as a result they also have different nationalistic attachments to their understanding of Arab heritage. A second problem arises between immigrant parents and their American-reared children. The children may participate in American culture to a greater extent than their parents, and they are constantly faced with the conceptual need to accommodate potentially conflicting points of view. Effective identity transmission requires the determination of the nature and extent of the different interpretations held by parents and their children and of the ways these interpretations

Special thanks are due to two persons who have contributed significantly to the shaping of ideas, statement of concepts, and reporting of results: Robert L. Bruce of Cornell University, my academic adviser, and the late Isma'il R. al-Faruqi of Temple University, an ad hoc member of my graduate committee.

Others have also contributed directly or indirectly to the outcome of my research. In particular, I wish to acknowledge Omar Afzal, Muslim adviser to Cornell University and surrounding communities; George J. Posner and David S. Powers, members of my graduate committee at Cornell; and Sid Doan, who helped me prepare the manuscript.

are reflected in their practice of Islam and association with the Arabic heritage.

This paper focuses on a small sample of Arab Muslim youth aged fourteen to twenty-two and their parents. They were a sub-sample of a larger group who participated in my study of North American Muslims' perception and practice of the Islamic belief system (see Barazangi 1988). These youth are first-generation children of immigrants who came to North America during the 1960s and 1970s. The aim of this effort is threefold:

1. To gain a greater understanding of the differences in the ways immigrants adjusted by examining the effects of preconception of identity on both the adjustment process of the immigrant parent and the transmission of identity to his or her children.

2. To explain the differences between the social (modification of behavior) and the conceptual (modification of world view) accommodation or assimilation process.

3. To explicate the role of the search for conceptual integration[1] as a more lasting factor than social integration, whether it is the parents' adjustment to the Western environment or the youths' attempt to acquire an Arab Muslim identity in the context of Western societies. The argument of this paper is built, therefore, on two propositions:

1. Not all immigrants—even those coming from the same region and adhering to the same religion—can be assumed to experience the same accommodation or assimilation process.

2. Conceptual accommodation and assimilation are the reverse of social accommodation and assimilation. People who assimilate socially may very well accommodate conceptually by modifying or changing their world view in the same way as they modified their behavior to fit the environment into which they assimilate. Those who accommodate socially and assimilate conceptually modify the environmental behavioral norms and world view.

I have concentrated on Arab Muslim youth who are children of the last wave of immigrants in order to examine the complexity of this identity problem at its roots, at the learning process. The basic questions are: What makes the present first generation of Arab Muslim youth associate with two conflicting, yet integrative, identities, Arabism and Islamic Muslim? And how do these youth perceive this dual-identity association in the reality of North American societies?

⚔ Styles of Identity Determination

Contemporary Arab Muslim immigrants may perceive themselves as having at least four different and simultaneous identity associations. They may identify themselves as Islamic, Muslim,[2] Syrian (or Iraqi, Yemeni, and so on), Arab, or American[3] at different times and in different contexts. These four aspects of identity can result in a minimum of twelve different combinations when the person attempts to describe his or her association, such as Arab Muslim American of Syrian descent or Muslim Arab Syrian who resides in America, and so on. The Iranian revolution indirectly added to the list of descriptive terms. With its emphasis on Shi'ism, a fifth identity association was added to the other four.

This complexity has had different social and political meanings since the early twentieth century, and particularly since the post–World War II growth of Arab nationalism and the Arab world's resistance to the creation of Israel. But even more interesting is the development of Islamicity[4] over the past decade. This term, which North American Muslims hitherto primarily used to refer to a religious affiliation, has now taken on a new religio-nationalistic and ideological meaning. (See Akbar Muhammad's account of the heightening and attraction of American Muslims to the political and religious sentiments of the Arabic-speaking world, 1984).

The establishment of sub-Muslim or sub-Arab organizations did not help resolve identity confusion, and, in fact, it may have added a new dimension to the problem. For example, the Muslim Arab Youth Association, the Malaysian Students Association, and others came into existence in the late 1970s, and since they differ in political tone, they also have different identity associations.

There is a wealth of studies treating attitudinal religio-social and behavioral adjustment (see, for example, S. Bochner 1983; R. Laurence Moore 1986; E. K. Lovell 1983; Abdo A. Elkholy 1966). Whether or not they relate specifically to immigrants, these studies are concerned mainly with the social accommodation or assimilation process of the individual or the group. Social accommodation is understood generally to indicate that the person modifies the new behavior, environment, or attitude instead of his or her own when attempting to integrate them. Social assimilation is understood to indicate that the person complies or conforms with the new behavior, environment, or attitude instead of modifying it.

Very few studies, however, have dealt with the conceptual aspects of attitudinal and behavioral adjustment. Baha Abu-Laban (1983) touches on this level when he suggests reviving *ijthad* (independent reasoning) to help reconcile Islam, as a body of theological doctrine and beliefs, with the new environment. This paper approaches the task by adapting from three sources—the reconstruction of religious thought (Iqbal 1962), the philosophy of science (Kuhn 1970), and conceptual change theory (represented in George J. Posner 1983; K. A. Strike and G. J. Posner 1983)—to construct a model of Islamic or Arabic integration within the context of North American societies.

⚶ *Conceptual Change Theory*

Evidence from recent work on the learning of concepts in science and mathematics suggests that beliefs about the nature of reality (metaphysical commitments) and about the nature of knowledge (epistemological commitments) may play a role in what is learned and how (see examples of these studies in G. J. Posner 1983; J. Confrey 1980; P. W. Hewson 1982). Although the mechanism of this interaction is unknown, the learning theory underlying these studies may be useful in understanding Arab Muslim youths' determination of their identity.

Conceptual change theory assumes that an individual's learning process is at least in part a rational process of altering or changing ideas or concepts (see K. A. Strike; G. J. Posner 1983).[5] To understand learning as a rational process, one must take into account a person's existing conceptual structure (what he or she already knows), his or her belief about the nature of reality (metaphysics), and his or her beliefs about the nature of knowledge (epistemology). Together, these may shape the reasons for what and how a person learns.

In contrast to Elkholy, Lovell, and other students of immigrant groups, who approach the adjustment from historical, anthropological, sociological, or psychological points of view, here these factors are taken into account, but within the framework of the learning and adjustment process (see, for example, Nathan Glazer 1972; Yih-Chyi Nina Lin 1978). That is, the parents who are attempting to maintain themselves in a new (Western) environment go through a learning process. Whether it is called adult learning or adjustment, it is a process of assimilating new concepts and accommodating previous concepts.

The same learning process applies to Muslim youth, with three differences. First, their epistemology (that is, belief or formative thinking) has not been fully established and is less complex or advanced than that of their parents. Second, they are being reared in two different environments at the same time, the familial and communal Muslim or nationalistic Arab and the school or host-societal secular. Finally, their social and conceptual accommodation and assimilation processes are interwoven in a complex balance that varies depending on their parents' adjustment process and transmission of the Islamic or Arab heritage.

It is essential to realize that both parents and youth but particularly parents, may have formed their epistemological view of Islam in another environment. It is possible, therefore, that they may go through an unlearning and relearning process when they have contacts with other Muslims and Arabs and are exposed to new conceptions of Islam and of Arabism.

Application to the Study

The theoretical question, hence, may be restated as concerning how an Arab Muslim's view of Islam and its different practices and of Arabism might affect how he or she learns the basic principles and their practice in a particular context. For example, Islam might be thought of as a faith in which the teachings are considered as an absolute list of "dos" and "do nots." A person with that view might accept and practice the codes and might think that they cannot be modified or changed to accommodate the new environment or way of life. On the other hand, Islam may be seen as an intellectual view of life that encompasses certain guidelines, and Arabic custom may be regarded as a tool or a manifestation of these guidelines. A person with that view might recognize not only the Islamic principal elements but also the variation in the ways they may be applied. He or she might take an approach to everyday activities that is different and perhaps less strict or dichotomous than that of the Muslim with an absolutist view. If however, a person chiefly thinks of Islam as codes representing the

Qur'anic teachings, he or she may learn them but keep them separate from or opposite to his or her practice in the real world. If this view is combined with a perception of Arab and Arabic as the only appropriate social manifestation of Islam, such a person may view Islam as being only the rituals and customs practiced by "Arab" Muslims.

✿ *Methods*

Members of fifteen Arab Muslim families of varied nationalities were interviewed in five major cities in Canada and the United States as part of a larger study. Seventeen parents (eight fathers and nine mothers) and seventeen youth (eight males and nine females) who could be matched for data analysis were interviewed and completed two sets of questionnaires. The criteria for selecting families in the sample were that they were willing to participate in the study and that they had children from fourteen to twenty-two years of age who were raised mainly in North America.

PARTICIPANT OBSERVATION

In many large North American cities Muslim groups have established centers and mosques where their major religious activities take place. Most Islamic or Arabic education programs also take place in these centers. The investigator spent at least a two-day weekend in Toronto, Montreal, Buffalo, New York, and Washington, D.C., to get a picture of community activities and to get acquainted with the people who associate with various centers. The weekend was chosen because most activities in Muslim centers take place then, beginning with Friday prayer, and most Muslim families can be reached easily only through these centers.

QUESTIONNAIRES

Two sets of questionnaires were used. In the first, closed and open-ended questions were developed to gather information about the individual's age, sentimental attachment to the culture, identification preference, nature of education, family status, patterns of practice, length of residence in America, and exposure to mass media.

In the second, forced-choice and open-ended questions tested the hypothesis that perceptual differences among Muslims, parents and youth alike, are associated with their understanding of the principles in Islamic teachings. The belief items tested were: monotheism and human role; prophethood and sense of mission; the Hereafter and accountability; the pillars of Islam and significance of application; the Scriptures; moral teachings, social systems, and social institutions; and beliefs about knowledge, inquiry, and education.

Focus-Group Interview

Four basic principles of Islam—Allah (God), Islam (as a world view), *taqwa* (consciousness of Allah), *islah* (construction), and eight other issues, such as why teach/learn the Arabic language, what do you mean by "practicing Islam"? and so on, were probed in taped focus-group interview sessions. Fathers, mothers, and youths who responded to the questionnaires individually were interviewed in small groups of like members. Also, each interviewee was asked, at the beginning of the interview, to write on an index card what he or she thinks, feels, or does when each of the above principles is mentioned.

ﷺ *Findings*

A model of Islamic or Arabic integration guided the analysis and the interpretation of data.[6]

The results are summarized under two major headings, the parents' responses and the youths' responses.

Parents' Conception and Practice of Islam

Although the parents in this study tend to regard themselves as "Arab Muslim" or "Muslim Arab," the majority of them identify primarily with their countries of origin. Yet, most do not want to be identified with their country of origin within the general context of American society.

In response to the question "What is your cultural heritage?" 82 percent identified themselves with their country of origin. Only 11 percent identified themselves with pan-Arabism, and 6 percent identified themselves with Islam.

In response to the question "How do you see yourself when you are among non-Muslims?" only 11 percent identified themselves as "Arab first," and no one identified him- or herself as "Muslim first." The majority of parents identified themselves as "American."

Most of these parents practiced Islam as a "religious" duty (in the narrow sense) before their arrival in North America. When they expressed some identity association with Islam, it was mostly a reflection of their idealized view of the past or of ethnic customary experience.

In response to the question related to family practice, emphasis, and reaction to their children's obedience in practicing "religious" obligation (conditional concepts), the majority agreed with their family's emphasis on religious obligations and supported a strong reaction when these religious practices become lax.

In response to questions related to family emphasis on scholastic and professional achievement, the majority of these parents agreed that their family valued such achievements. Yet, when they were asked about valuing Islamic knowledge of moral and social principles, very few indicated that their families emphasized this practice, but they had no quarrel with it.

In response to the question "What does practicing Islam mean to you?" the predominant themes among parents were related to overt behaviors that accompany beliefs such as behaviors "the Prophet used to conduct himself and deal with others," or outward appearances, such as dressing Islamically (60%), and the basics or the Pillars of Islam, such as "following *al sunnah* (footsteps) of the Prophet," or *salah* (prayer), *zakah* (tax on wealth), "read and learn Qur'an" (30%).

When parents join organizations with Islamic, Muslim, or Arabic names, they tend to politicize "Islamic" ideals or "Arabic heritage" in order to advocate personal views that are mostly the result of abstract nationalistic, ethnic, or sectarian sentiments.

For example, in response to the question "Why do you value teaching Arabic to your children?" only 25 percent of the parents emphasized the value of Arabic for understanding the Qur'an. Fifty percent emphasized Arabic as a means of keeping the heritage and for reading Arabic history books, and 25 percent emphasized the spoken dialect for easy communication with grandparents and relatives.

As Table 1 shows, parents in the study tended to score higher on questions that asked them to state Islamic central concepts and human interrelation concepts (82 percent in each case had mean scores at or above

TABLE I

PARENTS AND YOUTH FREQUENCY ON CONCEPTION AND PRACTICE

DOMAIN—CONCEPTION

	PARENTS		YOUTH	
	HIGH (%)[a]	LOW (%)[b]	HIGH (%)	LOW (%)
Central Concept	82	18	88	12
Conditional Concepts	70	30	53	47
Human Interrelation Concepts	82	18	88	12

DOMAIN—PRACTICE

	PARENTS		YOUTH	
	HIGH (%)[a]	LOW (%)[b]	HIGH (%)	LOW (%)
Central Concept	18	82	—	100
Conditional Concepts	82	18	82	18
Human Interrelation Concepts	18	82	24	76

[a] High: at or above mean score 4.5 on a 6-point scale.
[b] Low: below mean score 4.5 on the same scale.

4.5 on a 6 point scale) than on the practice of those same concepts, on which the great majority of scores fell below 4.5. This trend was reversed, however, in the case of the conditional concepts, on which the majority of the parents scored below 4.5 on conception and at or above that level on practice.

When these parents attempt to transmit their Islamic or Arabic heritage to their offspring, they transmit either definitions of principles and ideals or a mixture of socio-cultural customs of religious practices.

In response to the question "If you were to present the concept of 'Allah' to your youth, what are the first four meanings that you think of?" 90 percent responded with themes related either to the description of Allah's characteristics (for example, Creator, Master of the Universe, has no partner) or to the relationship of the concept "Allah" to the Hereafter (for example, "because we have to return to Allah one day, and we have to give an account of what we do, then we have to follow his instructions"). Only 10 percent responded with themes related to the human role in relation to the conception of Allah (for example, "God gives you guidance that, YOU can follow"; "because you need something to love and something that you can depend on").

In response to the question "If you were training your youth to become 'muttaqi' (to be conscientious about Allah and to practice the role of vice regency), what are the first two meanings that you would stress?" 50 percent replied: "Think that this is not the real world, what's after is," and the other 50 percent responded: "Feels good by doing what you're supposed to be doing, such as a prayer, fasting, etc."

In response to the question "If you were teaching your youth to be a 'muslih' (a person who undertakes constructive acts), what are the first three actions that you would produce as a role model?" 60 percent of the responses were related to the Hereafter (for example, "realizing accountability for constructive acts in Hereafter helps present society"), and 40 percent were related to worship (for example, "prayer is for your own soul, between me and God").

YOUTHS' CONCEPTION AND PRACTICE OF ISLAM

Parents' idealization or abstraction of "Islamic Muslim" and Arabic is reflected in the youths' confusion concerning identity association. In response to the question "What is your parents' cultural heritage?" 35 percent of the youth identified themselves as being of Arabic origin, 29 percent identified themselves as being of Muslim or Islamic origin, and 18 percent identified themselves with the country of their parents. The remaining 18 percent responded by checking "None of the Above."

The variation among siblings is interesting and indicates some uncertainty and confusion. For example, in one family, the oldest, who was in his mid-twenties, identified himself as Arab. The second child, who was in her early twenties, did not respond to the same question: "How do you see yourself when among non-Muslims?" The third child, who was in his late teens, identified himself as Muslim.

In response to the question about practicing Islam, the predominant theme among youth was to identify themselves as Muslims among non-Muslims (55 percent). There were two aspects to this identification, a positive one, such as "You have to identify yourself as a Muslim among non-Muslims by telling everyone you have a separate identity," and a negative aspect, "You can't pray five times a day in front of others."

The same theme, "being different," dominated the responses to the question "What does it mean to you to dress Islamically?" Yet, Muslim youth of Arab descent are more uncertain about being different than non-Arab Muslims who participated in my larger study. All the Arab girls who responded to this question agreed with the observation: "It is hard for us girls to dress Islamically because people will make fun of us."

The youth responses also reflect different perceptions from those of the parents even when they have scores similar to those of their parents. As can be seen in Table 1, youth tended, like their parents, to score higher on questions that called for them to state an Islamic central concept or human interrelation concepts (88 percent in each case had mean scores at or above 4.5 on a 6-point scale) than on the practice of those same concepts, where the great majority of scores fell below 4.5. The youths scored higher than their parents on questions related to the conception of human interrelation and on questions that called for them to state an Islamic central concept, but lower on questions that called for them to state conditional concepts. The youths' trend was, like that of their parents, reversed in the case of conditional concepts, where 47 percent scored below 4.5 on conception and 82 percent scored at or above that level on practice.

As these youth attempt to conceptualize and practice Islam and the Arabic heritage as presented to them by their parents within the framework of Western secular society, they tend to become confused by their parents' application of the Islamic principles or of the "Arabic heritage."

In response to the question concerning the meaning of Allah, for example, 65 percent of the youth responded with themes related to the human role (for example, "It is the concept of wrong and right. Right is what God wants you to do. It is the only way you can identify with Him [God]").In response to questions related to the meanings and actions toward the concept *taqwa*, 80 percent of youth responded with themes related to inner consciousness (for example, "It is the inner conscience and not the external factors that make one act rightly or wrongly") and to human interrelationship (for example, "It is always in the back of my mind that I'll be judged by my actions").

In response to the question on *islah*, 60 percent responded with themes related to worship as a reminder for human interaction (for example, "Prayer is a reminder that we are watched by Allah, so we should keep in mind [His orders] before acting").

🖾 Implications for Intergenerational Transmission of Islamic or Arabic Identity

Social assimilation of Arab Muslim youth in North America is only a symptom of a more basic problem, namely, conceptual accommodation. Their inability to perceive Islam as a system and Arabic heritage as one manifestation of this system is a probable reason for their difficulties in practicing that system in the new context.

The assumption that the group's cultural heritage can be preserved by maintaining the socio-cultural customs of the old country, though not unique to Arab Muslim immigrants, is seen here as one of the reasons for the inability of American Muslim immigrants to span the gap between the old and the new generations. That is, no matter how tolerant the old are to the young or how compromising the young generation is to their parents' socio-cultural customs, they will never be able to meet on the ideational level. The parents' ideas, sentiments, traditions, and interests are not the same as those of their American-reared children.

The parents' perception of Islam as abstract and as religious duties (in the narrow sense) is a central factor in their children's confusion in identifying with and practicing the "Arab Muslim" cultural heritage. The meanings, weight, and articulation the youth attach to the concepts "Arab" and "Arabic heritage" and to the Islamic system is another leading factor in the process of identity transmission.

This confusion suggests that the youth will either reject the parent's beliefs about Islamic or Arabic practice and the principles or the world view that come with them; continue to have unresolved conflicts between cultures and belief systems; try to compartmentalize by having two or three sets of behavior, namely Islamic or Arabic and Western; or reject the advocated practices and attempt to find, by themselves, a new means by which they can apply Islamic principles and the Arabic cultural heritage.

It follows that any attempt to reverse the situation requires first a change in decision makers' or in parents' perceptions of "Islamic" and "Arabic." This change in perception may be achieved by one or all of the following strategies:

1. Bring to the attention of decision-makers or parents the fact that as long as their conception and practice of Islam are limited to some rituals or to the Five Pillars only, they will not be able to relate these practices to their day-to-day interactions with the Western environment. Moreover,

youth may not be able to relate to this limited perception because they are mainly raised in the Western way of life.

2. Help decision-makers or parents as well as youth gain a realistic view of Western values, their consequences in practice, and the ways they actually differ from or resemble identical Islamic values.

The second prerequisite is to recognize the socio-political changes that are occurring rapidly in the countries of origin as well as in North America and how these changes are reflected in the immigrants' adjustment process. Parents need to address the practice of Islam and the achievement or retention of Arab Muslim identity in the North American context. The strategies may include:

1. Helping parents acquire the skills and understanding needed to deal with the Western environment so they will not have to compartmentalize conceptually the three aspects of cultural interaction, the Islamic, the Arabic, and the Western.

2. Making parents and youth aware that Islamic or Arabic identification and world view can be integrated into the Western environment without compromising Islamic principles or divorcing oneself from Arabic heritage.

Because of the small sample, this study can only be suggestive. Further research is needed on North American Arab Muslim youth who are in the second, third, or fourth generations of immigrants from the Arab regions and who adhere to Islam as a religion or world view. It is clear, however, that the conceptual change approach used here provides both explanations and guides to practice.

It is equally clear that unless Arabs and Muslims in general, and Arab Muslims in particular, identify and reconcile the ambiguities that exist in the conception and practice of Islam and in its relationship to the Arab heritage, attempts to transmit the Arab Muslim identity to the next generation will falter. Some parents succeed despite the difficulties described above. Understanding why they do may contribute to modifying the conceptual framework proposed and open the door for more sophisticated research on this key socialization issue.

ᅒ References

Abu-Laban, Baha. 1983. "The Canadian Muslim Community: The Need for a New Survival Strategy." In *The Muslim Community in North*

America, ed. Earle H. Waugh, Baha Abu-Laban, and Regula B. Quershi. Edmonton: University of Alberta Press.

Barazangi, Nimat Hafez. 1988. *Perceptions of the Islamic Belief System: The Muslims of North America*. Ph.D. diss. Cornell University, Ithaca, N.Y.

Bochner, S., ed. 1993. *Cultures in Contact: Studies in Cross-Cultural Interaction*. Vol. 1 of *International Series in Experimental Social Psychology*. New York: Pergamon Press.

Confrey, J. 1980. *Conceptual Change Number Concepts and the Introduction to Calculus*. Ph.D. diss., Cornell University, Ithaca, N.Y.

Elkholy, Abdo A. 1966. *The Arab Moslems in the United States: Religion and Assimilation*. New Haven: College and University Press.

Glazer, Nathan. 1972. *American Jews*. Chicago: University of Chicago Press.

Hewson, P. W. 1982. "A Conceptual Change Approach to Learning Science." *European Journal of Science Education* 3, no. 4: 383–396.

Iqbal, Sir Muhammad. 1962. *The Reconstruction of Religious Thought in Islam*. Lahor, India: Muhammad Ashraf.

Kuhn, T. 1970. *The Structure of Scientific Revolutions*. Chicago: University of Chicago Press.

Lin Yih-Chyi Nina. 1978. *Educational Needs in Intergenerational Conflict: A Study of Immigrant Families in New York Chinatown*, Ph.D. diss., Cornell University, Ithaca, N.Y.

Lovell, E. K. 1983 "Islam in the U.S.: Past and Present." In *The Muslim Community in North America* ed. Earle H. Waugh, Baha Abu-Laban, and Regula B. Quershi. Edmonton: University of Alberta Press.

Moore, R. Laurence. 1986. *Religious Outsiders and the Making of Americans*. New York: Oxford University Press.

Muhammad, Akbar. 1984. "Muslims in the United States: An Overview of Organization, Doctrines, and Problems." In *The Islamic Impact*, ed. Yvonne Haddad et al. Syracuse, N.Y.: Syracuse University Press.

Posner, George J. 1983. "A Model of Conceptual change: Present Statues and Prospects." In *Proceedings of the International Seminar on Misconceptions in Science and Mathematics*, ed. H. Helm and J. Novak. Ithaca, N.Y.: Department of Education, Cornell University.

Strike, K. A. and Posner, G. J. 1983. "Understanding from a Conceptual Point of View." Paper presented at the meeting of the American Education Research Association, Montreal, Canada.

LINDA S. WALBRIDGE

Sex and the Single Shi'ite
Mut'a Marriage in an American Lebanese Shi'ite Community

Soon after I began my study of the religious life of the Lebanese Shi'a residing in the eastern section of Dearborn, Michigan, I occasionally heard rumors that *mut'a* (temporary or pleasure marriage) was being encouraged by the religious leaders (*shaikhs*) in the community. To be more specific, young men in public places were discussing the matter in terms that suggested that the *shaikhs* (the *imams* of the mosques) were saying that the young men could have affairs with American girls as long as they formed a contract with the girl making her a *mut'ee*.

Dearborn has the largest population of Arab Muslims in America, and of these Arab Muslims, the majority are Lebanese Shi'a. Hailing mainly from the Beka'a region, they are concentrated in the northwest quarter of the city, which is adjacent to Detroit. Over the past decade or so the Lebanese Shi'a community have developed a prosperous commercial district. Three mosques, or mosque-like facilities, serve the spiritual and social needs of the community.

Defining Mut'a

According to Shahla Haeri (1989), *mut'* is a temporary marriage, "a contract between a man and an unmarried woman, be she a virgin, divorced, or widowed, in which both the period of the marriage shall last and the amount of money to be exchanged must be specified." Witnesses are not required for such a union, nor is it usually registered. A Shi'i man may contract as many temporary marriages as he wishes. The unions can be formed consecutively or simultaneously. For a woman, however, the rules are different. She may form only one union at a time after which she must abstain from sex until she knows whether or not she is pregnant.

Khomeini's 1984 book, *Resaleh Towzih al-Masael* (*A Clarification of Questions*), gives the following instructions for a temporary marriage:

> When a woman and a man themselves want to read the (impermanent) contract's formula it is correct if the woman, after determination of the length of period and the dowry, says I married myself to you for the specified length and the specified dowry" and the man says immediately, "I accept." And if they deputize another person and first the woman's deputy says to that of the man "I merchandised (made available for pleasure) my principal to your principal for the specified length and specified dowry" and then the man's deputy says immediately "I accepted that for my principal," it is correct (313).

Haeri (1989) states that the Ayatollah Khomeini, after the Iranian Revolution, issued a *fatwa* (religious edict) stating that a virgin must have her father's permission for a first marriage, be it permanent or temporary. Issues such as parental consent for a virgin to enter into a *mut'a* marriage might be under dispute among the Shi'i *ulama* (learned men), but the legitimacy of *mut'a* is not. While Khomeini may have encouraged the practice more strongly than other contemporary *mujtahids* (Shi'ite jurisconsults), they are all in favor of the use of this kind of marriage.

The topic of temporary marriage has been debated throughout the centuries, largely because the Sunnis reject it. The second caliph, Omar, who is widely hated by the Shi'a as the great usurper of the Imam 'Ali's position, abolished the practice, although it appears that it was permissible in the time of the Prophet. The *imams*, those descendants of the Prophet's daughter, Fatima, and her husband, 'Ali, who became the religious leaders of the Shi'a community until the occultation of the twelfth *imam* in the ninth century, have elucidated on this subject. The belief that *mut a* is acceptable, and actually encouraged, is part of Shi'i dogma. Haeri (1989) offers an excellent account of the practice of *mut'a* in the shrine cities of Iraq and Iran and explains the rationale behind the practice.

Mut'a marriage is an institution in which the relationships between the sexes, marriage, sexuality, morality, religious rules, secular laws, and cultural practices converge. At the same time it is the kind of custom that puts religion and popular culture at odds. Whereas religiously there is no restriction for virgin women to contract a temporary marriage, popular culture demands that a woman be a virgin for her first permanent marriage (3).

It is this tension between religion and popular culture that is my concern here.

I have not elected to focus on *mut'a* because it is a practice that is rampant in this community. Rather, it is because people's reactions to this institution reveal so much about their attitudes towards religion.

✿ *The Practice of* Mut'a *in Dearborn*

I had lived in the community over a year before I actually encountered Shi'a who claimed to have formed *mut'a* marriages. The first was a middle-aged woman who had just fled her husband, leaving behind her older children. She claimed to be homeless and through neighbors I learned of her problems. When the issue of legal assistance came up, she said that she was actually divorced from the man from whom she just had fled. However, some time after the divorce, she returned to him as a *mut'ee* and had lived with him since. Various members of this family had problems with the law and had been imprisoned, mostly for drug dealing. My impression is that this woman simply returned to her former husband and now refers to their relationship as *mut'a* to preserve some sense of dignity before her God-fearing neighbors. Judging from the overall disfunction of this family, it is highly doubtful that any contract was ever involved.

The second case was of a young man, Mahmoud S., who, as he told me, simply wanted sex. He said it was futile in his circumstances to hope that a Lebanese girl would marry him because he was still a student and had no job. He approached American women and asked if they would agree to a *mut'a* marriage. He reported that all of them laughed at him, except one. This woman, a divorcée, married Mahmoud temporarily. She eventually converted, at least nominally, to Islam, and they have since married permanently in the presence of a *shaikh*. I am told by one informant that temporary unions becoming permanent marriages is not uncommon.

In 1989 Shaikh Berri, the *imam* at the Islamic Institute in Dearborn, wrote a book entitled *Temporary Marriage in Islam*. Its existence indicated the level of concern regarding this issue, at least in some circles.

As time passed, I began to realize that, aside from attitudes toward religion, the issue of temporary marriage would also help illuminate this community's attitudes towards women and marriage. While initially I feared that people would not be forthcoming on this subject, I found, to the contrary, that there were many who were willing to discuss on the subject and share their personal views.

Shaikh Berri's Text

Shaikh Berri formulates his treatise in a conventional style used in Shi'ism. The English translation of Berri's text does not do justice to his facility with language. He is known for his exquisite Arabic, and though he has become quite facile with English, he did not use it to write this book.) This book is based on questions he has received on the subject. The answers are framed as responses to the concerns of one young man who says that "in his heart (he feels) it (temporary marriage) is an immoral act." The young man goes on to say that he would not accept *mut'a* for his sisters and doesn't believe that the other *maumineen* brothers (good Muslims) would do so either.

Berri prefaces his comments with a scenario about a beautiful girl (whom one presumes is American) who has seduced a believer and given him AIDS. In this way, he couches his argument in favor of *mut'a*, substantiated by the sayings of the early Shi'ite religious leaders (*imams*), in terms of its being a solution to the pressures of a highly sexualized environment.

Berri condemns Caliph Omar for having made *mut'a* illegal. He cites proof from the Qur'an that it was permissible in the times of the Prophet. But he still seeks logical justification for the practice in these modern times. He says:

> Isn't corruption to let the young men and women fall in the traps of adultery, weird sex, and homosexuality? Or is it maybe to seek God's protection, words, and his laws of

marriage and the organization of sexual relationship the corruption.

Therefore temporary marriage is one of chastity and love, and a form of decency and conservatism and is not an indecency. Nor is it like the "friendship" of boys and girls which was known before Islam, and is revived by the western culture (17–18).

He goes on to address the issue of a man allowing his sister to form a temporary marriage.

Is the standard that the brother accepts or rejects?

Isn't it first the satisfaction of Almighty God's will and then the sister herself?

Or maybe the religion of God should submit to the desires of the brother and his jealousy. Anyway some brothers do accept. Also, why would a brother in many cases allow himself to do things he prevents his sister from doing? Doesn't he do that to protect "himself" from social shame? And that "shame" is not it a fake and an improper one? And did it not originate from "tradition" not the right sensing? If not, why then would he do things that he does not allow her to do (19)?

While one should not forbid *mut'a* for virgins on general principles, Berri does not condemn the father who will not permit his virgin daughter to form a *mut'a* marriage, as long as permission is denied on the grounds that he is safeguarding her well-being.

Berri continues, "temporary marriage is seen as a way of avoiding sinfulness, especially during young maturity" (25). It is also a means of protecting oneself from sexually transmitted disease because a man is supposed to choose a "virtuous woman" as his *mut'ee*. He dispels the idea that this type of union is purely for sex, but that love can exist in a temporary union, as it can in a permanent one.

He also states that "temporary marriage is not encouraged when the continuous (marriage) is available" (33). Addressing the issue of "how many" temporary wives are allowed at one time, he cites some sources saying that four is the limit (as it is in so-called continuous marriage) and other sources saying there is no limit.

The young man inquiring about the practice of *mut'a* has strong misgivings. The idea of *mut'a*, especially for a virgin, runs contrary to the value Lebanese culture places on virginity. Sheikh Berri claims that the Qur'an allows the practice, but Lebanese culture does not. But Berri is himself a Lebanese and the father of daughters. He finds a loophole that is satisfactory both religiously and culturally. A father can reject *mut'a* for his daughter on the grounds that it is personally not good for her. In doing this, he rejects the notion that culture is more powerful and important than religion, while at the same time, he protects the cultural norm of virginity for unmarried women. Furthermore, he reinforces the Islamic (and cultural) prerogatives given to the male head of the household.

It is, indeed, striking that he ascribes to a sister the same rights held by her brother in matters of sexuality (although he also indicates that the father has authority to forbid the union.) It can be argued, of course, that he is simply giving the *mujtahid's* opinions on the matter. But Berri has carefully selected what he has presented about *mut'a*. What he has given us is not a hodgepodge of quotes from the *imams* and the *mujtahids*. Indeed, Khomeini and other ayatollahs are far more ardent in their encouragement of the practice than is Berri. Rather, Berri is responding to issues of Lebanese culture and the problems he is having to deal with in the United States. By saying that a girl can elect to form a *mut'a*, he is giving a way out to the headstrong girl, who, defying her parent's authority, has a sexual relationship with a man outside of marriage. Meanwhile, he is still protecting the rights of the father.

When I interviewed Husein[1], a man affiliated with the Shaikh Berri's mosque and one who has a close ear to the ground in the community, he said that, while it is not recommended that a young girl form a *mut'a* marriage, he could see that in the case of a rebellious girl who wanted to have a sexual relationship, *mut'a* could be a solution. By Shaikh Berri's stating that the possibility exists for a girl to form a temporary union, he is discouraging families from taking drastic measures against her. By drastic measures, I am referring to the possibility of killing the girl, something that was not unusual in Lebanon, especially in the Beka'a. In fact, in 1987 in Dearborn, a Shi'i man killed his teenaged daughter on the grounds that she was having an affair with a man and destroying the honor of the family.

In this text Berri is addressing young, unmarried men who are not yet in a position to marry. He is attempting to discourage casual sex and is encouraging sex within religiously sanctioned parameters. When he ad-

dresses the issue of married men forming *mut'a* marriages, he cites traditions that discourage the practice for married men, though he could easily
have found ones that do the opposite. He chooses to quote from the Imam
Al-Rida, who is reported to have said "but do not persist on pleasure
marriage where it would keep you occupied from your continuous wives.
Then they would reject the faith, complain, and then accuse us and curse
us" (34).

Shaikh Berri has given us the legalistic view, albeit a relatively
conservative one in comparison to that of other *ulama* of the practice of
mut'a. The question now arises as to how this view fits with that of the
community.

⚙ *Community Attitudes toward* Mut'a

For elderly Hajja Fatma, the worst thing a person can do is to commit
stupid acts - things that are *haram* (forbidden) - stealing, drinking, becoming *mut'ees*. Like Fatma, young Nadia is also from the Beka'a and also
hates *mut'a*. "It should never be allowed," she says. Nisrene, from the
religiously strict village of Nabitiyyeh, doesn't like it either. "If you want
to get married, do it the ordinary way." From Bint Jubeil in southern
Lebanon, Leila, still in her teens but married with a baby, says that *mut'a* is
haram. Only Hizb Allah (the militant Shi'ite forces who favor an Islamic
republic in Lebanon) have *mut'a*." In her home village in the Beka'a,
'Aiya has heard that *mut'a* is now practiced and is causing a great deal of
trouble in families. "It's all because of Hizb Allah, she said. We never had
mut'a there before. Elderly Um 'Ali, who recently made her pilgrimage to
Mecca, and who originates from Ba'albek and a Beirut suburb, says that
mut'a is "against religion."

Khadija dissents from this view. A "born again" young woman, who
spent her school years in America wearing blue jeans and listening to rock
music, heartily approves of the practice. Now wearing a gigantic scarf and
flowing coat she lectured me on the virtues of *mut'a*, which she supports
"100 percent." She said, "it is a rule sent by God to man. We cannot forbid
it because of this." I asked her for her personal opinion on the matter, but
she said she could not give me one, that she must tell me only what is
written in the books.

Mut'a is to protect society. It is for married men, but not married women because man and woman are different. Man has a much stronger sex drive. A woman isn't always interested in sex like a man is. When a woman is pregnant or menstruating she has to refuse her husband because it is *makruh* (undesirable but not prohibited) to have sex during these times, at least during menstruation. After all, you can have a deformed child if you get pregnant during your period. So, a man can get a *mut'a*. She cannot stop her husband from doing this. She should not ask him about it even.

Having rejected everything American, and with a young convert's single-mindedness, Khadija is ardent in her "fundamentalist" approach to Islam and considers an Islamic republic to be the ideal form of government. There are others in this community who share her religious/political views, but I have yet to hear such a forceful defense of *mut'a* from any other woman. Those who follow Islamic law carefully tend to pay lip service to the practice. And they all agreed that it was not for a virgin and did not see it as being for married men either. Zahra, also part of the earlier immigration and, who, like Khadija, has opted for a strict interpretation of Shi'ism, tended to justify *mut'a* on the grounds that it was part of religious dogma. She realizes that her husband is entitled to have a *mut'a*, and they have discussed the subject. He, apparently, has no intention of getting one, which Zahra admitted was good because she would "probably kill him," if he did. She also said that she saw it being abused by young, single men, and she was not hesitant to chastise them for this.

It was almost unanimously held that *mut'a* was not for virgins. The dissenting view came from an interesting source. The one woman I interviewed who rejects religion for leftist ideology, said that she saw *mut'a* as a good way to legitimize sex for unmarried women, though, she added, such a thing wouldn't be socially acceptable.

Amal, a woman who follows Islamic law carefully, but avoids the political aspects of religion, claimed that she does not agree with *mut'a*. This raised the hackles of an Iraqi woman who asked, "how can you not agree with something your religion preaches? You might not like to practice it, but to say you don't agree with it is wrong." This is the "religiously correct" response for the Lebanese women, but, apparently, they do not all hold it yet. Most of them reject the practice quite emphatically.

How do these responses fit with those of the men? The following selections give the range of comments.

'Ali S., a young, married, college-educated man from the south of Lebanon said, "Perhaps *mut'a* was a reasonable practice in the early days of Islam, but it has lost its purpose as far as I am concerned. It is no different than dating. Just because the name of God is said, doesn't make it good."

Khalid, also from south Lebanon and with a college education but more religiously learned than 'Ali, replied initially, "it is legal prostitution." He then retracted this statement and admitted he was confused about the issue. "It is supposed to be a religious thing, and I guess I am leaning towards accepting it, but I don't quite see how a man can have more than one wife." He found it more acceptable for a single than a married man. But he thought that only a divorced or widowed woman should be a *mut'a*.

'Ali H., a college student from the Beka'a, said that he disliked *mut'a* and that it was something of which only Hizb Allah approved. Ashraf, a college graduate who grew up in the Beirut suburbs, could not find a justification for *mut'a* but was being pressured by a relative sympathetic to Hizb Allah to form a *mut'a* marriage.

Muhammad T., who grew up in the United States and worked in a factory all his adult life, sees *mut'a* as a good idea especially in view of the current conditions in America. "Every man can have a *mut'a*," he said, but quickly added that he has never had one. (His wife was in the other room at the time watching TV and seemed not to be listening. However, when he made this last comment, she looked at me with a smile that said, "he knows what's good for him.")

But there are men who both approve of the practice and follow it. Muhammad F., a college student, is one of them. "It is a good solution for us because we are young students and it is our only choice." This way, he said, they could have sex and not go against Islam. I asked Muhammad if it was possible to form *mut'a* marriages here with Lebanese girls. He said that a man could form a temporary marriage with a free woman—one who is divorced, widowed, or a virgin over eighteen, if, that is, she is living in the United States. If she is in Lebanon she is under her father's or brother's guardianship, but not so here." He added that he rejected the Lebanese cultural attitudes against virgins being *mut'ees*.

Muhammad, young, serious minded and pro-Iranian, serves as a model for the sort of person who will form a *mut'a* marriage in this community. But he is not the only type.

Selim, unmarried, and a nightclub swinger on Saturday nights, but in the mosque[2] on Sunday mornings, was, in some respects, more liberal in his interpretation of *mut'a* than anyone else with whom I spoke. Any man, whether married or not, according to him, can have a temporary marriage, though he should "know the woman first" and not just walk up to her and propose *mut'*. The woman, he believes, should be divorced or widowed.

Selim parts company with almost everyone else I interviewed. According to my findings, those who believe a married man can form a *mut'a* relationship, nonetheless do not usually form them themselves. *Mut'a* remains, for them, a theoretical proposition, so to speak. A few older men, and I noted that they were ones who had spent long periods of time away from their wives at certain points during their marriages, said that *mut'a* was a way for them to meet their sexual needs while remaining within the law of Islam. Generally, though, those who do form *mut'a* relationships are the unmarried young men who do not see themselves as able to take on the responsibilities of marriage, but are eager not "to sin." However, as college student Issa added, *mut'a* is not to be taken lightly. If the woman becomes pregnant, it is up to the man to support the child.

Nuri's case was quite exceptional and indeed most surprising. Around forty years of age and the image of the Lebanese nightclub entertainer, he was married to and had children with a Muslim woman. Having spent most of his life in America before the new wave of immigrants arrived, he had adjusted to American society more than many. Therefore, I was startled to learn that he himself had a *mut'a* wife. He told me that she was also Muslim and Arab, but not Lebanese. Furthermore, this union was formed in the presence of the *shaikh* and people were invited to the occasion. However, the marriage was not a legal one in American law. He told me that a man is entitled to up to four wives if he can treat them all equally. He assured me he could treat his two wives, one of whom he referred to as a *mut'a* wife, equally. Actually, I believe he has confused the two types of marriage, permanent and temporary. However, by calling his second marriage, *mut'a*, he has found a way around the American law against polygamy.

❦ *Discussion*

While the views expressed here are admittedly diverse, there are some definite themes.

It is apparent that *mut'a* was not a burning issue in Lebanon before the Iranian Revolution. A number of the people with whom I spoke had only become aware of it recently and since they had come to the United States. It is certainly not viewed as being a Lebanese tradition. The fact that Fatma knew of the practice, as did the older woman who returned to her divorced husband as "a *mut'ee*, suggests, though, that the idea is not completely foreign to the Lebanese. In fact, it was probably only practiced by *shaikhs* and women who somehow found themselves on the periphery of society, much like Haeri discovered in Iran. In Lebanon, though, far away from the shrine cities, it was presumably practiced on a much smaller scale.

The overall consensus of the community is that, at best, *mut'a* is a hard pill to swallow. The women I spoke with, both formally and informally, overwhelmingly tended to express their dislike for the practice, and I often heard it said that it is against religion. Some women, who themselves are strict in their adherence to religious law, have brothers who have formed *mut'a* unions, and they were quick to justify their brother's behavior. However, they also mentioned the limitations imposed on the union. They want *mut'a* to be seen as a serious matter and something very different from the "boyfriend-girlfriend" relationships found in the United States.

While more men tended to accept the practice as being justifiable, there was still no overwhelming praise of the practice. Mr. S., a mechanic from the Beka'a said that it was acceptable for a man to form a *mut'a* marriage if he were going to be away from his wife for a long period of time. However, he added that it was far preferable for him to be loyal to her.

Only those who had completely accepted the "new" Shi'ism from Iran would contemplate the notion of a virgin as a temporary wife. And not even all of them would. Husein is a case in point. While he knew such a thing was religiously permissible, his Lebanese values kept him from truly accepting this idea.

Shaikh Berri's book on the subject of temporary marriage has not become a best seller in this community. Except for women such as Khadija and her close acquaintances, the few women whom I have known who are curious to know what is contained in the book are too embarrassed to go to the bookstore to purchase it. They fear that the shop owner will think they want to apply the practice themselves.

Whether or not people read the book, or even know of its existence, there is obviously a growing awareness of the practice as well as a growing concern that young men will "misinterpret" the use of *mut'a*, that is, seduce Lebanese girls into forming temporary unions. Um Hamood, well-educated in the teachings of Islam and very strict in her interpretation of the Islamic law, scolded a young man who formed a *mut'a* marriage with a girl. She asked him if he would allow his sister to form such a union. She said that "this shut him up." She conceded that it was acceptable to form a *mut'a* if one cannot marry but added that, "we really hate this practice." Though I have been led to believe that most of these *mut'a* marriages are with Americans, it is obvious from the comments of Um Hamood and of others that some Lebanese girls are involving themselves in these unions. Should the girls in this community see *mut'a* as a way to legitimately fulfill their sexual needs, this community could face extraordinary turmoil in the near future; turmoil that, I believe, would ultimately force the extinction of the practice in Dearborn.

✿ References

Berry, Abdullatif. 1989. *Temporary Marriage in Islam.* Dearborn, Mich.: Az-Zahra International Co.

Haeri, Shahla. 1989. *Law of Desire: Temporary Marriage in Sh'i Iran.* Syracuse, N.Y.: Syracuse University Press.

Khomeini, Ruhollah Mousani. 1984 . *A Clarification of Questions*, trans. J. Borujerdi. Boulder, Colo.: Westview Press.

Walbridge, Linda S. 1991. *Shi'i Islam in an American Community.* Ph.D. diss., Department of Anthropology, Wayne State University, Detroit.

NILUFER AHMED, GLADIS KAUFMAN, AND SHAMIM NAIM

South Asian Families in the United States

Pakistani, Bangladeshi, and Indian Muslims

South Asia Asian Muslim families are relative newcomers to the United States, and little has been written about them despite their increasing numbers. Highly educated, often with careers in medicine, engineering, and science, they live primarily in our larger cities but also in smaller population centers, brought there by jobs. Their major concerns are the socialization of their children in the Islamic faith and finding suitable matches for their children of marriageable age. Arranged marriages are still typical, but adjustment problems have led to some divorces. Extended family households are unusual, though extended kin ties are emphasize.

Though still a small group compared to Arabs and Iranians in the United States, the number of Muslim families of South Asian origin has been steadily increasing. Precise numbers are impossible to obtain, since U.S. census data lump Pakistanis and Bangladeshis into an "other group" category, while East Indians, whether Hindu or Muslim, are grouped together. In 1981 Ghayur estimated that there were over 45,000 Pakistanis, 4,500 Bangladeshis and 25,000 Indian Muslims in the United States. Using a variety of sources and assumptions, he had, by 1984, estimated 96,537 persons of Pakistani origin alone in the United States, but his figure

The authors' names are listed alphabetically. No ranking is implied. Two of the authors are of South Asian descent and this paper is based on their years of observations and contacts with members of their community. Informal interviews were also conducted by all authors.

includes students, diplomats, and other temporary workers and visitors. The 1990 census counted 815,447 East Indians in the United States; if immigrants reflect similar population ratios as in India, than 11 percent, or at least 89,000, are Indian Muslims. Statistical yearbooks of the U.S. Immigration and Naturalization Service (INS) show a total immigration up to 1993 of 36,579 Bangladeshis, 136,538 Pakistanis, and 600,035 Indians (see Table 1). Almost all Bangladeshis and Pakistanis are Muslim. When taking into account natural increase and a small number of illegal immigrants, we estimate the South Asian Muslim population in the United States to be well over 300,000 in 1995.

A short history of the South Asian area is useful in understanding its ethnic divisions. When India gained independence from the United Kingdom in 1947, deep antagonisms between Hindus and Muslims resulted in the partitioning of India and the creation of new national boundaries. India remained predominantly Hindu, while Pakistan, formed out of its northeast and northwest sections, called East Pakistan and West Pakistan respectively, was mostly Muslim. East and West Pakistan were nine hundred miles apart but united under one government. At this time several million Hindus left Pakistan for India, and about seven million Muslims left India for Pakistan, especially West Pakistan. Some Muslims remained in India, primarily rural farmers whose only security lay in their land, but also some professionals and other intellectuals who believed, as Gandhi had, in a united India. The latter have been the source of recent Muslim emigrations from India to Canada, Great Britain, Australia, and the United States. Many who had originally moved to Pakistan have also relocated in these western nations.

Within the Islamic Republic of Pakistan, the capital and most governmental power, are in West Pakistan, much larger in area, but slightly smaller in population than the eastern province. Political conflict between the two sectors resulted in the creation of Bangladesh as an independent nation in 1971. Thus, anyone who migrated from the Bangladesh area before 1971 would have been listed as a Pakistani. The Bangladeshi people have a common language, Bengali, but Pakistan is divided into five main languages, and India has sixteen distinct linguistic groups as well as three main religions: Hindu, Muslim, and Sikh (Ghayur 1981; Hossain 1982). These divisions have created a special problem for Indian Muslims, espe-

TABLE 1

NUMBERS OF IMMIGRANTS ADMITTED TO THE UNITED STATED
BY COUNTRY OF BIRTH

	BANGLADESH	PAKISTAN	INDIA[a]
Before 1971	—	5,179	44,068
1971	—	2,125	14,317
1972	—	2,480	16,929
1973	154	2,525	13,128
1974	147	2,570	12,795
1975	404	2,620	15,785
1976	590	2,888	17,500
1977	590	3,183	18,636
1978	716	3,876	20,772
1979	549	3,967	19,717
1980	532	4,265	22,607
1981	756	5,288	21,522
1982	639	4,536	21,738
1983	787	4,807	25,451
1984	823	5,509	24,964
1985	1,146	5,744	26,026
1986	1,634	5,994	26,227
1987	1,649	6319	27,803
1988	1,324	5438	26,268
1989	2,180	8000	31,175
1990	4,252	9,729	30,667
1991	10,676	20,355	45,064
1992	3,740	10,214	36,755
1993	3,291	8,927	40,121
Totals	36,579	136,538	600,035

[a] Reflects *total* Indian immigration population. Muslims make up approximately 11 percent of the Indian population.

SOURCES: Statistical yearbooks for the U. S. Immigration and Naturalization Service (1976–1993).

cially students in U.S. universities where nationalism is more intense. Indian Muslims constitute a small group in the United States, and Pakistanis tend to see them as Indian citizens who may not even be "true" Muslims. And since most Indians are Hindu, they tend to regard themselves as quite different from Indian Muslims.

☙ *Immigration History*

Pakistani and East Indian Muslims began coming to the United States in small numbers in the early 1900s. Ghayur (1981) mentions that one Indian-Pakistani community has existed in California for four generations, and Khan (1984) reveals that several hundred Pakistanis of farming background had settled into agricultural jobs in the Sacramento Valley and the Southwest in the 1910–1920 period. It is also known that Ahmadiyya missionaries, belonging to an offshoot of the Shi'ite sect of Islam, had migrated from what is now Pakistan to several major U.S. cities by the 1920s (Holmes 1926; Mohammed 1984). Informal sources reveal that a small number of Bangladeshis of basically working class background jumped ship in Detroit in the 1930s and 1940s and took up various occupations ranging from shopkeeper to security guard. The second generation is not highly educated and have similar occupations. Khan (1984) mentions Pakistani seamen who overstayed their shore leaves and a few who crossed the Mexican border during this period. Numbers of students began arriving in the 1950s, along with other educated and professional people, as part of what Haddad (1987:14) calls the "fourth wave" of Islamic migration to the United States.

Most South Asians, however, immigrated after changes in the immigration laws in 1965 gave preference to relatives of U.S. citizens and to professionals and others with skills needed by the United States. (See Khan 1984 and Hing 1993 for a more detailed discussion of U.S. policies and their effect on South Asian immigration.) The vast majority of those arrivals were well-educated persons of middle-and upper-class background, though Haddad (1987) mentions groups of semi-skilled workers from Pakistan. New York has a small but growing Bangladeshi community of similar background. Since the 1960s many South Asians who originally came as students or tourists chose to remain in the United States.

The 1986 immigration data,[1] for example, show that the majority (63%) of Bangladeshi aliens who adjusted to permanent resident status were students. For Pakistani and East Indian aliens who have stayed, roughly half were tourists while 20 to 25 percent were students. A similar pattern can be observed in the earlier 1980s immigration data. Many of the immigrants from these years were professionals: doctors, pharmacists, engineers, computer scientists, chemists, and businessmen. In 1982 Hossain estimated that 90 percent of the total population of Pakistani and Bangladeshi immigrants were professionals: however, immigration data suggest smaller estimates. For example, 1986 data show that for those Bangladeshi and Pakistani immigrants who stated an occupation, only 22 percent entered the country as professionals, though the comparable percentage for East Indian immigrants was 39 percent. "Executive, administrative, and managerial" occupations accounted for 17 to 22 percent for each country. Among Bangladeshi immigrants, 41 percent entered as "service" workers, compared to 27 percent of Pakistanis, and only 12 percent of East Indians. It should be noted that the largest category from each country both in the 1980s and the 1990s has been "no occupation or not reported," which can include homemakers, students, unemployed, or retired persons. In 1993 this category had reached 78 percent for Bangladeshis, 72 percent for Pakistanis, and 65 percent for Indians. The numbers declaring a professional, technical, executive, or managerial classification had declined to 9 percent from Bangladesh, 15 percent from Pakistan, and 25 percent from India in 1993.

Recently many South Asian immigrants have come as relatives of the 1960s and 1970s immigrants who have become permanent residents or naturalized citizens. This process of chain migration has brought in not only spouses and children, but also brothers, sisters, and parents, who generally do not have as high an educational level or as prestigious an occupation as the earlier migrants. Under immigration law, these relatives can enter the United States for "family reunification" and are not subject to the same numerical limitations as nonrelatives. For many years, from both Pakistan and Bangladesh, the largest percentage of such immigrants entered the United States as spouses of U.S. citizens. In 1985 and 1986, for example, 57 percent of Pakistanis and 69 to 71 percent of Bangladeshis who entered without numerical limitations were classified as spouses of U.S. citizens. For India, however, a different pattern was observed. The largest proportion entered the United States as parents of U.S. citizens: 62 percent in 1985 and 59 percent in 1986. A similar pattern was also found in the 1980 immigration data. This reflects the fact that East Indians have been migrating to the United States for a longer time and were older, with parents of retirement age. By 1993, 74 percent of Bangladeshis, 77 percent of Pakistanis, and 68 percent of the East Indians were entering the United States through immediate relative-and family–sponsored preference rather than through employment-based preferences. Parents outnumbered spouses in 1993 by 521 to 408 from Bangladesh, 6029 to 4111 from India, but 982 to 1449 from Pakistan.

During the past five years citizens of Bangladesh and Pakistan have also entered the United States through programs aimed at diversifying immigration. Indian citizens are not eligible, since the programs are for nations with lower numbers of immigrants. The most recent program is informally called the "visa lottery." An individual enters this lottery by sending his/her name and address to the National Visa Center, which then randomly draws an allotted number of names of individuals who are eligible for immigrant visas (for the 1995 fiscal year, 55,000 immigrant visas were made available under this program, close to 7,000 from Asia).

Anecdotal evidence suggests that many who have entered the United States through this system have low educational levels and few work skills. Many live in New York, New Jersey, Texas, and Illinois—states with fairly large concentrations of Bangladeshis and Pakistanis. This is not surprising, since this has allowed many to find jobs working for better–off immigrants in their small businesses as gas-pump attendants, waiters, construction workers, and sales help.

The total numbers of emigrants to the United States from all three countries have steadily increased over time (see Table 1). In 1993 Bangladeshis officially numbered four times the number of 1983 and twenty-one times that of 1973. The number of Pakistanis entering the United States increased from 2,525 in 1973 to 4,807 in 1983 and 8,927 in 1993. In the same years, Indians numbered 13,123, 25,451 and 40,121.

The data also illustrate that male immigrants have outnumbered female immigrants. For every Bangladeshi woman that migrated in 1986, there were almost two Bangladeshi men; there were 1.3 Pakistani men for every Pakistani woman. However, by 1992 males were only 54 percent of the immigrants from Pakistan and in 1993 women (51.8%) outnumbered men. Indian men and women immigrated in the 1980s in almost equal proportions, though by 1993 women (53.1%) were again outnumbering men.

In nearly every ten-year age group, male immigrants outnumbered female immigrants from all three countries throughout the 1980s. The exception to this pattern was for the 50- to 59-year-old age group, where women outnumbered men by a fairly large margin. For example, the 1986 data show that for India, 984 men ages 50 to 59 immigrated, compared to

1,587 women, while for Pakistan the numbers were 192 men and 248 women. Since the age group 60 and above again shows a preponderance of men it is difficult to explain this exception.[2] In 1993 men over 70 outnumbered women, but women were more numerous in the categories from 45 to 69 from India. From age 20 to 24 women outnumbered men by 3163 to 941, indicating the many brides who were coming from India. The same age group from Pakistan was 68 percent female, while males were more numerous in the age ranges from 0 to 19, 30 to 44, and over 65.

South Asian immigrants from Bangladesh and Pakistan are from diverse regions within their home countries, though generally of urban background. Indian Muslims also come from various regions, but significant numbers are from Hyderabad, a former Muslim princely state. With independence, Hyderabad was conceded to India, and as a result many Muslims left. Some went to Pakistan, but being a highly educated group, many also migrated to Great Britain, Canada, and the United States.

Occupational preferences by the United States have played a role in determining who can immigrate and have sometimes influenced the educational choices of individuals in their home country. In Bangladesh, for example, in the early 1970s, pharmacy was listed as a favorable occupation for individuals wishing to immigrate to the United States. Signs around the pharmacy school proclaimed "Join Pharmacy: Fly to the U.S.A." The first group with either bachelor's or master's degrees in pharmacy came from Bangladesh in 1972. This initial contingent consisted of only five individuals, but the numbers grew as ensuing classes graduated and immigrated. The peak years were 1974–1976 when approximately a hundred came. Informal estimates put the total number of such professionals at five hundred. In 1985 the immigration of pharmacists ceased when the occupation was taken off the preferred list.

The majority of Bangladeshi pharmacists settled in New York City, though there are several in Philadelphia and other cities, primarily on the east coast. Many have finished higher studies in pharmacy in the United States, and most have obtained their professional licenses. A significant number, however, have not continued in their profession, usually because they were unable to continue their studies or they could not obtain their licenses. These have joined the business world and are presently found in retail pharmacy, management of fast food restaurants or ethnic restaurants, and food management in hospitals.

ᛖ *Marriage*

Nearly all of these pharmacy immigrants were men. Most of them came alone and later went back to Bangladesh to marry and bring their wives to the United States. Many of these wives are presently holding jobs in department stores, travel agencies, insurance companies, and the like. The parents of the few women with pharmacy degrees did not want their daughters to emigrate alone, so, often, marriages were arranged with male pharmacy students in the same or a very close cohort. A few women did migrate alone, but soon married male pharmacy students whom they had known at school. Many of these couples have children, the most common number being two, which is also typical of the other South Asian groups discussed below.

Divorce is still rare in this group. The very few that have occurred are reportedly due to adjustment problems between the couples where the men, after several years here, went back to Bangladesh to get married and then brought their wives over. Some of these wives are lonely here and some feel that life in the United States requires too much independence— that there is too much to take care of. When the wife has a job, she often feels burdened by the housework and child care, for husbands tradition- ally do little of this work. The aid of the extended family, so available in the home country, does not exist here.

The men who came to the United States in the earlier 1900s generally could not bring over wives because of U.S. immigration policies and often married women of Anglo-American or Spanish-American backgrounds, or remained single (Khan 1984). Once the laws changed in 1950, men most often wed women from their home country through arranged marriages, as in the above-mentioned pharmacy group. Now that the children of 1960s–1970s migrants are reaching marriageable age, one of the main problems facing parents is finding suitable mates for their sons and daugh- ters. Although parents of boys would like their sons to marry within the Islamic faith, this is not considered as essential as for daughters.[3] Since children usually follow the father's faith, a daughter's children could lose their Islamic affiliation. Therefore, boys are more free to marry girls from other religions, such as Christian or Jew. The divorce rate among these marriages, however, is quite high. Also, since daughters typically go where their husbands live and parents would like to continue seeing their daughters and grandchildren, finding a mate for a daughter is usually more problematic than for a son.

One solution has been to arrange a marriage to a young man from the home country and bring him over here. Some of these marriages, however, are likely to end in divorce since there are difficult adjustment problems associated with young men from the home country. They find it hard to accept the way of life followed by American-raised women and are more likely to think a woman's place is in the home and to resent a wife's freedom of mobility, outside activities, independence, and late working hours. It is often hard for these young men to get decent jobs, which adds to their economic and emotional pressures. Women who are brought over to marry American-raised men are often lonely, but generally adjust better to their new environment than do men.

There is great fear that children who grow up in the United States will marry someone of whom the parents do not approve. The parents feel they have no say in such matters if they remain in the United States. In a few cases parents have taken a daughter home, arranged a marriage for her, and the parents then returned to the United States without their daughter. In one family the oldest daughter married a Hindu, which so upset her parents that they took their second daughter to Bangladesh and quickly arranged a marriage. In another family the oldest son married an American woman without even informing his parents, who became so distraught that they took their younger, nineteen-year-old son to India and married him to an Indian Muslim woman.

If the marriage is arranged in the home country, the visiting parents try to find suitable mates for their offspring by looking into the community and talking to their friends and relatives. Parents will try to find out all they can about the family background, possible health problems, social status, and economic position of the prospective spouse's family. After they are satisfied, the proposal will be made through a third party to both concerned families. If all the parents agree, then the young men and women usually have a chance to meet to see if the match is mutually agreeable to them. If they too desire the marriage, wedding arrangements will be made. Some marriages take place within the extended family, so families generally know each other well and only the consent of the involved children is needed. The marriage of first cousins is traditionally a preferred marriage choice, though this is becoming much less common in the United States.

The best solution, when possible, is to find suitable mates within the community here in the United States. When both partners are raised in the United States they tend to have good jobs and stable relationships. Since the South Asian Muslim community is still relatively small, such marriages are difficult to achieve. The matrimonial advertisements in South Asian immigrant newspapers and magazines (such as *New Horizon*, *India Abroad*) indicate that similar nationality is no longer as important, but Islamic faith is, along with a preference for beauty, fairness, university education and/or a green card. To find suitable matches, parents again seek information from friends and relatives. Other sources of information on marriage availability are Islamic organization meetings and even professional conferences. For example, the meetings of the Islamic Physicians Association of North America is attended by many doctors who are looking for matches for their children.

Once marriages are arranged, families like to go back to the home country for the wedding ceremony. If it takes place in the United States several possible procedures can be followed. After getting the civil license, the ceremony may be performed in a mosque by a *qazi* who has the legal authority to solemnize marriage, but *qazis* are usually found only in large cities. In the smaller cities and towns, where the mosque or Islamic center does not have the necessary legal authority or where there is no center at all, the ceremony will be performed by a Justice of the Peace and then it may also be performed by "religious right."[4]

The wedding is an occasion of much happiness and festivities that take place both before and after the ceremony. The ceremony itself is a two-minute affair, but the festivities depend on the traditions of the particular home country and the economic status of the parties. Usually the bride's parents will give whatever presents they can in cash and kind to ensure her a smooth start without too many deprivations.

Divorce (practically unknown in the home country) is still rare, but increasing in the United States community. In one case, the wife went to live with her sister because of physical abuse. In several others, professional working wives divorced because of the pressures of the "double day" and the husband's continuing demand for special services. Economically independent wives are less likely to tolerate excessive male authority. Men sometimes do not want their wives to work for fear of divorce.

☙ *Elderly*

Among the young adults who have settled in the United States, much concern centers around their parents still in the home country. Many here have good incomes and can afford to bring their parents to the United States. They would have more peace of mind if their parents were here where they could take care of them and see that their needs are met.

However, they realize that the parents would face relative isolation here, especially when the children live in areas where there are few or no other families of their background. Here the parents might have neither friends nor extended family, and language would be a problem. At home they have an important role to play in their community, have friends and relatives, and see themselves as being needed. Generally, the parents do not want to come, saying they do not want to be a burden. Many of the children send money and goods back to their parents and bring their parents over for visits, which often reinforces the feelings of the parents that they do not want to live here. The extended-family household is also becoming less common in cities back home due to the internal demands of relocation for job opportunities.

Some families, over the years, have been able to create the extended family here. In New York City, two Bangladeshi brothers in their thirties bought a large three-story house, brought their parents and a married sister here, and proceeded to renovate the house for extended family living. The inside walls have been knocked out on the second floor to create a large dining/kitchen/family room. The daughter and husband live in a basement apartment, one son and his family are on the first floor, while the second son's family and the parents live on the third floor. The sons and son-in-law are doctors, while the daughter is a pharmacist. However, one son would like to move to a new area in order to get a better job. The son also resents the authoritarian attitude of the father, who does not think the son should leave and "break up the family."

In another case a Chicago Pakistani married couple sponsored the husband's two sisters with their families, and the wife's sister, brother, and mother. Other cousins are also in the Chicago area. So family gatherings are quite large, but most live in nuclear households.

Another Pakistani engineer has sponsored three brothers, one sister, and his parents. One brother married an American Christian woman and another is dating a Christian. The sister married a Pakistani Muslim, but divorced within one week. The engineer himself worries about whom his two sons will marry. The older parents often blame their son for bringing them to the United States and "destroying the family."

As the first generation immigrants are growing older, there are also concerns about their own old age, nursing homes, and homes for the elderly. Almost all are against staying in nursing homes and would like their children to care for them but know this may not happen. Most hope to be able to live near their children so they can be looked after. Some would like to go back home, especially the Pakistanis. A few have substantial homes in Karachi, Pakistan, that are unoccupied and looked after by caretakers until the owners can retire and return. Those who do not wish to return are starting to talk of nursing homes for Muslims, and several Muslim communities here have bought their own burial grounds.

❦ *Community Relations*

South Asian Muslims are concentrated primarily in several large urban centers like New York, Los Angeles, San Francisco, Philadelphia, and Chicago, although a sizeable number are found at smaller academic centers such as Ann Arbor, Urbana, Madison, or College Park, Texas, primarily as students and faculty members, and in some smaller cities and towns as professionals such as doctors, professors, and engineers. Community relations vary with the size of the population, the ethnic makeup, and the distance from a large community. Hossain (1982) has described the South Asians of southern California, and several studies of Canadian Pakistanis exist (Siddique 1983; Qureshi and Qureshi 1983). Chicago and Peoria, Illinois, provide a good example of two different size populations interacting within themselves and outside the community, and will be described in more detail in the following section.

The Chicago community is typical of large urban centers with a large South Asian population. There are several mosques and Islamic centers in

Chicago catering to the needs of different ethnic groups such as Black Muslims, South Asians, and Middle Easterners. The Muslim Community Center and Islamic Foundation, as well as the Islamic Society of the Northwestern Suburbs have mostly South Asian Sunni members. While most active members of the Muslim Community Center are of Indian origin, those of the Islamic Foundation are primarily from Pakistan. There is a small population of Bangladeshi Muslims, but they have no separate organization. The South Asian Chicago community also has a large Shi'ite population, many of whom are members of the Midwest Association of Shi'ite Muslims and the Hussaini Association of Greater Chicago.

Preservation of religious and cultural identity is a prime concern for all South Asians, so, whenever possible, families get together. There are regular Sunday schools where children are taught to read the Qur'an in Arabic and learn how to pray. Other Islamic values are taught in English, so all South Asian children, whether they speak Urdu, Bengali, Punjabi, or any other regional language, have a common instructional language with which they feel more comfortable. While children attend Sunday schools, prayers are held for adults. After prayers, discussions are usually held in which contemporary problems are analyzed in relation to Islamic values.

In addition to these regular meetings, on various festivals and religious occasions, like the month of Ramadan and *aftar* (breaking the fast at sunset), prayers are held every night, followed by *taravih* (recital of Qur'anic verses). Special prayers are offered at *Eid-ul-Fitr* (marking the end of the month of Ramadan), and *Eid-ul-Adha* (commemoration of the pilgrimage to Mecca). These prayers attract people not only from the city of Chicago and its suburbs, but also from communities as far as central Illinois, for family reunion is one of the most important needs at such times. After the prayer, families get together at each other's homes to celebrate the occasion. As the growing population in the city has created overcrowding, suburban centers are emerging as smaller satellite centers for such special occasions. "*Milad-un-Nabi*" and "majlis" are also becoming fairly common in Chicago. "*Milad-un-Nabi*" is usually a gathering of Sunni Muslims, to which they recite and recall the teachings of the Prophet, passages from the Qur'an and illustrations from the Prophet's life. "*Majlis*" is a get–together of Shi'ite Muslims that concentrates on recital and remembrance of the deeds of Imam Ali and his son Imam Husain and the Tragedy of Karbala. These gatherings are usually very selective and consist of family and close friends.

While mosques and Islamic centers provide opportunities for religious gratification, conventional educational needs are fulfilled by American institutions. This trend is reflected in the fact that even though Chicago has an Islamic University, most South Asians feel that the curriculum is not geared towards modern-day living in America and prefer that their children go to prestigious U.S. universities. Education is considered extremely important.

Civic organizations in Chicago, like their religious counterparts, cut across national boundaries. Since most Urdu-speaking *mahajir* (foreign Muslims) of Pakistan and Biharis (Muslim immigrants from Bihar province, India) in Bangladesh have common ties with the Urdu-speaking population of India, especially from North India and the former state of Hyderabad, the cultural organizations have members from all three countries. The organizations arrange meetings, community picnics, and literary functions, host dignitaries, artists, and scholars from the home countries, arrange for the showing of home movies on a regular basis, and organize programs like *mushairas* (recital of Urdu poetry), musicals, and dramas. The efforts of these organizations have also succeeded in providing radio and television programs each week for South Asian populations. Devon Street in Chicago has several blocks of stores where South Asian videotapes, clothing, foods, and special 220 electronics to take as presents for home visits can be obtained.

Peoria, Illinois, represents a smaller city with fewer South Asians. About twenty-five families who live in Peoria, and nearly twenty additional families in a surrounding fifty-mile radius, come to the Peoria Islamic Center for Sunday prayers and attend meetings to discuss contemporary religious and social problems, while their children attend Sunday school and learn Islamic values. The smaller community structure provides a friendly relationship among the members. After *zuhr* prayers, a potluck dinner is served, and then *asar* prayer is performed before participants leave. While Peoria's Islamic Center satisfies the religious needs of the community, the urge to unite and celebrate with even distant relatives and friends brings many of these isolated families to Chicago for *eid* prayers and celebrations.

Besides these religious meetings, five or six families often meet at homes and socialize. Dinner is served by the host family or a potluck might be planned. Indian and Pakistani films are shown and, in some cases, slumber parties for teenagers occur on weekends. Parents feel it important for their children to socialize with others of similar cultural background, and the teenagers enjoy these weekend meetings. Those who can afford it take their children to their home country every two to three years to emphasize their cultural background.

Most community news is exchanged via telephones and much information is gathered through radio and television broadcasts from Chicago. Cultural events in Chicago are well publicized and are often attended as two or three families make plans to drive to Chicago for the occasion.

Muslim schools have been started in all communities with a sizable South Asian Muslim population, even small university cities like Ann Arbor, Michigan. The schools are open on Saturdays and evenings to teach children basic religious practices such as how to pray and how to read the classical Arabic of the Qur'an. Some parents have expressed dissatisfaction with the religious education their children are receiving but feel the school is better than nothing. In their home country children would learn from the entire extended family, which is not available in the United States.

South Asian Muslims vary from the very religious to the non-practicing Muslim who does not participate in religious observances but who would still practice certain cultural customs, such as a distaste for pork and/or avoidance of alcohol. Some families are placing more emphasis on Islamic teachings here than they would in their home country as a way of retaining their heritage and culture. Haddad (1987) found this to be especially true among Pakistanis when compared to non–South Asian Muslims.

Depending upon individual feelings about religion and its importance, the lack of religious training and practices for young people can be a concern. One couple, both of whom are highly educated professionals, would like to return to their home country because they feel their two young sons, both under five, will not know their religion if the family remains in the United States. The mother, who is very religious, is especially eager to return. They hope that one or both of them can obtain jobs at a university and are actively pursuing this goal.

Several families would like to return for other reasons. Sometimes it is to ensure a Muslim marriage for their children but also because they have friends and relatives there, they feel a sense of responsibility for their parents, if they are at home, and life would be easier because there would be less job stress and not so many hours of work. Many are men who originally came to the United States as graduate students and chose to stay because of job opportunities and sent for their wives and children. Although some would like to return, they remain here because there are few job opportunities for them at home and because of better educational opportunities for their children, especially sons who are urged to set Harvard or MIT as their goal. Increased unstable conditions at home have also made some more reluctant to return.

Conclusions

The family is a significant institution among South Asian immigrants, and marriage problems and adjustments are one of their prime concerns. Finding suitable matches for young people is more difficult in the United States, and almost every kin group is "looking for someone" for a young man or woman of their extended family. The most important criterion is similar religion, though the same ethnic and linguistic background are desirable. Parents are also concerned with Islamic training for their children, and community religious and civic organizations have been organized to meet these needs. Though generally quite successful economically, the South Asian Muslim population faces some stress in maintaining cultural traditions and values in family life. Some welcome change, but others view it with hostility.

Little has been written on South Asians Muslims in the United States. Hopefully, our limited study of Bangladeshi, Pakistani, and East Indian Muslims will help to alter this situation, for further information and analysis is greatly needed.

References

Ghayur, M. Arif. 1980. "Pakistanis." Pp. 768–770 in *Harvard Encyclopedia of American Ethnic Groups*, ed. S. Thernstrom. Cambridge: Harvard University Press.

————. 1981. Muslims in the United States: Settlers and Visitors. *Annals of the American Academy of Political and Social Science* 454: 150–163.

————. 1984. "Demographic Evolution of Pakistanis in America: Case Study of a Muslim Subgroup." *American Journal of Islamic Studies* 1:113–126.

Haddad, Yvonne Y. and Adair T. Lummis. 1987. *Islamic Values in the United States*. New York: Oxford University Press.

Hing, Bill. 1993. *Making and Remaking Asian America through Immigration Policy 1850–1990*. Stanford, Calif.: Stanford University Press.

Holmes, Mary. 1926. "Islam in America." *Muslim World* 16: 262–266.

Hossain, Mokerrom. 1982. "South Asians in Southern California: A Sociological Study of Immigrants from India, Pakistan, and Bangladesh." *South Asia Bulletin* 2, no. 1:74–82

Jensen, Joan M. 1980. "East Indians." Pp. 296–301 in *Harvard Encyclopedia of American Ethnic Groups*, ed. S. Thernstrom. Cambridge: Harvard University Press.

Khan, Salim. 1984. "Pakistanis in the Western United States." *Journal Institute of Muslim Minority Affairs* 5: 36–46.

Kurian, George and Ratna Ghosh. 1978. "Changing Authority within the Context of Socialization of Indian Families." *Social Science* 53: 24–32.

Mohammad, Akbar. 1984. "Muslims in the United States: An Overview of Organization, Doctrines, and Problems." Pp. 195–218 in *The Islamic Impact*, ed. Yvonne Yazbeck Haddad, Byron Haines, and Ellison Findly. Syracuse, N.Y.: Syracuse University Press.

Nagarajan, R. 1988. "Essential Role of the Family." *India Abroad* 10 (June): 3.

Nanji, Azim. 1983. "The Nizari Ismaili Muslim Community in North America: Background and Development." Pp. 149–164 in *The Muslim Community in North America*, ed. E. H. Waugh, B. Abu–Laban, and R. B. Qureshi. Edmonton: University of Alberta Press.

Nyang, S. S. and Mumtaz Ahmad. 1985. "The Muslim Intellectual Emigre in the United States." *Islamic Culture* 59: 277–290.

Qureshi, Rezala and Saleem Qureshi. 1983. "Pakistani Canadians: The Making of a Muslim Community." Pp. 127–148 in *The Muslim Community in North America*, ed. Earle Waugh, B. Abu–Laban, and R. Qureshi. Edmonton: University of Alberta Press.

Rahim, Enayetur. 1980. "Bangladeshi." Pp. 172–173 in *Harvard Encyclopedia of American Ethnic Groups*, ed. S. Thernstrom. Cambridge: Harvard University Press.

Siddique, Muhammad. 1983. "Changing Family Patterns: A Comparative Analysis of Immigrant Indian and Pakistani Families in Saskatoon, Canada." Pp. 100–127 in *Overseas Indians*, ed. George Kurian and Ram Srivastava. New Delhi: Viking.

U.S. Bureau of Census. 1992. *Statistical Abstract of the United States, 1990.* Washington D. C. : U. S. Government Printing Office.

U.S. Immigration and Naturalization Service. 1976–1994. *Statistical Yearbook of the Immigration and Naturalization Service.* Washington, D. C.: U.S. Government Printing Office.

GLADIS KAUFMAN AND SHAMIM NAIM

An International Family
A Case Study from South Asia

International mobility has resulted in the scattering of families throughout the world for many South Asian Muslim kinship groups. This paper
will trace the history of one such family, which originated in India and
now has members in Pakistan, the United Kingdom, the Middle East, and
North America. Political, economic, and cultural factors have all played a
role in the dispersion and continued unity of this extended kin group.

This is the story of Razia and her family. Born in India fifty-one years
ago, Razia now resides in the United States where she teaches at a
midwestern university and lives with her husband of twenty-six years.
They have a twenty-three-year-old son graduating from a U.S. university
this year, and a twenty-five-year-old married daughter who lives in England. Razia phones her daughter once a week and they see each other,
often for extended visits, at least once a year. Their closeness illustrates
the central place of family in the lives of most South Asian Muslims, and is
indicative of the ties that still bring cohesion to an extended family network spread throughout the world.

When Razia was born in the northern region of India, her family was
known as one of the wealthiest and most prestigious in the area. Not only
were they considered of noble background, but her grandfather had made
a fortune in the late 1800s and early 1900s through commerce. He worked
with German merchants importing machinery, especially sewing machines, and exporting leather. With the advent of World War I, his

German partners left and he took over the business himself. Family legends tell of the servants who not only fanned him as he slept, but also stood outside his windows to shoo away the birds so their noise would not disturb his rest. The home he had built, intended to be the family compound for generations, consisted of eight connected houses. It was so large that one section of it is now used as a high school. The family also had many hundreds of acres of orchards and cropland, as well as houses in the city about fifteen miles away.

Razia's father was the third of four children born in this house. Having no interest in his father's business, he was sent away for a university education and there found his calling in the Indian independence movement. An older brother had died when in his twenties, and the business was taken up by a son-in-law. When the grandfather died around 1930, however, the management of the lands and family compound was taken over by Razia's grandmother. Though strong and capable, she was not formally educated and could read only the classical Arabic of the Qur'an. She valued education, however, and saw to it that all of her grandchildren were educated, girls as well as boys. Though she stayed in the village where the family lands brought in an income from crop production and rentals, the younger families spent the school year in the city where the children attend a Christian school with western-style educational policies resented by some of their neighbors, who were especially upset at the education of girls. When they confronted grandmother, asking, "Who will marry them?" she replied, "When I ask you to marry your sons to my daughters, then you can complain."

Razia started school when she was four years old, being driven each day in a family car with her brother, sisters, and several cousins. By 1953 she had graduated from high school and began attending a junior college for women. After two years at this institution she went to a university and, by the age of twenty-one, had obtained a master's degree. (Even today only 19 percent of all women are literate in India.) Razia then taught on the college level for ten years.

Indian independence, gained from Great Britain in 1947, had caused many changes for Razia's family. Her father had believed in and worked for a united India and did not leave when Pakistan was created from the northern part of India as an independent Islamic nation, in 1947. His sister's husband, however, belonged to a family that wanted a separate

Pakistani nation and they moved to the newly created country. The family of Razia's mother were also devout advocates of Pakistan and her mother's seven brothers and one sister and their children moved upon partition. Many of the native Islamic Pakistanis resented the influx of several million *muhajirs* (foreign Muslims) from India, and prejudices and factional disputes led one brother to return to India. Thus politics and religious ideals provided the impetus for the first international migration among Razia's kin group. As Pakistan's government changed to a military dictatorship, many of the younger generation began to migrate to the West, and several of Razia's cousins were incarcerated, and one killed, in a Pakistani jail.

The second change brought by Indian independence was economic. Land-reform laws were passed giving property to those who worked the land, and Razia's family thus lost ownership of the lands that had been rented to or worked by others. While able to maintain control over several hundred acres of the property, the traditional family income from rentals was gone. Her father had spent his life in idealistic political activity and had never held a salaried job. Faced with a sudden loss of income, but still owning village lands as well as rural and city houses, the family began to sell segments of their property and lived on the proceeds. Today only a few houses and village lands are still in family hands.

Continuing friction between Hindus and Muslims within India also influenced family life. Even though he had spent his life working for Indian independence, her father was regarded with suspicion by many of the predominately-Hindu government officials. Repeated snubs led to his resignation from political activity.

When she was twenty-four, Razia married a man of her own choice, though approved of by her family. She continued to teach until she was eight months pregnant with her first child and went back to work when her daughter was six months old. She stayed home for several years from the time of her second pregnancy until her children were in school. Her husband taught at a university that had been established by American Presbyterian missionaries. He was also in the college administration, which was having increasing difficulties with the government. Some of the local conflicts led to personal and even physical attacks, so a Lutheran program sent him to the United States for a year of study in his specialty. In his last month there Razia came to visit him, became acquainted with several university people in her field, and was invited to study for her

Ph.D. She accepted, though her husband went home, and they were separated for several years while he cared for their two children in India. In 1981 they were all reunited when her children and husband came to the United States. She finished her degree and eventually found a university faculty position.

Razia's daughter married a first-cousin (Razia's sister's son) living in the United Kingdom. Several first- and second-cousin marriages have occurred in Razia's extended family since this has long been regarded as a preferred marriage arrangement. The two families know each other well, and trust and familiarity are believed to promote good marriages and family unity. Though the marriage took place in the United States, wives generally go to their husband's home, so Razia's daughter has lived in London since her marriage.

Though marriage has caused the international movement of several young women within the family, in recent years economics has become the predominant cause for migration to the West. Razia's cousins, nieces, and nephews can be found in Virginia, Illinois, Iowa, California, Ohio, Florida, and Texas; as well as in Canada; several places in the United Kingdom such as London, Birmingham, and Dundee (Scotland); and even in the Middle East. Most of this migration has been for educational and economic opportunities. Some people have moved several times, as the scientist who left Pakistan to first attend school in Turkey, then in Illinois, and now works in Virginia; or the cousin who first left India to work in the Middle East, then got a job as a bartender on a cruise ship, jumped ship in Florida, married an American girl, and now lives in Connecticut. Perhaps the most traveled is Razia's older sister's husband, who went from India to Pakistan at the time of partition. After trying several business ventures he went to Bangladesh, then on to Kuwait, and finally settled in London. Another family member went to the American University in Turkey, found both a job and a wife in Finland, and now lives in Sweden. Razia has eighty-four first cousins: seventy-one are in Pakistan, five in India, two in the United States, one in England, another in Canada, and four in the Middle East. She also has four sisters in Pakistan, two in the United Kingdom, and one sister and brother, along with her mother, in India. The children of these siblings have migrated even further, and several have come to the United States.

This international mobility has been typical for many South Asian

Muslims of middle- and upper-class backgrounds with high levels of education. In a National Science Foundation survey from 1973, only 52 percent of Indians and 51 percent of Pakistanis had come to the United states directly from their home countries. U.S. immigration statistics from 1986 show that 17 percent of immigrants from Pakistan had been born elsewhere. Such figures suggest that many Indian-born Muslims first immigrated to Pakistan and then re-immigrated, often to Western countries.

Migration to the United States has also increased since the 1960s when U.S. immigration laws were changed to give preference to those with occupations and job skills needed by the U.S. economy. This has brought many highly-educated people to the United States; Razia's family has been a part of this immigration trend. The occupations of her uncles, cousins and nephews include nuclear physicist, engineer, and medical doctor, as well as businessman and professor. Although most of the women are housewives, those who do work are primarily in academic positions.

Razia knows where most all of her relatives are living. Addresses and phone numbers are exchanged and contacts renewed by phone calls and visits. All of those kinfolk living in the United States were invited to the marriage of Razia's daughter; such events are welcome reasons for getting together. When Razia or her daughter plan their trips they consider where family members and friends are living. Marriage planning also unites them. Razia always has a few nieces, nephews, or cousins for whom she is "looking for" suitable matches. Information on available young women and men is exchanged, but Razia does not want to find a match for her son, as she feels he is too Americanized to accept such a process. The aid that family members in different countries can provide is diverse and mutually beneficial. Sometimes it reflects the political turmoil of the South Asian region. For example, when there is increased friction between Pakistan and India, mail between the two countries is often unreliable. So kinfolk in these countries send letters to their relatives in England to be forwarded back to relatives in South Asia. When Razia's father died in 1979, relatives phoned her sister in England who then called Razia who was alone in the United States. All such contacts and instances of mutual assistance and support have ensured the cohesiveness of this family. The traditional joint family no longer lives together, but their unity has continued. Razia's family is large and international, and she knows she can call most any one of them and receive a supportive response.

🦜 *References*

National Science Foundation. 1973. *Immigrant Scientists and Engineers in the United States: A Study of Characteristics and Attitudes.* Washington, D. C.: U.S. Government Printing Office.

U. S. Immigration and Naturalization Service. 1987. *Statistical Yearbook of the Immigration and Naturalization Service: 1986.* Washington, D.C.: U. S. Government Printing Office.

PLATE 2. *Belal and his grandmother. Dearborn, Michigan, 1980.*

PLATE 3. *The Reverend Imam, M. Karoub, conducting a Muslim marriage ceremony at home. Michigan, 1995.*

PLATE 4. *The extended family at home celebrating the Atassi-Abdulhak marriage. Michigan, 1995.*

PLATE 5. *Karoub family reunion.*
The family immigrated from Lebanon early in the twentieth century.

PLATE 6.   *Women demonstrating after the Israeli invasion of Lebanon in 1982.*
Dearborn, Michigan.

PLATE 7.   *Helen Okdie Atwell at the Dearborn, Michigan, mosque her family
helped to establish.*

PLATE 8. *Isam, an Iraqi refugee, and his nephew Sadoon, 1994.*

PART TWO

Practical Issues for Families

ANAHID KULWICKI

꧁꧂

Health Issues among
Arab Muslim Families

G rowing concern about the declining health status of ethnic minorities
in the United States has led many nurse leaders to challenge the
quality of health care provided to culturally diverse populations.
Nurses who work with ethnic minorities have long recognized the role of
cultural factors in the provision of holistic patient care. Theorists and
practitioners of transcultural nursing, a subfield of nursing, have sought to
develop culture-specific nursing-care modalities that take into account the
beliefs, values, and practices of their clients (Leininger 1978). The primary goal of transcultural nursing is to improve clients' health-care status
by providing culturally sensitive nursing care.

Arab-Americans form one of the largest and most neglected minority
groups in Michigan. In order to provide culturally congruent care to
Arab-Americans, nurses need to understand the lifeways, social structure,
and environmental factors that affect on their health and well-being.

This paper describes issues related to health-care beliefs, values, practices, and expectations among Muslim Arab families of Dearborn, Michigan. The information presented in this chapter is derived from the author's
experience as a researcher in the areas of AIDS (Kulwicki 1989), teen health
(Kulwicki 1988), prenatal health-care practices, cardiovascular risk assessment (Kulwicki 1990), and an ethnographic study of illness perceptions and practices of Yemeni Americans (Kulwicki 1987). My Middle
Eastern background, knowledge of the Arabic language, and twelve years

of professional nursing experience with the Arabic community of Dearborn have contributed to the interpretation of significant cultural factors.

The Arab community in Dearborn is comprised predominantly of poorer immigrants from Yemen, Palestine, and South Lebanon. Many health issues and attitudes found here also will be common among Arabs from many areas of the Arab world. It has been observed that Middle Easterners, whatever their national, religious, regional, ethnic, or language background, share broad features of a common culture. This similarity is due in part to a common knowledge of Arabic, even if it is not the mother tongue. Among most ethnic and religious minorities in the region, it is the language of commerce, education, and law. It is also partly due to the cohering influence of the Abrahamic religious tradition, which is shared by the major religions of the Middle East: Judaism, Christianity, and Islam; to a shared political history, which, with the exception of Israel, includes four hundred years under Ottoman Turkish rule and a century under European colonialism; and partly to a pervading attitude, derived from Islam, stressing social cohesion over individualism. Thus, many of the attitudes, behaviors, and customs described here will be familiar to those with experience with other immigrant communities from the Middle East, including Chaldeans and Assyrians, Persians, Turks, Kurds, Copts and other Christians, and Jews. Nonetheless, this chapter to describes specifically only attitudes and situations of the Muslim Arab-American community of Dearborn.

🎋 *The Dearborn Arab Community*

The metropolitan area of Detroit has a larger concentration of Middle Eastern peoples than any other metropolitan area in the country. High estimates for the number of Arab-Americans living in the Detroit area range from two hundred thousand to two hundred fifty thousand; the earliest of these estimates was made in 1978 (Abraham 1983; Naff 1983; Abraham and Abraham 1983). The *1980 Census of the Population* counted fifty-two thousand eight hundred Arab-Americans in metropolitan Detroit; according to census data, another twenty-two thousand live in other parts of the state, bringing the total to some eighty-five thousand Arab-Americans in Michigan (U.S. Bureau of the Census 1983; Sands 1986). The 1980 census used ancestry codes to determine Arabic ancestry, although the use of such codes has been criticized (Kayal 1987; Jabara and Abraham 1986).

The Arab community in the greater Detroit area is composed of people from numerous and diverse national and religious affiliations. The major groups include Lebanese/Syrian, Iraqi/Chaldean, Palestinian/Jordanian, and Yemeni. The major religious affiliations of this Arab population include Arab Christian, Arab Muslim, and Chaldean Christian of several traditions (Abraham 1983).

The first immigration from the Middle East to Detroit began in the 1890s. The Southend community in Dearborn was at that time, and still is, the principal point of entry (Abraham and Abraham 1983; Aswad 1974). A 1979 survey found that two-thirds of the Arabic respondents were born overseas and had emigrated to the United States after 1974 (Bowker 1979). It is expected that immigration will continue as it has occurred in the past, although fluctuations may occur from time to time according to political and economic conditionsin Middle Eastern countries and shifts in the economic conditions in the greater Detroit area.

Residential patterns further stratify the Middle Eastern population, creating distinctive, cohesive Arab communities in the greater Detroit area. One of the main reasons for this cohesiveness is the presence of quite a number of extended families, which, on the average, contain three to five adults per household. Concentrations of Arab-Americans are found primarily in Dearborn and southwest Detroit, the east side of Detroit, Grosse Pointe and its environs, southeastern Oakland County, and southern Macomb County. The Muslim population is found mostly in the Southend area of Dearborn, whereas the Arab Christian population can be found throughout the greater Detroit area.

According to the 1980 census, the Middle Eastern population differs from the general population in that Arab-Americans tend to be younger (median age is 23.2 years). Roughly 54 percent of the population is male. A larger number of males is due to the high incidence of immigration into the United States by single men as well as married men who reside here on their own for a short period of time. Arab Americans rank below the general population in educational attainment; their mean number of years of schooling is 9.2, and many report that they have only completed high school. Their mean level of income also is rather low.

The mosque is one of the principal gathering places for both men and women in the Southend of Dearborn. It not only facilitates social interaction among members of the community, but it also serves the traditional function of providing religious orientation for the community (Naff 1983). The importance of the mosque to the Arabic community has been described by Elkholy as follows: "The mosque institution plays a vital role in the life of the entire community, for religion's vital psychological functions integrate the individual personality with that of the surrounding society" (1966: 134).

The Southend of Dearborn is characterized by neighborhoods comprising different Arabic groups which coalesce to form an ethnic community that shows clear indications of customs and culture from Middle Eastern countries. The majority of the Arabic population in the Dearborn area is working class, a number of whom are employed in the nearby automobile industry. Economic recession during the decade of the 1980s, however, has brought the experience of unemployment to the Arabic population, as it has to many others in Michigan. The community is considered poor since its residents earn little in comparison to the general population, but also because many of them arrive in this country with little or no resources. Economic considerations, then, are very crucial when seeking to identify the needs of the Arab-American population. A recent survey by the Wayne County Health Department found that 45 percent of the respondents interviewed reported an annual income of less than $10,000. Compared to roughly 5 percent of the general population in the greater Detroit area who fall below the poverty level, some 27 percent of the Arabic population reported earning wages below poverty (Gold 1987). According to another study, nearly 45 percent of the Arabic community are unemployed. Lack of education is one factor that contributes to the unemployment. Only half of the Arab-American population in Dearborn have received a high-school diploma. Approximately a third of the immigrant community speak no English and some 66 percent speak a limited amount of English. Twenty percent read and write a limited amount of Arabic (Abraham, Abraham, and Aswad 1983).

❆ Health Issues

The ability and willingness of Arab-Americans to access and have a favorable experience with the American health-care system is dependent on a number of factors. These factors include English language proficiency, family finances, socioeconomic background, level of education, religion, and other cultural values.

The language barrier is probably the most difficult health issue facing the Arab community of Dearborn. Many have limited proficiency in spoken English. The acquisition of English reading and writing skills is, therefore, very difficult. Many Dearborn Arabs, particularly women, are also illiterate in their native Arabic. Many Arab patients are incapable of reading medical instructions even if written in Arabic. Since many of the Arab residents of the Southend are recent immigrants, only the passage of time will improve their mastery of English. The only immediate resolution of this problem would be greater availability of bilingual translators or bilingual health-care providers.

Another major health issue is family finances, which can limit access to health care. The Southend is a relatively poor community with a heavy concentration of families at or below the poverty level. While some wage earners are employed by auto companies and receive good health benefits, many more are employed in the restaurant industry or at menial jobs in which health-care benefits generally are not provided. Poverty is exacerbated by a lack of familiarity with public assistance programs and, in some cases, ineligibility for such programs or for social security because of their recent immigration. There is also resistance among male members of the community to accepting public assistance because it is perceived as a negative reflection on them as economic providers. Language, financial, and cultural factors combine to restrict access to public transportation for unescorted females.

Lack of education is another health issue for Arab Muslims in the Southend. Most are from comparatively deprived backgrounds in their native countries. Yemeni, Lebanese, and Palestinian residents are almost exclusively from poorer agricultural areas in which educational opportunities are limited. Few have an education that extends beyond primary school. Among the problems this poses is that Arab patients lack a knowledge of body parts and body functions. Knowledge of germ theory is frequently lacking, and competing folk theories of illness sometimes exist. Concepts such as liver and glandular function, blood circulation, bacterial and viral infection, immune response, and disease prevention and health promotion may not be understood well. Culturally sensitive health education within the health-care setting is a remedy to this barrier to health-care access. Improvements in general educational levels may be expected to solve the problem over time.

Differences in customs, values, and beliefs between Arab Muslims and mainstream Americans represent sources of potential conflict and misunderstanding in the health-care setting. Significant Arab Muslim customs and beliefs are discussed below and grouped in the following broad categories: religious beliefs and practices, family roles, sexual roles, knowledge and superstitions, and social mores. These categories do not present a comprehensive view of Arab or Muslim life, but highlight points of divergence from conventional American values and beliefs.

Religious Beliefs and Practices

Islam is the predominant religion of the Middle East and North Africa. It is a monotheistic religion whose chief article of faith is "There is no God save (the one) God and Muhammad is his Prophet." Muslims believe that the religion of Islam was revealed in its complete form to Muhammad, the last of the prophets. However, the message of Islam is that it is not only a religion, but also a comprehensive way of life. As such, it has a pervasive and deep influence on Muslim attitudes and conduct. For Muslims, all acts that are necessary to human life are given a religious meaning and direction by the *Shari'a* or Islamic religious law. The *Shari'a* sets forth rules of religious observance and practice, marriage and family law, rules for social conduct and interaction, dietary regulations, and general rules for cleanliness. Islamic practices and beliefs described below may influence Arab Muslim contact with the health-care system.

FATALISM

Muslims find offensive the popular Western perception that Islam is a fatalistic religion. Indeed, the charge of fatalism has been used for centuries in attacks on Islam by Christian antagonists who have overdrawn its significance. An understanding of Islam would leave no doubt that a concept of human free will and initiative is central to the faith. Humans have a rational mind endowed with decision-making and problem-solving capabilities. Humans have the duty to follow the demands of the faith and bear responsibility for their actions. However, Islam also emphasizes that freedom in an absolute sense belongs to God alone. In matters of health and illness, Muslim attitudes generally allow a more limited sphere of influence to human action than is common in the United States.

These attitudes manifest themselves in the feeling that the health-care system has a narrowly defined role to play in matters of health and illness, and life and death. Muslims believe they have a religious obligation to seek a cure for an illness. However, some Muslim patients are often brought into the health-care system at an advanced stage of illness. Likewise, if Muslims determine that medicine does not have an easy answer to a health problem, they may show a greater inclination to resign themselves to God's care. Muslims view illness as God's test of man's faith in Him. God is the ultimate causation and cure of illness. Those who suffer in this world and keep their faith in God will find their reward in the afterlife. A common Arabic expression, *in sha' Allah* (if God wills), implies that one's ultimate fate rests with God.

Since God makes the final determination in life and death, Muslims are offended by diagnoses that predict death within a defined period of time or, conversely, that predict recovery with certitude. In cases where medical professionals predict a time of death or a point of recovery, Muslims may cease to cooperate in the medical care or withdraw from care completely. For example, in the local community, the Lebanese mother of a heart patient ceased visiting her ailing son in the hospital because of her distress over repeated dire prognoses by hospital personnel. Although the father prevailed in keeping the son under hospital care, greater sensitivity on the part of doctors and nurses might have prevented the withdrawal of the mother at a critical point in her child's recovery.

CLEANLINESS

Islamic tradition records the Prophet Muhammad as saying, "The religion (of Islam) is based on cleanliness." Precise rules for cleanliness are contained in Islamic law. According to the *Shari'a*, there are things that are, by nature, unclean and, therefore, to be avoided by Muslims, especially in prayers and eating. The major categories of unclean things include: urine and stool; blood and semen; corpses; unclean animals such as pigs and dogs; intoxicating liquids; and non-Muslims. Attitudes toward contact with non-Muslims vary widely in the Muslim world. For example, a conservative Yemeni woman, the daughter of a *sayyid* (a man revered as a descendent of the Prophet and endowed with special spiritual skills), withdrew from a hospital after a Christian minister, in attempting to comfort her, patted her arm. Treatment in a non-Muslim setting had not overly concerned her until this intrusive and unsolicited action occurred.

Muslims are required to clean their faces, arms, and legs up to the knee prior to the prayers to be undertaken five times daily. In addition, Islamic law is specific on the ablutions required after urination and defecation and after sexual relations. Muslims from impoverished backgrounds, or from countries where water resources are scarce, are often scrupulous in fulfilling ritual cleansings but sometimes leave unwashed important areas of the body such as under the axilla, breasts, and navel areas. Hygiene is a matter that needs to be handled delicately through education and demonstration.

DIETARY RESTRICTIONS

Islamic dietary regulations forbid the consumption of blood or blood products, pork, and alcohol. Meats should be prepared in the *halaal* method with all blood removed. Insofar as *halaal* meats are not available, kosher prepared meats may be substituted. All pork products including bacon, ham, wieners, and baked goods and crackers prepared with lard are forbidden. Foods should not be prepared in containers that have held pork or pork products. Muslims may often reject hospital foods for religious reasons and may seek to bring home-prepared meals to hospitalized family members. Institutions with a high percentage of Arab clientele can address this issue by providing special meals. Alternatively, hospitals can be more tolerant or even encourage Muslim families to bring meals from home.

RELIGION AND MENTAL ILLNESS

Arab Muslims believe that illness may befall an individual because of his or her loss of faith in God. The most common illness attributed to this is madness (*jinaan*). The word *jinaan* is derived from the Arabic word *jinn* or demon. *Jinn* is the source of the English words "genie" and "genius." The word *majnuun* (a mad individual) means in its original sense "one possessed by the *jinn*." *Jinn* may be either good or evil. Other names used for the evil jinn are *shaytaan* (Satan or devil), *zaar* (a male demon), and *qariina* (a female demon).

Madness is, perhaps, the illness most feared by Muslims. Since humans are considered the highest form of life because of their possession of a rational faculty, loss of reason is the most serious illness that can befall them. The only cure for illnesses caused by possession is for victims to reaffirm their belief in God. This may be done directly or through the assistance of a religious intermediary or folk healer. The treatment for such mental illness is by some form of exorcism of the evil. Muslims of the Southend believe knowledge of illnesses caused by possession is outside of the realm of the American medical or mental practitioner and, therefore, seek a remedy from a folk healer.

۞ Family Roles

Family and kinship ties are highly valued among Arabs. Members of the extended family are expected to take part in all aspects of an Arab's life, including financial matters, marriage, family birth, illness, and death. The sharing of experiences with immediate and extended family is necessary, not a luxury, for Arabs and Arab-Americans. At times of crisis, family members are expected to show support by their presence and the offering of financial assistance. The strong affinity and need for family support is apparent when an Arab-American client is cared for in a hospital setting. Some American health-care providers view Arab-Americans as imposing and non-compliant with visitation rules. Arab-American clients, on the other hand, view limitations of family visitation as violation of a basic right and so may ignore regulations. Arab-Americans consider family support essential to the health and well-being of an individual. The hospitalized Arab seeks strength and comfort in the support and presence of family members. Denying Arab-Americans such support by setting rules and limitations on visitation creates tensions between health-care providers and health-care recipients and often leads to confrontation.

Nurses and social workers in the Detroit metropolitan area frequently express concern about violations of visitation rules by family members of Arab clients. On the other hand, Arab clients complain of limited hospital hours. Compromises that meet with some success include taking the patient to an area where family members have gathered or amending the rules to permit longer visitation or visits by more family members than rules generally allow. Clearly a balance must be found between the needs of the Arab patient and family and that of the hospital clientele as a group. Within the extended family, there is a sense of openness and shared experience. Family members express pride in the family and are protective of its members. An aspect of this pride and protectiveness is that family members may be secretive about illnesses or health matters that are perceived to bring shame and dishonor to the family. Family members might be secretive about family histories of mental illness, mental retardation, genetic, or reproductive disorders, and chronic illnesses such as cardiac disorders and seizures. A major factor in this concealment is that knowledge of these health matters may interfere with the marriage possibilities of the person in question or other family members. Information regarding such health problems may be withheld from health-care professionals for fear that they will become public and harm the family. For example, a Lebanese woman related that her mother concealed a family history of a rare blood disorder until after her grandchildren were diagnosed with the ailment. The mother was concerned that knowledge of the disorder would limit the woman's potential for marriage.

Arab Muslims have great respect for elders. Children are raised to be obedient to parents and elder sisters and brothers and never to question elders. Talking back to parents or elders is considered a sign of a poor upbringing. However, children and teenagers who have been exposed to American values for a period of years may become resentful of their parents' traditional value system. They may exhibit embarrassment over their parents' traditional clothing or demeanor. In the health-care setting, this may lead to conflict in a number of ways. The children may be translators for ill parents and may not convey the full content of parent responses to the health-care providers. In other cases, children may be abrupt with parents to limit their contact with outsiders.

Family ties may also mean that families reject medical advice for specialized care or institutionalization for the elderly or handicapped. The elderly are held in high esteem by the family. It is the duty for the family to provide care in the home, typically until death. Even though the family may lack the resources to provide proper care for a disabled individual, there is a feeling that life outside the family is not worth living.

🐚 *Sexual Roles*

Arabs maintain strict sex-role differences. Traditionally, Arab males are the providers and in charge of social and political affairs. Women, on the other hand, are the childbearers and rearers, and are in charge of household activities. Although economic pressures are slowly changing sex roles, Arabs continue to view men as decision makers for matters outside the household. This is due to their greater experience with and exposure to public life. Women make decisions about child-rearing and household matters. This does not mean that decisions are made without consultation between partners. What it implies is that final authority and responsibility rests upon the individual who has experience, knowledge and authority in his or her respective role.

In the health-care setting, the male is responsible for the final decision and signing consent forms and surgical permits. This is because the male head of household is responsible for decisions outside the home and generally has the best command of English. Often during emergency situations, the male Arab guardian is not available to sign consent forms for treatments or surgical procedures. Female Arab guardians, therefore, are pressured by health professionals to sign these informed consent forms without consulting with their spouses. This frequently becomes a source of later conflict between the spouses or guardians because the female failed to understand some of the procedures or the implications of a contractual agreement, or because she entered into a field beyond her authority.

Sex-role differences extend to the notion of the male being the protector of family members from outsiders and the female being the nurturer and carer for family members. Islamic and Arab traditions value female purity and virginity prior to marriage. The male who is usually the father or an older brother is expected to protect the family honor by ensuring that female members of the family preserve the notion of chastity and purity. In the health-care setting this extends to the notion of protecting females from being exposed to strangers of the opposite sex. Male kin may feel embarrassed and powerless when female kin are exposed to male professionals. Consequently, to protect the family honor, some males may forbid their sisters, spouses, or daughters to be examined by males. In one case, a Palestinian father refused an examination for his prepubescent daughter who was suffering from a vaginal infection. Permission was refused because it was felt that the exam jeopardized the daughter's virginity and, hence, marriageability. A solution was found when a doctor agreed to prescribe a treatment based on the symptoms without benefit of a physical examination.

Sexual matters are considered exclusively single gender topics of conversation. Males and females do not discuss sexual matters with members of the opposite sexes, and this is true even between spouses. However, intimate sexual concerns are openly discussed between people of the same sex. Contraception, infertility, or matters concerning family planning often are not discussed between partners and, in some instances, females may make decisions about family planning without the knowledge or consent of their spouses.

Differences in sex-role behaviors are also apparent during childbirth and delivery. Childbirth is a female experience and often is shared with midwives or close female members of the family such as mother, mother-in-law, or an experienced sister-in-law. Traditionally, Arab males are excluded from the birthing process. Expectations within the United States health-care system that a father be present or assist in the delivery may cause confusion, embarrassment, or irritation to the father. Conversely, exclusion of a pregnant woman's mother or sisters from a delivery room may be a source of consternation and increase the anxiety of delivery.

Differences in role expectations also create difficulties for women whose children are ill and need hospitalization. This is particularly true for women who do not have an extended family in the United States. Mothers are expected to be with their ill children during hospitalization. However, with a lack of availability of child-care services and a negative attitude towards leaving children with paid baby-sitters, women find themselves in conflict. If they remain in the hospital to care for the ill, they are not available at home to tend to other children. This is further complicated by the fact that women lack communication skills and, hence, their concerns often are not understood by the health-care professionals. The helplessness of mother and child in coping with a strange hospital environment may lead to conflict. Often mothers resort to avoiding the hospital. Arab children may become uncooperative and noncompliant because of their separation from their mother and fear of strangers. The impact of such experience both on the child and the mother is so devastating that anger, discomfort, and impatience about treatment often occur. Delays brought about by the absence of parents or noncompliance of patients may cause further tensions between hospital personnel and Arab-American clients.

⚕ *Social Mores*

Arab-Americans value hospitality and generosity highly. Personal relationships are preferred to impersonal ones. Hospitality serves a social purpose in allowing one to get to know an individual personally in a context of sharing food or gifts. Although these characteristics are much valued and greatly admired by Arabs, in a health-care setting they delay the sharing of vital information, creates greater time demands from Arab-Americans than from other clients, and cause a feeling of discomfort with gifts that are considered overly generous and imposing by American standards.

CONFORMITY

Arab-Americans are generally conformist by nature. This is due to Arab family life-styles and religious orientation. Because most Arabs come from extended families, group cohesiveness and conformity to family and cultural norms is important for an individual to be able to live with others harmoniously. Nonconformity with family values and cultural norms is undesirable. In addition, Islamic law dictates a uniform life with the roles and responsibilities of individuals well delineated so that harmony with surroundings and religious life-style is maintained. This explains why Arab-Americans are compliant generally in the health-care setting and do not express any disagreement they may have with health-care professionals for fear that they may be labeled as nonconformist or rude.

However, in spite of the willingness of Arab-Americans to conform to rules and regulations of the American health-care system, there are instances when Arab-Americans are unable to adhere to hospital routines because of cultural and social barriers. One of the greatest areas of difficulty is Arab-American's lack of familiarity with the American health-care system. Many immigrants who have come from rural or economically depressed backgrounds have had limited or no experience with the American health-care system. This is further complicated by a lack of knowledge of English, and often by an inability to read in any language. Language deficiencies cause difficulties in following directions, understanding instructions, communicating needs and concerns, and arriving at appointments at scheduled times.

EMOTIONAL BEHAVIOR

While Arab Muslims are emotive in the family context, they tend to be reserved in public or in a strange environment. However, in certain situations, highly emotional behavior is socially approved. For example, the death of a child or dear one may lead a woman to wail, tear clothing, and lose physical control. In another example, pregnant women may react to labor pains with unrestrained emotions. In the American health-care context, such emotional behavior in public is often frowned on and may be considered disruptive.

SOCIAL INTERACTIONS

Arabs tend to consider current matters and contacts as more important than matters and persons at a distance. What and who are present is more important than what and who is away. For example, it is considered rude and inconsiderate to rush away from a friend or associate even though another appointment or obligation may be delayed. There is a general sense that timing is "flexible." Consequently, in the rural Middle East, formal medical appointments generally are not made. Rather, a client is asked to return in a few days or weeks. In Detroit and Dearborn, Arab clients are often perceived as unreliable or non-compliant because they often fail to keep appointments. Although reserved in strange surroundings, Arabs or Arab-Americans tend to be more demonstrative among one another than most Americans are. The arrival and departure of family or friends is accompanied by hugs and kisses on the cheek. Conversation can be animated and often loud.

MODESTY

Muslims are modest in dress. For example, both males and females typically cover their extremities in public. Some Muslim women wear a form of veil, which may vary from a simple head scarf to a complete, full covering. A sensitivity to this higher level of modesty is crucial to the provision of successful health care. The male head of household may forbid a female member to be examined by a male professional. The presence of female members of the household may be helpful in these circumstances.

𝕰 *Attitudes toward Modern Medicine*

Arab culture shows great respect for knowledge and science. Most Arabs are aware of Arab historical contributions to science and medicine in general terms and take considerable pride in them. The knowledge held by a healer is thought to convey power and authority. Islamic jurists who have an expert knowledge of religious law have unquestioned authority in matters of interpretation and execution of the law. Similarly, doctors and other medical experts are viewed as having a power and authority emanating from their knowledge of science and medicine. For Arabs without formal education or from less educated backgrounds, there may be an exaggerated respect for the powers held by a physician. However, because the medical process is not well understood, if the healing powers are not exhibited in a direct, obvious, and effective manner, Arab may resort to traditional practices that are perceived as more efficacious.

Because of their profound respect for medical experts, Arab-Americans have difficulty questioning medical authorities and being actively involved in medical decision making. Arab-American clients often expect doctors to make medical decisions without the need for the collection of a medical history and without consultation with the client. In cases in which clients are asked to participate in the decision making about their medical regimen, Arab-Americans may lose trust in the medical experts and discontinue treatment.

Arab-Americans value Western medicine and consider themselves privileged to use facilities that were, in many cases, inaccessible to them in their countries of origin. Physicians are often consulted for physical disorders or ailments. Highly technical and invasive therapies are considered superior over noninvasive therapies. Surgery is preferred to oral medications. Therapies that aim at eliminating, cutting, or eradicating by burning or purifying are desired more than therapies aimed at prevention or promoting health. Arab-Americans often expect cure from medical treatments regardless of its acuity or the chronicity of the condition. This creates a problem in instances in which treatment is aimed at prevention of a recurring disease, or prevention of further complications in chronic illnesses such as diabetes, heart disease, epilepsy, and hypertension. In many instances Arab-Americans will discontinue treatments based on their perception of being cured from a disease. When they find that the condition recurs, they will sometimes reject further treatment and follow-up care, and resort to folk remedies. One informant gave this account of the experience her neighbor had with *tarfa* (stroke):

> The woman was sitting out on the porch. Suddenly, her son looked at her and told her that her face looked funny. The woman asked her son what he meant. He said her nose and mouth had gone to one side of her face. The woman rushed into the house and looked at her face in the mirror. She found her son was right.
>
> She then went to the doctor. The doctor told the woman she needed an operation in her head. The woman refused to have the operation done. One of her neighbors then told her she will do *al-makwaa* on her if she would allow her to do so. The woman had a *makwaa* done. The hot metal was applied on both sides of the woman's mouth. You can still see small scars from the burns, but the woman's face became straight. She would have gone through all that operation when something simple like *al-makwaa* could treat her.

Arab-American clients often expect doctors to diagnose and treat illness without time consuming and painful diagnostic procedures. Arab-Americans often become impatient when they have submitted to a battery of laboratory procedures. They also tend to develop distrust for doctors who need to rely on such measures before treatment. Moreover, Arab-American clients may change doctors frequently if they are not satisfied with the speed of recovery while undergoing treatment. Arab-Americans make active use of emergency-room services when conventional clinic care would be suitable. Several factors influence the use of emergency services. First, Arab-Americans lack an understanding of the role of emergency services. They perceive emergency facilities as a convenient place to take any ill person. They may consider Americans lacking in spontaneity by developing rigid criteria for use of such services. Second, Arab-Americans avoid medical treatment until a condition is too severe to continue avoiding its expense. This may reflect their current financial condition or a lack of medical insurance. It may also be a conditioned response based on their customary use of health-care facilities in their countries of origin. Third, women, who are the primary carers for family members, may lack available transportation or a translator to assist in taking the sick person to a doctor or a clinic. They may need to wait until their spouses return from work, which may be after normal clinical hours.

FOLK MEDICINE

Under certain circumstances, Arab clients are more inclined to resort to traditional healing practices. In general, if an illness is thought to have a cause that is outside the realm of knowledge of a doctor, Arab clients may seek out traditional healers. Traditional healers are often consulted in the treatment of mental disorders such as madness (*jinaan*), depression, and schizophrenia because medical interventions are often inconclusive or ineffective. Arab clients may also resort to a traditional healer to treat illnesses caused by evil-wishers who cast the evil eye ('*ayn al-hasad*) or who use sorcery.

Arab Muslim informants in Dearborn identified three kinds of folk healer: a *sayyid*, a *faatiḥat al-kitaab* (literally, opener of the book or spell, and '*ajami* literally a foreigner, a blind and mute man who roamed rural Yemen).

THE EVIL EYE

Folk beliefs and traditional healing practices regarding health and illness are still found among Arab-Americans of Dearborn. For instance, many Arab-Americans believe that hatred and jealousy can cause illness to beautiful and healthy children. Jealously is often expressed by casting the evil or envious eye.

Victims of the evil eye ('*ayn al-hasad*) are generally children or young adults who are healthy and considered beautiful. Informants report that the eye is typically cast by women jealous of the good fortune of another who has beautiful and healthy children. In admiration, they praise the beauty of a child or youth, but fail to mention the name of God or the Prophet. (People are advised always to mention the name of God when admiring others because it gives horror to the evil spirit and prevents it from doing harm.) The evil eye is believed to cause vomiting, gastrointestinal disorders, and, on rare occasions, death.

Various amulets are used to ward off or distract the eye, and may include the use of blue stones or verses from the Qur'an which are placed on the child, the child's clothing, or on a crib. The treatment of an illness caused by the evil eye is usually *tabkhiir* (fumigation). *Tabkhiir* involves the burning of frankincense and an article of clothing or personal effects from the caster of the evil eye. The frankincense and article of clothing are burned in a small container over charcoal. The victim of the evil eye is asked to bend over the fumes of the burning items.

SORCERY

Hatred is usually expressed through the use of spells or sorcery (*sihr*). Illnesses caused by sorcery are often manifested in mental and emotional disorders. In sorcery, an individual plotting harm to another hires a sorcerer (*sahar*) to cast a spell on the intended victim. The spell causes illnesses that make a sudden appearance such as seizures and madness. Typically a sorcerer casts a spell by preparing a *kitaab* (a writing) that contains the curse. At times the curse is prepared in a series of symbolic knots tied in thread or animal or human hair. The *kitaab* is generally concealed in or near the victim's home or place of work. In the Middle East, the *kitaab* is often thrown into the sea or concealed in the mountains where it cannot be recovered easily. Some believe that curses hidden in this way cannot be undone. *Kitaabs* that are recovered may be undone by a folk healer skilled in such matters. An example of the ability of a folk healer to heal a victim is described below:

> I know a woman in Yemen who became mad. People believed that her father did the *sihr* on her because he opposed her marriage to a person he very much disliked. The woman used to run to the hills and spread her arms as if she was flying. She also would call "ah-ah" like an eagle would do. This madness could not be cured because the *sihr* was fed to the eagle. After it ate the *sihr*, the eagle could not be located. The woman remained mad all her life. People thought after the death of the eagle that the spell would go away. I don't know if that ever happened.

🐚 *Conclusion*

The experience of Arab Muslims within the American health-care system is similar to that of many urban ethnic minorities. Language, culture, and economics represent barriers to access to this system. Optimally, a culturally informed, bilingual representative or ombudsman should be available in each health-care setting with a substantial minority clientele, although as a practical matter, individuals with a full bicultural understanding may not be available. Nonetheless, promotion of a general knowledge of minority values and beliefs among health professionals is a helpful first step in the successful provision of health-care services.

Based on difficulties Arab-Americans experience in receiving health-care services in hospital settings, there is a need for culturally specific health promotion and disease prevention educational materials to be developed and disseminated to state and local health agencies, nonprofit health organizations and community health centers in order to resolve some of the issues Arab-Americans face in the American health-care system. Other useful community-wide educational approaches include:

1. Health officials, service providers, and community groups need to develop and implement programs directed toward health promotion and risk reduction among the Arab-American population.

2. Comprehensive bilingual health-education programs need to be developed for those who are illiterate or have only a rudimentary education.

3. Educational materials should be targeted to promote healthy life style behaviors such as yearly physical examinations, diet, exercise, and stress-reduction programs among Arab-Americans.

4. Mass media education campaigns through television and visual aids should be utilized in educating the Arab public about the most common preventable disease conditions.

5. Culturally aware individuals should be employed in the integration of health education information within the cultural context of Arab-American women. Female bilingual health-care professionals should be utilized to provide health-care services in obstetrics and gynecology.

The best and most holistic paradigm for creating an effective health-promotion behavior among Arab-Americans would be the establishment of a systematic, comprehensive approach addressing social, economic, cultural, and health concerns. In the case of Arab Muslims, a basic sociocultural understanding is a prerequisite to the provision of quality health-care services.

Ō *References*

Abraham, S. Y. 1983. "Detroit's Arab-American Community: A Survey of Diversity and Commonality." Pp. 84–108 in *Arabs in the New World: Studies on Arab-American Communities*, ed. S. Y. Abraham and N. Abraham. Detroit: Wayne State University Press.

Abraham, S. and Abraham, N., eds. 1983. *Arabs in the New World: Studies on Arab-American Communities.* Detroit: Wayne State University Center for Urban Study.

Abraham, Samcer Y.; Abraham, Nabeel; and Aswad, Barbara. 1983. "The Southend: An Arab Muslim Working-Class Community." Pp. 153–184 in *Arabs in the New World: Studies on Arab-American Communities,* ed. S. Y. Abraham and N. Abraham. Detroit: Wayne State University Press.

Aswad, B., ed. 1974. *Arabic Speaking Communities in American Cities.* New York: Center for Migration Studies.

Awada, F., 1985. *Teen Parenting Study.* Report written for ACCESS. Dearborn, Mich.

Bowker, J., 1979. *Health and Social Services Needs Assessment Survey.* Unpublished manuscript, Department of Sociology. Ann Arbor, Mich: University of Michigan.

Elkholy, A. A. 1966. *The Arab Moslems in the United States: Religion and Assimilation.* New Haven: College and University Press.

Gold, S. 1987. *Wayne County Health Department Infant Mortality Demonstration Project: Preliminary Report.* Detroit, Mich.

Jabara, A. and Abraham, N. 1986. "Numbers Game: Detroit's Arabs Lose." *Detroit Free Press.* June 19.

Kayal, P. M. 1987. "Counting the Arabs among Us." *Arab Studies Quarterly* 9: 98–104.

Kulwicki, A. 1987. *An Ethnographic Study of Illness Perceptions and Practices of Yemeni Arab-Americans.* Ph.D. diss., School of Nursing, Indiana University, Indianapolis.

———. 1988. "Hot Iron Treatment among Yemeni Arab Americans." *The Journal of Nursing Science and Practice* 1, no. 3: 20–21.

———. 1989. *Executive Summary: Arab Teen Health Survey.* Final report, Michigan Department of Public Health, Bureau of Community Services, Lansing, Mich.

———. 1990. *The Arab AIDS Knowledge and Belief Survey.* Final report, Arab Community Center for Economic and Social Services, Dearborn, Mich.

Leininger, M. 1978. *Transcultural Nursing.* New York: John Wiley & Sons.

Mackie, N. 1985. *The Arab-American Parenting Study*. Unpublished manuscript. Detroit: Wayne State University, School of Social Work.

Meleis, A. 1981. "The Arab American in the Health Care System." *American Journal of Nursing* 81, no. 6: 1180–1183.

Meleis, A. and Sorrel, L. 1981. "Arab American Women and Their Birth Experience." *Maternal Child Nursing*, 6 (May–June): 171–176.

Mesa, V. 1987. *Infant Mortality Demonstration Project: Dearborn Arab Community Survey*. Unpublished preliminary report, Wayne County Health Department. Detroit.

Michigan Department of Public Health, 1988. *Minority Health in Michigan: Closing the Gap*. Lansing, Mich.: Department of Public Health.

Naff, A. 1983. "Arabs in America: A Historical Overview." In *Arabs in the New World: Studies on Arab-American Communities*, ed. S. Y. Abraham and N. Abraham. Detroit: Wayne State University Press.

Paine, P. 1985. *A Study of the Middle East Community in the Detroit Metropolitan Area*. Detroit: United Community Services.

Penchansky, R. 1972. *Study of Southeast Dearborn*. Unpublished study. University of Michigan, School of Public Health, Ann Arbor, Mich.

Qur'an. Egypt: Dar Al-kitab Al-Masri.

Sands, G. 1986. *An Estimate of the Arab Population of Metropolitan Detroit*. Census discussion paper no. 6. Michigan Metropolitan Information Center, Wayne State University, Detroit.

U. S. Bureau of the Census. 1983. *1980 Census of the Population: Ancestry of the Population by State: 1980*. Supplementary report, PC 80-S1-10. Washington, D.C.: Government Printing Office, table 3.

Wigle, L. 1974. "An Arab Muslim Community in Michigan." In *Arabic Speaking Communities in American Cities*, ed. B. Aswad. New York: Center for Migration Studies.

ANAHID KULWICKI AND PENNY S. CASS

Arab-American Knowledge, Attitudes, and Beliefs about AIDS

Little has been written about the impact of Acquired Immune Deficiency Syndrome (AIDS) on Arab-Americans. Conditions that arise from being immigrants, mostly male, mostly young, among whom high levels of unprotected sexual activity may be acceptable, place a portion of the Arab-American population at risk to AIDS, if their behaviors expose them to HIV. Added to these conditions are little fluency in English and low rates of literacy, which inhibit the use of HIV education strategies that have been designed for educating the mainstream English-speaking population about precautions to prevent exposure to HIV.

The purpose of this study of members of the Arab-American community living in Dearborn, Michigan, was to identify levels of knowledge, attitudes, and beliefs related to AIDS and the transmission of HIV and to elicit opinions on educational strategies. These community-based data were essential for developing educational and preventative strategies and implementing the language-appropriate, culturally sensitive AIDS risk-reduction program for the Arab-American population, known as the Wiqaya Project—*wiqaya* means prevention in Arabic (De La Cancela 1989).

The seriousness of the threat of HIV infection and AIDS to Arab-Americans is unknown. Since there currently are no procedures by which Arab-American AIDS cases can be extrapolated from national data reporting systems, neither the prevalence rate nor the incidence of HIV infection

For full statistical information see Kulwicki, A. 1990. *Arab AIDS Knowledge, Attitudes, Beliefs and Behaviors.* Executive Report, Office on AIDS Prevention and Intervention. Michigan Department of Public Health, Lansing, Mich.

among Arab-Americans in the United States is known. For the city of Dearborn, which has one of the largest concentrations of Arabs outside the Middle East, several cases of AIDS have been identified since 1989, the first year the Wiqaya Project was implemented. It is not clear whether HIV infection among Arab-Americans will follow what the World Health Organization has described as a "Pattern I" or a "Pattern II" profile (Adrien et al. 1990; Haverkos and Edelman 1988; Larson and Ropka 1991), each of which implicates a separate trajectory of exposure. No single mode of transmission has been identified as the predominant route among cases of AIDS in the Middle East (Huxley 1989).

☙ *Target Population*

Estimates of the number of Arab-Americans living in the Detroit area range from two hundred thousand to two hundred fifty thousand (Abraham 1983; Abraham, Abraham, and Aswad 1983; Sands 1986). Concentrations of Arab-Americans are found primarily in the city of Dearborn, but there are other communities elsewhere in the tricounty area of southwest Detroit, the east side of Oakland County, and southern Macomb County. It has been estimated that of the more than eighteen thousand who live in Dearborn, there are over six thousand who live within a five-mile radius of each other. The Arab community in Dearborn is composed of Muslims and Christians of Lebanese/Syrian, Yemeni, Palestinian/Jordanian, Iraqi/Chaldean backgrounds, but the majority are Muslim (Abraham 1983; Naff 1983).

Residential patterns further stratify the local Middle Eastern population and create distinctive, but cohesive Arab communities throughout the neighborhoods. One of the main reasons for this cohesiveness is the presence of extended families, which may contain three to five adults per household. A significant portion of the Arab-American community is young and male, living as single men, or separated from their wives and families. Marriage occurs early among Arab-Americans. Pregnancy is frequent among young married women, and infant mortality is high (Mesa 1988).

Arab-American men living in Dearborn frequently experience underemployment and even periods of unemployment. Two factors are important for the present study: a higher rate of sexual activity among adolescent males (34%) than among adolescent females (14%), which places boys at greater risk than girls of acquiring sexually transmitted diseases (STDS) and HIV infection; and a slightly lower rate of drug use among Arab-American teens (3.3%) than that of the general population (Kulwicki 1989a).

A basic problem of providing health-care services to the Arab-American community is lack of baseline information by which to assess the community's health-related needs. Cultural values related to religion and sex roles play an important part in health-seeking behaviors (Kulwicki 1987; Lipson and Meleis 1983). Religion has been implicated in inhibiting the development of programs for AIDS education (Huxley 1989). Arabic culture demonstrates a bias against planning for health care because planning suggests defiance of God's will (Kulwicki 1987; Lipson and Meleis 1983). How the cultural practices related to these values can be translated to develop strategies for HIV risk—reduction education is not addressed in the literature. Despite the need for language-appropriate, culturally sensitive health-care services in Dearborn, many Arab-Americans lack an awareness of the community resources available and demonstrate a limited knowledge of health problems (Kulwicki 1987, 1989a). On the positive side, Western medicine is highly valued by Arab-Americans (Kulwicki 1987; Lipson and Meleis 1983; Meleis 1981).

✿ Methods

An Arabic/English AIDS questionnaire was developed from Centers for Disease Control models for knowledge-attitude-belief surveys (Dawson, Cynamon, and Fitti 1987), reviewed by experts from the Arab-American community and the local health department, and then revised and submitted for approval to the Special Office on AIDS Prevention, Michigan Department of Public Health. Once approved, this interview guide was translated into Arabic and pretested with 53 respondents. Bilingual interviewers were then recruited and trained in survey techniques for administering the survey questionnaire.

SAMPLE AND SETTING

A random sample of 411 households was selected from a telephone listing of Arab-American residents in Dearborn and surveyed regarding their knowledge, attitudes, and beliefs about AIDS, transmission of HIV, and HIV

TABLE 1
PROFILE OF SURVEY RESPONDENTS

NATIONALITY
Lebanese	65%
Yemeni	23%
Palestinian	9%
Syrian	2%
Other	1%

PRIMARY LANGUAGE SPOKEN AT HOME
Arabic	51%
English and Arabic	42%
English only	7%

MARITAL STATUS
Married	65%
Single	25%
Other	10%

EDUCATION
Completed elementary school	34%
Completed high school	32%
Completed college	11%
Completed some college or technical school	9%
Completed vocational school	3%
No school at all	12%

GENDER
Men	41%
Women	59%

Age ranged from 13–85 years, two-thirds were between 15–39; mean age was 32.8 years.

risk–reduction education. Contact was made with one person from each household. Those able to complete the questionnaire on their own did so and returned it in the envelope provided, but face-to-face interviews in the respondents' homes were held with those unable to read and write. This method was the most effective way to gather information due to low levels of literacy, in English and Arabic, and a reluctance within the Arab community to answer health-related questions over the phone when the caller was a stranger (Lipson and Meleis 1989; Meleis 1981). Confidentiality of respondents was assured by recording no names. Forty-six women indicated they had no knowledge of AIDS or HIV and, therefore, were excused from completing the questionnaire.

Sample parameters (see Table 1) approximated those of previous studies of the Arab-American community in Dearborn for national origin, language spoken at home, marital status, and education (Kulwicki 1989a, 1989b; Rice and Kulwicki 1992). Of the 411 respondents who were interviewed, 65 percent identified themselves as Lebanese, 23 percent as Yemeni, 9 percent as Palestinian, 2 percent as Syrian, and 1 percent as other. Some 51 percent spoke Arabic as their main language at home, 42 percent spoke English and Arabic at home, and 7 percent spoke only English. Some 65 percent were married, 25 percent were single, and 10 percent were other. Some 34 percent had completed elementary school, 32 percent had completed high school, 11 percent had completed college, 9 percent had completed some college or technical school, 3 percent had completed vocational school, and 12 percent reported no schooling at all. Respondents ranged in age from thirteen to eighty-five years, of whom two-thirds were fifteen to thirty-nine years old. Their mean age was 32.8 years. Women were 59 percent of the sample and men were 41 percent.

▓ *Results*

There were few significant differences between the men and women in their responses to the survey. However, there were significant differences of greater magnitude on general level of AIDS knowledge among respondents by age, education, and, to a lesser extent, marital status.

SELF-ASSESSED KNOWLEDGE

To measure self-assessed knowledge (see Table 2), respondents were asked to select one of the four items that best described their level of knowledge about AIDS. Some 39 percent said they knew very little about AIDS and 7 percent said they never heard of AIDS, but 37 percent reported they knew quite a bit and 16 percent said they knew a great deal about AIDS. There were significant differences in self-assessed knowledge between the younger and older respondents and between the more and less educated. Respondents under twenty-five said more often than older respondents that they knew quite a bit or a great deal about AIDS, and the more educated reported more often than the less educated that they knew quite a bit or a great deal about AIDS.

TABLE 2

SELF-ASSESSED KNOWLEDGE REGARDING AIDS

STATEMENT	DEARBORN[a] ARAB- AMERICAN	MICHIGAN[b] GENERAL POPULATION	U.S.[c] GENERAL POPULATION
I have never heard of AIDS	7	1	10
I know very little about AIDS	39	26	24
I know quite a bit about AIDS	37	60	46
I know a great deal about AIDS	16	14	19

[a] AIDS knowledge-attitude-belief survey of Arab-American community in the city of Dearborn (present study).

[b] AIDS knowledge and attitude survey of general population in Michigan, conducted by Special Office on AIDS Prevention, Michigan Department of Public Health (unpublished data).

[c] Data on AIDS knowledge and attitudes among the general population in the United States, from the Nation Health Interview Survey (Dawson 1988).

SOURCES OF INFORMATION

Television was reported to be the major source of information about AIDS (51%), more than friends (11%), school (6%), newspapers (4%), or other sources that provide educational information.

GENERAL KNOWLEDGE

Respondents, for the most part, were familiar with the primary routes of transmission but were less familiar with what cannot transmit HIV (see Table 3). A large percent of respondents thought that a person can get AIDS from having sex with a man who has AIDS (86%), having sex with a woman who has AIDS (83%), receiving a blood transfusion from someone with AIDS (79%), or sharing an injection needle with someone who has AIDS (77%). Fewer respondents denied that a person can get AIDS by working or going to school with someone who has AIDS (52%); donating blood (44%); sharing a toilet seat (46%), food utensils (45%), razor (36%), or toothbrush (33%) with someone who has AIDS; or from mosquito bites (39%).

TABLE 3
KNOWLEDGE ABOUT AIDS

A PERSON CAN GET AIDS FROM . . .	ARAB-AMERICAN			GENERAL MICHIGAN		
	YES	NO	DON'T KNOW	YES	NO	DON'T KNOW
Sitting on a toilet used by someone who has AIDS	36.6	45.8	17.6	2.8	89.5	7.7
Donating blood	37.9	44.3	17.8	10.7	85.9	3.3
Working or going to school with someone who has AIDS	26.7	51.9	21.3	1.6	95.2	3.2
Sharing food utensils with someone who has AIDS	29.7	44.8	25.6	8.9	77.8	13.3
Mosquitoes	27.0	38.8	34.2	7.6	67.9	24.5
Having sex with a man who has AIDS	86.0	4.1	9.9	97.3	1.5	1.3
Having sex with a woman who has AIDS	83.0	7.6	9.4	97.3	1.5	1.3
Blood transfusion from someone who has AIDS	78.6	10.1	11.3	97.4	2.0	0.6
Sharing an injection needle with someone who has AIDS	77.3	7.8	14.9	98.3	1.2	0.5

Men and women did not differ significantly in their knowledge about AIDS, but subjects did differ significantly by age and level of education. Those under twenty-five years of age knew significantly more about the disease than older respondents. They were more likely to respond correctly that HIV can be transmitted by a blood transfusion from someone infected with the virus, sharing infected "drug works," and having sex with a man or a woman who is infected. They also knew that HIV cannot be transmitted by working or going to school with someone who has AIDS; sitting on a toilet seat; sharing food utensils, toothbrush, or a razor with someone who has AIDS; mosquito bites; or donating blood.

Respondents with higher levels of education showed significantly more knowledge about what can and cannot transmit HIV than less educated respondents. The more educated were more knowledgeable about the risk of HIV-infected blood transfusions, the risk of getting AIDS after having sexual intercourse with a man who is HIV positive, and the risk of having sex with an HIV positive woman.

Single respondents demonstrated significantly greater levels of knowledge about what can and cannot cause AIDS than the married respondents. They knew more often than married respondents that a person can get AIDS by sharing "drug works" and having sex with an infected man or woman and that AIDS cannot be transmitted by working or going to school with someone who has AIDS or by sitting on a toilet seat used by someone who has AIDS. There were no significant differences in the levels of their knowledge about HIV between married men and married women.

ATTITUDES AND BELIEFS

Subjects were asked to indicate the extent to which they agreed or disagreed with statements about AIDS and the AIDS epidemic. Nearly half (49%) agreed that the AIDS virus was easy to transmit. Only 23 percent of subjects felt that enough was being done about AIDS in Michigan. Nearly half of the respondents (48%) agreed that children with AIDS should be permitted to attend school. Most subjects (79%) reported being very worried about AIDS, and most (74%) did not believe they were personally at risk for AIDS. However, 4 percent indicated being at high risk. When asked about the seriousness of AIDS in the Arab community, only 27 percent thought it very serious, 20 percent serious, 20 percent not very serious, 16 percent not a problem at all, and 18 percent did not know. Most respondents (80%) saw men as being most at risk for AIDS, 17 percent believed women are most threatened, and 6 percent believed children were at risk to acquire AIDS.

More single than married subjects believed that children with AIDS should be permitted to attend school. Also, respondents with higher levels of education were more likely than those with less education to believe that children with AIDS should be allowed to go to school. Respondents with higher levels of education were more likely to believe that AIDS is a serious epidemic.

EDUCATIONAL STRATEGIES

Considering prevention and education strategies, 34 percent of the subjects reported that children between ages 10 through 13 should receive AIDS education; 22 percent indicated six through nine as the most appropriate age for AIDS education; 21 percent indicated ages fourteen through sixteen; 12 percent thought education was appropriate anytime after twelve years; 8 percent did not know; and 3 percent would begin AIDS education efforts younger than age five.

Most respondents (68%) indicated that men should be educated not to have sex until they are married; not to share "drug works" (73%), to use condoms and contraceptives during sex (72%), to avoid contact with homosexuals (67%), to avoid contact with bisexuals (64%), and to avoid contact with women with multiple sex partners (74%). In turn, subjects indicated that women should be educated not to have sex until they are married (74%), not to share "drug works" (68%), to use condoms and contraceptives during sex (63%), to avoid contact with homosexuals (65%), to avoid contact with bisexuals (61%), and to avoid contact with a man with multiple partners (71%). Subjects supported various institutions and individuals as appropriate sources for AIDS information as follows: schools 75 percent; mosque or church 52 percent; parents 71 percent; and health care agencies 70 percent. Only 9 percent said that AIDS information should never be given.

In terms of educational prevention programs to help fight AIDS that are tailored for the Arab population, subjects 45 years old or older reported a willingness to teach Arab men to avoid sex before marriage, to avoid contacts with homosexuals, to avoid contact with bisexuals, and to teach men to use condoms and jellies. Respondents age twenty-five or older believed that Arab men should be taught to avoid sex with homosexuals, and demonstrated willingness to teach Arab women to avoid sex before marriage, not to share needles or drug equipment, to use condoms and jellies, to avoid contact with homosexuals, to avoid contacts with bisexuals, and to avoid contact with multiple partners.

Single subjects believed more often than married subjects that AIDS education should take place in schools, also more subjects with higher educational levels shared similar beliefs about children receiving AIDS information in school than the less educated subjects. There were differences in opinions between men and women about the age at which AIDS education should be provided. Men believed that AIDS education should begin at an older age (10–13) than women (6–9).

⚛ Discussion

The significance of this AIDS knowledge-attitude-belief survey is that it was administered in one of the largest Arab-American communities in the United States, and it provides one of the first reports on AIDS among Arab-Americans.

The major source of information about AIDS among the Arab-Americans who were surveyed is television (51%), as it is for other minority groups who are isolated from mainstream society by barriers of language, such as Native-Americans (Gregory et al. 1992) and Spanish-speaking migrant workers in Michigan (González 1992). Arab-American respondents in Dearborn were less dependent on television for information about AIDS than either the general population (Adams and Hardy 1991; Dawson 1988, 1990; Hardy 1992) or larger minority populations in the United States, such as African-Americans (Hardy and Biddlecom 1991) and Hispanic-Americans (Biddlecom and Hardy 1991; Dawson and Hardy 1989). More than 70 percent of the respondents from the general U.S. population over the past several years (and the African-American and Hispanic-American populations in 1990) report television as a major source of information about AIDS.

Public service announcements about AIDS and HIV have appeared on Michigan television in English since January 1989. These brief statements about AIDS and HIV, and even the longer programs that provide a more thorough discussion of issues, may lead to misperceptions, since cultural understanding of "what is really being said" among minority people may diverge from mainstream biomedical models of disease causation and preventive measures (Kuipers 1989).

Arab-American respondents generally had less knowledge about what actions can transmit HIV than the Michigan general population or the general U.S. population interviewed for the National Health Interview Survey. There were more misconceptions about the implications of casual contact and less knowledge about which actions cannot transmit the virus among Arab-American respondents than among respondents from the general population in Michigan or the general population throughout the United States (Adams and Hardy 1991; Dawson 1988, 1990; Dawson, Cynamon, and Fitti 1987; Hardy 1992). Arab-American respondents demonstrated less knowledge about the primary routes of transmission and more misconceptions about casual contact than other populations that have been surveyed, such as African-Americans in the United States (Biddlecom and Hardy 1991), Hispanic-Americans in the United States (Hardy and Biddlecom 1991; Dawson and Hardy 1989), Vietnamese women in Los Angeles (Flaskerud and Nyamathi 1988), high school students and adolescents from selected locales throughout the United States (Banner and Maire 1988; DiClemente, Zorn, and Temoshak 1986), and Haitian immigrants in Canada (Adrien et al., 1990).

There evidently was some confusion about the implications of AIDS for the Arab-American community. Respondents generally expressed confidence in their AIDS knowledge, indicating they now knew more about AIDS than a year ago (64%), yet nearly two-thirds (79%) were very worried about AIDS, and only 40 percent knew where to go or whom to call if they wanted a blood test. The higher percentages of Arab-American respondents who answered incorrectly that a person could get AIDS by donating blood, or from sitting on a toilet seat, working or going to school, sharing food utensils with someone who has AIDS, or from mosquito bites suggest that there are general misconceptions about these unlikely modes of transmission. These differences between Arab-Americans and respondents to other surveys further suggest that responses to questions on the more viable modes of transmission may not represent much certainty among the study population about what will and will not transmit HIV. These results form a call to action in the development of education and prevention strategies for Arab-Americans.

There were similar differences in self-assessed knowledge between Arab-American respondents and general population respondents from Michigan and the United States. Not surprisingly, the overall percent of Arab-American respondents who indicated that they had little or no knowledge was greater than for other populations. Not only has the present study found a low level of general knowledge and a number of misconceptions about AIDS and HIV among Arab-Americans, it also has found some indication of the recognition of a need for AIDS education and prevention within the community.

✂ References

Abraham, S. Y. 1983. "Detroit's Arab-American Community: A survey of Diversity and Commonality." Pp. 84–108 in *Arabs in the New World: Studies on Arab-American Communities*, ed. S. Y. Abraham and N. Abraham. Detroit: Wayne State University Press.

Abraham, S. Y.; N. Abraham; and B. Aswad. 1983. "The Southend: An Arab Muslim Working-Class Community." Pp. 164–183 in *Arabs in the New World: Studies on Arab-American Communities*, ed. S. Y. Abraham and N. Abraham. Detroit: Wayne State University Press.

Adams. P. F. and A. M. Hardy. 1991. "AIDS Knowledge and Attitudes for July–September 1990: Provisional Data from the National Health Interview Survey." *Advance Data from Vital and Health Statistics* no. 198. Hyattsville, Md.: National Center for Health Statistics.

Adrien, A.; J. F. Boivin; Y. Tousignant; and C. Hankins. 1990. "Knowledge, Attitudes, Beliefs, and Practices Related to AIDS among Montreal Residents of Haitian Origin." *Canadian Journal of Public Health* 81: 129–134.

Banner, D. and J. A. Maire. 1988. "HIV-Related Beliefs, Knowledge, and Behaviors among High School Students." *Morbidity and Mortality Weekly Reports* 37, no. 47: 718–721.

Biddlecom, A. E. and A. M. Hardy, 1991. "AIDS Knowledge and Attitudes of Hispanic Americans: United States 1990: Provisional Data from the National Health Interview Survey." *Advance Data from Vital and Health Statistics*, no. 207. Hyattsville, Md.: National Center for Health Statistics.

Dawson, D. 1988. "AIDS Knowledge and Attitudes: August 1988: Provisional Data from the National Health Interview Survey." *Advance Data from Vital and Health Statistics*, no. 163. Hyattsville, Md.: National Center for Health Statistics.

———. 1990. "AIDS knowledge and attitudes for July–September 1989: Provisional Data from the National Health Interview Survey." *Advance Data from Vital and Health Statistics*, no. 183. Hyattsville, Md.: National Center for Health Statistics.

Dawson, D. A.; M. Cynamon; and J. E. Fitti. 1987. "AIDS Knowledge and Attitudes: Provisional Data from the National Health Interview Survey: United States, August 1987." *Advance Data from Vital and Health Statistics*, no. 146. Hyattsville, Md.: Public Health Service.

Dawson, D. A. and A. M. Hardy. 1989. "AIDS Knowledge and Attitudes of Hispanic Americans: Provisional Data from the 1988 National Health Interview Survey." *Advance Data from Vital and Health Statistics*, no. 166. Hyattsville, Md.: U. S. Public Health Service.

De La Cancela, V. 1989. "Minority AIDS Prevention: Moving beyond Cultural Perspectives towards Sociopolitical Empowerment." *AIDS Education and Prevention* 1: 141–153.

DiClemente, R. J.; J. Zorn; and L. Temoshak. 1986. "Adolescents and AIDS: A survey of Knowledge, Attitudes, and Beliefs about AIDS in San Francisco." *American Journal of Public Health* 76, no.12: 1443–1445.

Fernea, E. W. and R. A. Fernea. 1979. "A Look behind the Veil." *Human Nature* 2, no.1: 68–77.

Flaskerud, J. H. and A. M. Nyamathi. 1988. "An AIDS Education Program for Vietnamese Women." *New York State Journal of Medicine* 88 632–637.

González, R. M. 1992. *AIDS Education for Migrant Workers: An Experimental Evaluation of Changes in Knowledge, Attitudes, and Behaviors*. Ph.D. diss., Michigan State University, East Lansing.

Gregory, D.; C. Russell.; J. Hurd.; J. Tyance.; and J. Sloan. 1992. "Canada's Indian Health Transfer Policy: The Gull Bay Band Experience." *Human Organization* 51: 214–222.

Hardy, A. M. 1992. "AIDS Knowledge and Attitudes for January–March 1991: Provisional Data from the National Health Interview Survey." *Advance Data from Vital and Health Statistics*, no. 216. Hyattsville, Md.: National Center for Health Statistics.

Hardy, A. M. and A. E. Biddlecom. 1991. "AIDS Knowledge and Attitudes of Black Americans: United States, 1990: Provisional Data from the National Health Interview Survey. *Advance Data from Vital and Health Statistics*, no. 206. Hyattsville, Md.: National Center for Health Statistics.

Haverkos, H. W. and R. Edelman. 1988. "The Epidemiology of Acquired Immunodeficiency Syndrome among Heterosexuals." *Journal of the American Medical Association* 260: 1922–1929.

Huxley, C. 1989. "Arab Governments Wake up to AIDS Threat." *Middle East Report* 19. no. 6: 24–25.

Kuipers, I. C. 1989. "Medical Discourse in Anthropological Context: Views of Language and Power." *Medical Anthropology Quarterly* 3: 99–123.

Kulwicki, A. 1987. *An Ethnographic Study of Illness Perceptions and Practices of Yemeni-Americans*. Ph.D. diss., Indiana University, Indianapolis.

———. 1989a. *Adolescent Health Needs Assessment Survey: Executive Summary*. Technical report prepared for the Office of Minority Health, Michigan Department of Public Health.

———. 1989b. *Cardiovascular and Diabetes Risk Reduction Assessment Survey*. Technical report prepared for the Office of Minority Health, Michigan Department of Public Health.

———. 1990. *Arab AIDS Knowledge, Attitudes, Beliefs and Behaviors*. Executive Report, Office on AIDS Prevention and Intervention. Michigan Department of Public Health, Lansing, Mich.

Larson, E. and M. E. Ropka. 1991. "An Update on Nursing Research and HIV Infection." *Image: Journal of Nursing Scholarship* 23: 4–12.

Lipson, J. G. and A. L. Meleis. 1983. "Issues in Health Care of Middle Eastern Patients." *Western Journal of Medicine* 139: 854–861.

———. 1989. "Methodological Issues in Research with Immigrants." *Medical Anthropology* 12: 103–115.

Meleis, A. I. 1981. "The Arab American in the Health Care System." *American Journal of Nursing* 81: 1180–1183.

Mesa, V. 1988. *Infant Mortality Outreach Demonstration Project: The Dearborn Arab Community Survey*. Technical report prepared for the Wayne County Health Department, Detroit, Michigan.

Naff, A. 1983. "Arabs in America: A Historical Overview." Pp. 8–12 in

Arabs in the New World: Studies on Arab-American Communities, ed. S. Y. Abraham and N. Abraham. Detroit: Wayne State University Press.

Rice, V. H. and A. Kulwicki. 1992. "Cigarette Use among Arab Americans in the Detroit Metropolitan Area." *Public Health Reports* 107, no. 5, 589–594.

Sands, G. 1986. *An Estimate of the Arab Population of Metropolitan Detroit.* Census discussion paper no. 6. Michigan Metropolitan Information Center, Wayne State University, Detroit.

BARBARA C. ASWAD AND NANCY ADADOW GRAY

Challenges to the Arab-American Family and ACCESS

Muslim Arab immigrants experience great stresses on the family such as generation role reversals and gender strains. In addition the vacillating unemployment rate in the auto industry, particularly high in 1982, put many families onto public assistance. A local community center, Arab Community Center for Economic and Social Services (ACCESS) was organized to assist these families. This paper traces the origins and development of ACCESS from a grassroots organization and raises questions about its direction for the future. It examines the nature of the problems of the Arab family by examining first, all the cases brought to the family counseling mental health unit during one year and, secondly, sixty major cases during one year.

Origins and Development of ACCESS

ACCESS was established and located in southeast Dearborn, a working-class community near the Ford Rouge auto plant in 1971 by a group of people of Arab origin. It is a Muslim community and its members come from villages and small towns of south Lebanon, Yemen, and Palestine. The Detroit area has one of the largest concentrations of persons of Arab origin outside the Arab world or the twenty-one nations of the Arab league.

A core group of approximately ten people established a membership controlled board of directors as the basis for the constitution and bylaws of the organization. The provision of services or assistance to newly immigrated persons was clearly identified as the major goal in the original constitution. The primary services offered were English instruction, interpreting and assisting with daily problems. The organization has grown from serving one hundred twenty-five families in its first year to serving over several thousand people. It offered its services to 62,415 people in 1993–1994 through forty-two programs and a staff of forty-five with two hundred volunteers (ACCESS 1994: 2–3). The staff evolved from a basically volunteer force operating in a store front to one that includes many professionals and well-trained individual, offering services in a number of buildings. These currently house the main office, the family counseling center, the health center, and the employment program. The services offered by ACCESS vary from year to year depending on a combination of the availability of funding and the needs expressed by the community.

The unwritten, not so clearly identified goal of the early organization was the establishment of a strong, ever growing group of persons who identified with the importance of providing and promoting democratic, self- or community-determined services. The philosophical and ideological basis of the organization was to promote individual, family, and organizational economic integrity. Dependence on "outside" or governmental funding sources and on the traditional social agency tendency to "target the victim of personal or social distress" as the basis for action was opposed.

It is clear that the origins of ACCESS, as described in its constitution and bylaws, are a mix of motives. There was a desire and an organizational effort to be community based and to reflect and promote the strength and integrity of its constituency and community. There was also the more traditional service vision of assisting individuals and families who were in distress.

Blum and Regab describe the developmental stages of neighborhood organizations. Each of four organizations studied had stated purposes of empowerment of neighborhood residents through social action and negotiation. Each was structured as an "organization of organizations" rather than as individual membership organizations (1985: 21). The organizations had established a balance in their programs that included the day-today concerns of the residents, longer-term neighborhood revitalization activities, and selective involvement in citywide and national actions. Blum and Regab noted that "the organizations often did not know how to use [their] problem-specific funds as leverage for organizational recruitment or for pursuing their own agendas, but operated within the narrow guidelines of the funders" (1985: 21).

Over time, traditional social-agency funding sources that target the individual and family in distress but ignore the social and economic causes of the problems helped propel ACCESS away from its community base. However, the fact that the Center is located in the middle of the community, and that the staff speak Arabic, has meant that people came to it with their problems and, in many cases, the Center responded to client-sponsored needs such as language classes; a seven thousand volume library; job training, tutoring, health, recreation, and cultural arts programs.

Another organizational dilemma described by Blum and Regab is the potential for confrontation with the city and state, thus, threatening their service funding. The organization must decide how to select and time strategies so that they are not counter productive to funding sources while still maintaining its ideological focus of empowerment for its members.

To be reflective of the community, the board of directors has been composed of people of Yemeni, Palestinian, Lebanese, Syrian, and Iraqi national origin, often representing key social, village, or religious organizations from the larger Arab-American community. Several non-Arab professionals active in the community, have also been encouraged to join the board. There was a strong desire to promote community-based funding sources. However the low income of the local area and general diversity of the various Arab groups in the Detroit area, both from a class basis and an ethnic basis (Aswad 1974; Abraham and Abraham 1983), made fund raising more difficult than among some other ethnic groups. Since 1986 local telethons have raised from sixty to eighty thousand dollars. The realities of community needs and the resulting tendency to rely on paid, rather than volunteer, staff pushed the organization toward traditional social services and categorical funding, specifically delineated for particular services, such as surplus food distribution, emergency rent or mortgage payments, mental-health counseling, and assistance with completing or translating forms. The emergence of another Arab agency, competing for state social-service funding, precipitated an accelerated individuation of funds.

The role of the state in the agency's funding was ambivalent, but with the Arab population increasing, Arabs were eventually given status in funding for special populations in Michigan. It has taken a major effort by the administrative staff and others to make state politicians aware of the needs of this low-income community, since Arabs do not have official minority status. The role with the city of Dearborn has been more complex. Because ACCESS is a service agency, primarily funded by the state, it never experienced the confrontational problems with the city as were experienced by another grassroots organization, the Southeast Dearborn Community Council (SEDCC).[1]

The wars in the Middle East, particularly the Israeli-Palestinian wars, and the wars in Lebanon, added to the need for a center, and the sheer increase in the number of immigrants and refugees added to the state's awareness and support of the Center. It should be added that, although the Palestinians and Lebanese were indeed refugees from wars, they were not granted official refugee status by the U.S. government, as were the Iraqi Chaldean population, which had this status from the early 1960s until 1991. Refugee status is particularly beneficial since one can immediately obtain welfare rights, whereas other immigrants must wait three years before receiving such benefits. In the late 1980s Lebanese were granted temporary protected status by the state of Michigan, which authorized work permits but not immediate welfare provisions. In 1992 this special status was terminated.

During the initial fifteen years of ACCESS numerous programs were implemented. But during the early years of community mental-health funding, begun in 1986, problems were revealed that came as a shock to many Arab-Americans. The ACCESS community mental-health program has three service components. The category of funding was originally identified as "consultation, education, and prevention." The implementation of mental-health services resulted in a market-based needs assessment. In the process of identifying the appropriate and effective means of mental-health service delivery, the response and expression of personal, family, and social problems were identified. The combination of services were direct bilingual counseling; mental-health education for the Arab-

American community; and descriptions of the Arab family, culture, religions, and community to human-service providers and professionals.

A link with a local university to provide cross-cultural training to human-service providers alerted the ACCESS staff to the importance of identifying the strengths, as well as the weaknesses, of a particular cultural group. Human-service workers are often confronted with human suffering. If they are not familiar or comfortable with other ethnic, racial, or cultural groups, personal, family, and social conflict can be misidentified as cultural pathology rather than as idiosyncratic or a defense against identifiable stress, conflict, and change. McGoldrick has written a classic article on this subject, and while decrying the fact that the mental-health field has paid most attention to the intrapsychic factors that shape life experiences and little attention to cultural influences, she states:

> It seems so natural that an interest in families should lead to an interest in ethnicity, that it is surprising this area has been so widely ignored. Ethnicity is deeply tied to the family, through which it is transmitted. The two concepts are so intertwined that it is hard to study one without the other, and yet we have done just that (1982: 3).

Since the Arab family typically tries to deal with its problems within the family, there was a great deal of skepticism initially about the degree to which counseling services would be used. The availability of bilingual, bicultural, trained therapists, and the attraction of a local community center that provided a meeting hall and basic survival services of English-as-a-second-language classes, translation of documents, immigration assistance, emergency food and rent or mortgage assistance, contributed to making the center an acceptable place to come for help. One cannot comfortably reach out at times of stress if there are language, transportation, and cultural barriers.

ACCESS is engaged in an ongoing effort to explain to its mental-health funding source why bilingual staff cannot be integrated into large, traditional, community mental-health programs, a reorganization that is seen as less costly. It seems clear that community members become comfortable in asking for and receiving assistance for a variety of their individual and family needs if the mental-health staff at ACCESS has the immediate support of a multiservice approach, providing for basic survival needs of its clients, and engaging religious and social leaders of the Arab-American community in its operation.

The staff includes both first- and second-generations Arabs. The first generation staff members have degrees from abroad or the United States. They are in direct contact with the clients because they speak their language. The second-generation staff members hold administrative positions and have the advantage of experience with and understanding of U.S. service organizations, funding sources, and bureaucracies.

The current challenge to the effectiveness and integrity of the organization remains its ability to maintain grassroots support. Can it add to the support of the community, village, national, and religions organizations of the Arab-American community.

Current funding sources, the departments of mental health, social services, and the United Way demand the maintenance of large numbers of individual client contact hours, making it difficult to identify and target the social causes of the individual, family, and community problems. Hence, the challenge is to promote a balance in programs to include the day-to-day concerns of residents, longer-term neighborhood revitalization activities, and involvement in city, state, national, and international issues.

As ACCESS became larger, with a budget of $1,500,000, it demanded a more complex organization. The challenge lies between a top down decision-making structure and one that involves staff and constituents, with their natural skills, and the organization of family, religious, village, and national groups in community issue problem solving.

🕱 Challenges to the Family

Entering a new environment can result in many stresses on the family. The Arab Muslim family is patrilineal, with an authority structure that favors men over women, and adults over children. It is characterized by extended kin relations, preferred marriage within kin units, the possibility of multiple wives, emphasis on female modesty and premarital chastity for women, and varying degrees of segregation of the sexes in public. Our understanding of some of the stresses placed on the family was gained through participant observation and the examination of data from two sources. The first is a general survey of all the problems brought into the

ACCESS Family Counseling Center by over one thousand people during the first year of its operation in 1986 (Aswad 1987). The second source is an evaluation of sixty major cases for which the clients came for counseling five or more times.

GENERAL SURVEY RESULTS

In the general survey, we found that the vast majority of clients were Arabs (95%) and that 10 percent more males than females came to the Center. This latter fact may seem unexpected, but the men who would come initially for help with immigration problems, would discuss their other problems and be referred to mental-health therapists. Most clients were between the ages of 20 to 34 years (43%). Close to 70 percent of the families earned less than $10,000 a year, and nearly 40 percent of the total clientele received some sort of financial assistance. Of this, 46 percent were on Aid to Families with Dependent Children (AFDC), 18 percent were receiving Supplemental Security Income (SSI), and 17 percent were being supported by their families.[2]

The community was directly affected by the auto depression of 1982, with unemployment rates reaching 35 percent in 1979 (Bowker 1979). Community leaders estimated it reached 40 to 50 percent by 1982 (Ahmed 1982). As a result, some individuals went back to the Middle East or went to California. Most, however, could not go back to south Lebanon or Palestine because of the wars there. As many were recent immigrants, they were not yet eligible for public assistance. Thus, the two factors of employment lay-offs and increasing immigration into the community put severe economic stress on its members. Employment increased again, but at the time of the survey, was still estimated by ACCESS leaders to be high.

Because of these stressful factors, the Center's economic-crises services were those most frequently requested. These include requests for general assistance, emergency food, and payment of housing and utility bills. Next were requests for counseling related to family crises. It is also important to note that counseling services require numerous visits, while economic assistance is often accomplished through temporary economic assistance followed by referrals to other appropriate agencies.

The use of public assistance has increased. Of the ninety families interviewed by A. A. Wasfi in 1964, only one (1.1%) was receiving AFDC. this increased to 13 percent of the random sample of two hundred families looked at by Barbara Aswad in 1971. Currently, of the families using the Center, 20 percent are receiving AFDC. The rate increase does appear to be due to difficult times. As in other low-income families, welfare is being used to supplement low wages, often with the family remaining intact. Aswad found that welfare may discourage women from seeking employment since a woman can contribute to the family income without leaving the home (1994).

Family crises accounted for 34 percent of the visits to the Center although only 17 percent of its total cases.[3] This is due to required repeated visits. Of these cases, about half related to acute marital problems, and the other half related to acute problems with children. Primary causes listed for the marital problems, were general arguments (38%), discussion of separation and divorce (14%), and separation (10%). Spouse abuse was mentioned in 7 percent of the cases. It is interesting to note that in the cases of female mistreatment, there were more reports of mistreatment by brothers and children than by husbands or in-laws of married women. Alcohol and drug abuse was listed as the cause of the problem in 10 percent of the cases. Other lesser causes related to death of a spouse and inadequate support by the spouse.

Of the family crises related primarily to children, causes included discipline (17%), the concern over children who were abroad (15%), the death of a child (14%), concerns over actual or possible suicides of children (9%), daycare while the mother works (9%), alleged mistreatment of children (8%), child custody (4%), and dating (4%). Very few young people or children came to the Center reporting problems with their parents. The few young persons who did come spoke of problems relating to planned marriages and religion. College age students also spoke of scholastic and language problems. The small number of children seeking help undoubtedly reflects the authority of the Arab parental generation.

Fourteen percent of the total visits related to health crises. Of those, close to 40 percent were referred to Arab doctors who provided free medical care, as many clients had no insurance. A significant number had problems related to pregnancy and abortion. In particular, a number of recent immigrant women who were pregnant had no insurance.

A small number (4%) of problems related to legal crises. These cases centered around political asylum, immigration, and law suits. The low rate of crime in the community has been reported previously and is reflected in these low statistics (Bowker 1979; Aswad 1974). Strong family pressures and control over family members through the concept of honor and shame help to limit the neighborhood crime rate, which is higher in nearby Detroit communities of a similar low-income level.

DISCUSSION OF MAJOR CASES

A survey of the sixty major family crises, in which there were five or more visits to the Family Counseling Center, was made to identify more specific causes of stress and crisis. If there were multiple problems, each was recorded.

In the area of marital problems, 80 percent of those seeking assistance were women. Fifty percent had problems related to husbands not paying the bills and restricting the wives' employment. The husbands did not want their wives to separate for the purpose of becoming eligible for public assistance (AFDC), rather they insisted that they could support their family; the women, on the other hand, desired a divorce and admission to AFDC. In view of the patrilineal nature of the Arab family, it is evident that the availability of welfare, which has traditionally been paid to women, can dilute the husband's role within the family, as it has done in other ethnic groups.[4]

Thirty percent came with some sort of immigration problem. These ranged from such experiences as the husband taking his wife abroad and leaving her with his parents, husbands bringing a second, new wife from abroad, wives deserting their husbands and going to their homes abroad, men marrying women for their green card and then deserting them. Problems reported to a lesser degree, but obviously not constituting less grief for the clients, involved spouse mistreatment, the wife not obeying, unfaithful husbands, alcoholism and mistreatment, and conflicts over children coming between the parents.

Trends in problems relating to children reveal that, as with the general sample, many report they cannot effectively discipline their children (38%). Cases of daughters rebelling and sometimes running away were mentioned. Due to the asymmetrical treatment, whereby daughters are more restricted than sons, this is understandable. The culture requires that girls be chaste at the time of their marriages. While this is also preferable for boys, it is not required. These requirements clash greatly with the premarital sexual permissiveness of the host culture. The fear is that daughters will date, and that boys will date non-Arab girls, get them pregnant, and perhaps fall in love with and want to marry them. There are also cases of parent-teenager role reversals, since the younger people often acculturate faster than their parents and, thereby, gain power. Sons may mistreat mothers, and daughters may also dominate mothers. When fathers are alone, they have reported difficulties controlling their daughters. The majority of cases reported were of difficulties between mother and daughter (43%), mother and son (36%), father and son (17%), and father and daughter (4%). Of course this trend also reflects the fact that the majority of clients are mothers, and the fact that a daughter's behavior is watched with more concern than is a son's. Mothers are held responsible for their children's behavior, and their daughters reputations are a major concern to the family name. The reported threat of suicide, previously discussed, in the general sample was primarily from teenage girls.

Twenty three percent of the sixty cases concerned separations or divorces. These clients also reported financial difficulties and difficulty in controlling their children. In many cases there are arguments over custody and conflict between the custody traditions of the Middle East and the United States. Traditional Middle Eastern rules typically specify that children join the father after the age of seven for boys and nine for girls, since they are members of his patrilineage. U.S. traditions, on the other hand, often favor the mother, award joint custody, or specify that the children join whichever parent provides the best care. Records show that some men want custody of their daughters to protect their reputation, others want the boys too. If mothers have had their children while on AFDC, they feel the children should stay with them. In another study by Aswad, 80 percent of the Lebanese, and 20 percent of the Yemeni women felt they should have custody of their children until the children reach eighteen (1991).

In 15 percent of the cases, the specific problems related to children who remained in Lebanon and Yemen, or to the fact that a husband or wife left the United States and the remaining spouse was having trouble controlling the children. In several of these cases, children had been killed in the Middle East, and parents felt great frustration, grief, and, perhaps, guilt. There were few cases reported of physical mistreatment. In 11 percent of the cases it was specifically mentioned, but in others it was inferred from descriptions of, for example, a husband screaming at the family constantly.

Some of the problems presented in these cases reflect the problems of migration and the disruption of the extended family. Since many of the people studied come from rural families in which extended families are traditional, entrance into the U.S. labor force may disrupt these alliances. Nervat Hatem, writing about the switch from rural extended families to urban families in Egypt, notes that the role of the mother changes. In the rural areas, mothering is only one of many tasks performed by a woman in an extended family, and it is shared with other women. When a woman moves to the city, the act of mothering alone feels unnatural. Hatem also points to the advantage of having several aunts or uncles to advise and protect their nieces and nephews in cases of disputes in their poor urban neighborhoods, where individualism is played down (1987). In Cairo, mothers were overburdened by poor incomes and harsh conditions. Aswad found that while a group of women may socialize the children in a village, children are often by themselves or entertained each other in groups but are seldom with their busy mothers, thus giving themselves space from authority. In Dearborn, as distinct from Cairo, women may not be overburdened and are sometimes bored. Certainly they are not used to only the mothering role, and they visit often, watch TV and videos, attend English classes, and desire employment (Aswad 1991).

Those who join a family group or grow into large family groups, such as many of the southern Lebanese, retain or build these extended ties. In other studies of Southend women Aswad found that most of the southern Lebanese women had from forty to two hundred relatives in the Southend. In contrast, Yemeni women had four to nine relatives in Dearborn, and they felt the separation significantly (1974; 1991). Yemeni women miss their mothers and sisters but not their mothers-in-law. Some recent Lebanese immigrants of the more educated, urban, middle class also have few relatives here and miss their families. For both the Yemeni and those Lebanese without kin, the very close knit primary neighborhood community substitutes for extended kin to some extent.

This bring us to the positive function of the family in acculturation. In a patrilineal family, such as the Arab family, every persons is assigned to a group at birth. Membership passes only through men, but passes to both sons and daughters. Therefore, no one is without a group that has some responsibility for him or her, and to which that individual must answer for his or her behavior. This group includes women, and women must answer to the people in their patrilineage as well as seek their protection in times of conflict with their husband or children. This contrasts with bilateral descent, which is common in the United States and Europe, whereby, individuals may ally with members of either their mothers' or fathers' side, or no side, and the situation is more ambiguous and flexible, allowing more individual choice. There are also fewer extended families in the United States. It is clear that U.S. social workers who are unfamiliar with Middle Eastern culture and unaware of the patrilineal principle, can focus their attention on the authority system that accompanies patrilineality, but miss the protective functions or the various rights and privileges that are also a part of it. Thus, they might overlook a chance to ask a brother of a woman who was being mistreated by her husband for assistance. The brother-sister relation is one of the strongest in the family. It is also strengthened in instances in which women give up their property to the brother in exchange for his protection.

American social workers may not understand why men feel that the children should stay with them after a divorce, yet, if they are part of his patrilineage and not their mother's, it is a perfectly logical arrangement to Arabs. Arab men often call America a country for women. With an understanding of the patrilineal principle, one can also understand why the concepts of adoption and foster care outside of the family are frowned upon and rare.

Beyond this extended family group, the patrilineage spreads out to include a larger group. The implications are that there is security in membership, few people feel alienated unless they are without members of their family, a rare and most unfortunate situation as viewed by those interviewed. Members assume responsibility and, in extreme situations may be responsible for the life or death of another member. If men or women misbehave, they shame their patriline first and their spouse or their spouse's patriline second.

The members of the larger family may not live in the same house, especially if the homes are small, but they interact frequently and try to live close to one another. Migration itself tends to disrupt these close living patterns, creating more dependence on non-patrilineal kin or neighbors than there was before.

Another advantage is the interfamilial exchange of economic favors.

This assists in initial settlement, providing loans of capital for investment, employment, and other favors. Lineages are also important units for arranging marriages. The favored spouse is a first cousin on the father's side, but second cousins, or others from within the home village or another related village are also favored. Parental involvement is usually an advantage since families become involved in protecting their children in marriage. But it can also be a disadvantage if the marriageable child is already in love or if parents use their power to force a marriage on the child, a situation all too often seen. Abu-Lughod has written about the poetry of Bedouin women who lament arranged marriages to men they do not want (1986). Because of polygamy, men living in the Middle East have the means of softening the dissatisfaction of arranged marriages, but women have no such option. There are, in fact, few polygamous marriages in the Middle East, and fewer still in the Dearborn community, because it is illegal in the United States. A few do exist however, primarily in situations in which a man has one wife in the United States and another abroad.

🎐 Nature of Services Offered

In view of the above-mentioned problems brought to it, ACCESS offers immediate, bilingual counseling. It also offers assistance with hospitalization and sees patients after they are discharged from referring public and private hospitals. The staff provides out-patient treatment, coordinates treatment with local mental-health facilities, and has an Arabic-speaking psychiatrist on staff, thereby helping to integrate patients back into the community. Because the Center is an integrated part of the community, cases can be brought to the attention of practitioners early, thus enabling detection and prevention of greater problems. ACCESS is currently being challenged to identify or develop bilingual group housing and vocational training to increase the options needed for successful mental emotional and social recovery.

The drawback to this close identification of the Center with the community is that, occasionally, people who know staff members as their neighbors may feel uncomfortable approaching them as professionals. For this reason, as well as the disparity in class and education, the vast majority of the Center's counselors and administrators do not live in the immediate community. Interestingly, there is a broad representation of staff from Iraq, Lebanon, Yemen, Egypt, and Pakistan; both Muslim and Christian.

Services are also offered to people with developmental and physical disabilities. The Center sees people with intellectual retardation; learning disabilities; epilepsy; and speech, vision, and hearing loss. In cooperation with school, medical, and financial assistance personnel, the Center offers programs and counseling geared to these special needs. Special and increased funding for services for these disabled people and their families is necessary to assist with the "shame" factor in Arab-American families. Access has used a cable television video series in Arabic to promote an improved awareness of developmental and handicapping disabilities.

In the area of marital problems, the therapist may actively reach out to involve both parties. The woman is assisted to be more assertive, to resist and check physical violence that typically accompanies alcohol or cocaine use by men. Bilingual counselors assist the spouse, usually the wife, and family members to take the necessary steps to halt physical aggression and to promote substance-abuse treatment of the addicted member. As a result of high unemployment, the Arab male is experiencing severe mental, emotional, cultural, and economic distress. This may bring on the use, sale, and abuse of drugs; physical violence; family distress; and the reversal of the traditional male and female roles of family leadership. This is particularly true if the wife has the option of receiving AFDC and can move out. We already mentioned problems with child discipline for women, it is also a problem for men.

For seven years, Access ran a teen-parenting program for young wives who became pregnant in their early teen years. While most U.S. teen-parenting programs are traditionally aimed at unmarried teenaged mothers, the Arab-American cultural code of modesty and chastity for young women usually prevents out-of-wedlock births. Early-teen marriages, however, do occur. When these marriages result in pregnancy, the mothers often drop out of school and have difficulty financing and obtaining adequate prenatal care. Consequently, the Access teen-parenting program was aimed at young wives. Access's teen-to-parent programs have sponsored seminars in the schools to promote an exploration of options for Arab-American youth and counseling for generational and cultural conflict between youth and their parents.

There are new innovative programs that include AIDS education, a well-baby clinic, a newly established addiction prevention and treatment program, a teen-health program, and a bilingual Alcoholics Anonymous group. Education programs include a library, a tutoring program, a learning abilities program, English-as-a-second-language outreach, a summer youth program, and home visits to assess student needs. A center in the more recently populated East side offers vocational training and job placement as well an Immigration and Naturalization Services officer.

A major program that assists the local community in preserving its culture and simultaneously extends to the non-Arab community is he Arab Folk Heritage Museum, which was opened in 1990 in the Center's main building and is the only museum of its kind in the United States. Many high-school and university students come to hear lectures and see the changing museum displays. Some of the exhibitions have been on Arabic calligraphy, Arab-American women, the Roman ruins of Syria and Lebanon, the history of Arab immigration to the Detroit area, and the history of Arabic coffee. Children are also taught traditional storytelling, embroidery, and classic Arabic music on the 'oud and other instruments.

Aswad found that despite the wishes of most of the women in this Arab-American community, few immigrant women are employed (1991). This is the result of many factors, such as their husband's rich-peasant mentality that emphasizes wives not working outside of the home, patrilineal and Islamic modesty codes, the male-dominated auto industry, and the women's own limited skills. Nonetheless, ACCESS established a day-care center in 1992 to assist them but found it too costly to run, and it was closed in 1994.

The large population of Arab-Americans in the Detroit area, upwards of two hundred thousand, provides for an ever increasing immigrant population. As many as ten thousand people emigrate from Yemen, Lebanon, Iraq, Palestine, and Egypt each year. As a result, immigration services provide a natural screening process to assess areas of emotional, educational, physical and, economic need. There has been no dearth of people seeking the services of ACCESS, and the challenge is to identify the most effective way to assist the community. An understanding of the dynamics of migration through social science studies can assist in this identification.

The very organization of ACCESS can become a model that promotes citizen involvement in individual, family, and community problem solving. Or, it could follow the path of least resistance and promote the dependency and weakness of the individuals, families, and community it serves through an authoritarian organizational structure and model of service delivery. If it follows the latter course it will have become a part of the problem for Arab-Americans in the United States, rather than part of the struggle to promote health and well-being in the larger culture.

ᛞ *References*

Abraham, N. 1989. "Arab-American Marginality: Myths and Praxis." *Arab Studies Quarterly* 11, nos. 2 and 3.

Abraham, S. and N. Abraham. 1983. *Arabs in the New World*. Detroit: Center for Urban Studies, Wayne State University.

Abu-Lughod, Lila. 1986. *Veiled Sentiments*. Berkeley and Los Angeles: University of California Press.

Alldredge, Elham-Eid. 1984. *Child-Rearing Practices in the Homes of Arab Immigrants: A Study of Ethnic Persistence*. Ph.D. diss., Department of Sociology, Michigan State University, East Lansing.

Arab Community Center for Economic and Social Services. 1993. *Annual Report 1993*. Dearborn, Mich.

———. 1994. *Annual Report 1994*. Dearborn Mich.

———. 1994. *Twenty-Third Anniversary Dinner Program* (April 9).

Aswad, Barbara C. 1974. "The Southeast Dearborn Arab Community Struggles for Survival against 'Urban Renewal.'" In *Arabic Speaking Communities in American Cities*, ed. Aswad, B. C. Long Island, N.Y.: Center for Migration Studies.

———. 1987. *Family Profile of Clients Entering the Family Counseling Program*. Mimeo. Dearborn Michigan: Arab Community Center for Economic and Social Services.

———. 1991. "Yemeni and Lebanese Muslim Immigrant Women in Southeast Dearborn, Michigan." In *Muslim Families in North America*, ed. Earl Waugh, Sharon Abu-Laban, and Regina Querishi. Alberta: University of Alberta Press.

———. 1992. "The Lebanese Muslim Community in Dearborn Michigan." In *The Lebanese in the World: A Century of Emigration*, ed. Albert Hourani and Nadim Shehada. London: Tauris.

————. 1994. "Attitudes of Immigrant Women and Men in the Dearborn Area Toward Women's Employment and Welfare." In *Muslim Communities in North America*, ed. Yvonne Haddad and Jane Smith. Albany: State University of New York Press.

Bowker, Joan. 1979. *Health and Social Services Needs Assessment Survey*. Mimeo. Dearborn, Mich.: City of Dearborn.

Blum, Arthur and Ibrahim Ragab. 1985. "Development Stages of Neighborhood Organization." *Social Policy* (Spring).

Cowen, Emory L. 1985. "Primary Prevention in Mental Health." *Social Policy* (Spring).

Elkholy, Abdo. 1981. "The Arab American Family." In *Ethnic Families in America*, ed. Charles Mindel and Robert Haberstein, New York: Elsevier Publication.

Haddad, Yvonne and Adel Lummis. 1989. *Islamic Values in the United States: A Comparative Study*. New York: Oxford University Press.

Haddad, Yvonne Yazbeck and Jane Idleman Smith. 1993. *Mission to America: Five Islamic Sectarian Communities in North America*. Gainesville: University of Florida Press.

Hatem, Nervat. 1987. "Toward a Study of Psychodynamics of Mothering and Gender in Egyptian Families." *International Journal of Middle East Studies*, 19.

Kirk, Jerome and Marc Miller. 1987. *Reliability and Validity in Qualitative Research: Qualitative Research Methods*, ser. 1. Beverly Hills: Sage Press.

McGoldrick, Monica. 1982. "Ethnicity and Family Therapy: An Overview." In *Ethnicity and Family Therapy*, ed. M. McGoldrick, J. Pearce, and J. Girodano. New York: Guilford Press.

Meleis, Afaf Ibrahim and Catherine Warsaw Lafever. 1984. "The Arab American and Psychiatric Care." *Perspectives in Psychiatric Care* 22: 2.

Naff, Alixa. 1985. *Becoming American: The Early Arab Immigrant Experience*. Carbondale: Southern Illinois University Press.

Nazzal, Laila. 1986. *The Role of Shame in Societal Transformation among Palestinian Women on the West Bank*. Ph.D. diss., Department of Sociology, University of Pennsylvania, Philadelphia.

Robinson, Richard. 1984. *The Process of Change in a Community Organization: An Anthropological Analysis of an Urban System*. Ph.D. diss., Department of Anthropology, Wayne State University, Detroit.

Stanley, Sue. 1988 "Psychotherapeutic Services for Ethnic Minorities: Two Decades of Research Findings." *American Psychologist* 43, no. 4 (April).

Wasfi, A. A. 1964. *The Dearborn Arab-Moslem Community: A Study of Acculturation.* Ph.D. diss., Department of Anthropology, Michigan State University, Ann Arbor.

JON C. SWANSON

Ethnicity, Marriage, and Role Conflict

The Dilemma of a Second-Generation Arab-American

Most Americans associate immigration with the beginning of the twentieth century when several hundreds of thousands of European immigrants arrived in the United States each year through Ellis Island. They are far less cognizant of the new immigration which has brought an average of four hundred thousand people to America every year since 1960.

Constituting about 6 percent of the U.S. population, the foreign born are an important cohort from the standpoint of social work, for immigrants and their children face significant problems adjusting to what is, for them, an alien American economy and society. Frequently these new immigrants come from less industrialized countries in the Eastern and Southern hemispheres and are often from rural peasant backgrounds (Borjas and Tienda 1987: 646). In most cases they arrive without English skills and must adjust to life and work in an urban industrial society. The children of such immigrants are usually fluent in English and far better integrated into American life. This in itself poses problems, however, for this new generation finds itself caught between the conflicting expectations of its parents and those of the dominant society. This chapter explores the issues of ethnicity and role conflict associated with marriage in one such group, Muslim Arab-Americans.

Monica McGoldrick (1984: 347) has observed that ethnicity, "by providing a sense of belonging and of historical continuity, . . . meets a basic psychological need." On the other hand, it may be argued that the tenacity with which an individual cleaves to his ethnic identity rests on more concrete considerations. Frederik Barth (1969: 14, 15, 28) suggests that whether a person maintains his identity is an individual decision that depends on both the perceived advantages of membership in the ethnic group and his ability to adequately perform the role associated with that ethnicity. Abner Cohn (1974: xxii), addressing the issue of the survival of ethnicity past the first generation, also emphasizes the importance of economics:

> If in a dynamic contemporary complex society a group of second- or third-generation migrants preserve their distinctiveness and make extensive use of their endoculture, then the likelihood that within the contemporary situation they have become an (economic) interest group is strong.

No doubt both psychological and economic dynamics are at play here. Certainly, for the first generation ethnicity offers not only psychological and spiritual support, but economic benefits as well. It is both more satisfying psychologically, and cheaper, to maintain loyalty to one's ethnic tradition. Indeed, for many migrants the ability to accumulate capital may rest on a rejection of the American consumer ethic. Subsequent generations enculturated with more American expectations may continue to derive psychological satisfaction from their ethnicity but perceive fewer real economic benefits.

Clearly new immigrants from the Arab Middle East derive many benefits from their ethnic identity and associations which help relieve the stress that accompanies settling in a new society. Arriving in the United States with no English and few skills, they invariably join an established community of kinsmen and fellow villagers who have shared the same experience.[1] Such relatives and friends are often prepared, not only to offer psychological support, but also economic support in the form of loans, employment, and housing. Thus, first generation Arab-Muslim immigrants enjoy the advantage, not only of being enculturated in a consistent and coherent cultural context, but of easing the stress of immigration by moving into a previously established support system made up of people who are culturally similar. By contrast their children are better educated, have access to a much wider range of economic possibilities, and are, therefore, far less reliant on the ethnic community for economic support.

While the second generation finds fewer economic incentives for maintaining their ethnicity, their psychological ties to their parents' tradition often remain strong. This can be a source of considerable role stress for, in contrast to their parents who were enculturated in only one cultural tradition, they are brought up simultaneously in two markedly different worlds. On the one hand they are socialized according to the norms and expectations of their parents, and on the other they are enculturated to the expectations of a wider cultural context, represented by their peers, teachers, and the media.[2]

It is not usually the first generation that bears the brunt of this transition. To the contrary, the first generation is secure in its identity and, moreover, often moves into an ethnic community of peers who share its values and can offer support in dealing with what are familiar problems of employment, housing, and the like in the new culture. Rather it is the second generation that faces the greatest obstacles in evolving an integrated identity. This group is trapped between two often conflicting sets of values, those of parents on the one hand and American peers on the other.

Elsewhere I have examined, in a more general way, the stresses besetting second-generation Yemeni-Americans (1988). Likewise Elkholy has noted, in writing of Arab-Americans in general, that "the second generation plays a transitional role between the old and the new cultures and is thus often the victim of both" (1981: 154–55). Erik Erikson has also written of the problems faced by the children of "minority groups of a lesser degree of Americanization" (1967: 217), and Ian Canino mentions behavioral difficulties associated with second generation ethnics (1988). Somewhat more empirical evidence of adolescent stress among ethnics is supplied by VerKuyten who found that, in Holland, ethnic adolescents scored lower on a test of happiness than their Dutch counterparts (1986). D. A. Rosenthal and C. Hrynevich examined the degree to which young Australian ethnics identified with their cultural traditions. They did not find evidence of identity conflict, but this was not the main focus of their research. Moreover they note, "awareness of differences between themselves and dominant Anglo society may increase as older adolescents face

developmentally salient choices, e.g. about vocation and intimate relationships" (1984: 738). Carlos Sluzki has also identified intergenerational
conflict as an important cause of stress in ethnic enclaves:

> This [intergenerational] clash is maximally apparent in fami-
> lies belonging to cultural groups that have been ghettoized by
> choice or by force in their country of adaptation. . . . If the
> process of socialization takes place in a milieu that reflects the
> norms and values of the new country, what has been delayed
> by the first generation will take the form of an intergenerational
> conflict of values (1979: 387).

One strategy for avoiding such conflicts is to shift back and forth
between roles. Speaking from experience, one forty-year-old second-
generation Lebanese-American informant noted, "they [Arab-American
children] are forced to be Americans by day and [Arabs] by night." Thus,
children play the role of Arab-child at home and the role of American-
peer outside of the home.

Edwin Thomas calls such vacillation "serial compromise" (1967: 27).
Such an adaptation is consistent with the tendency in Middle Eastern
culture to draw a sharp distinction between public and private behavior.
In this case the distinction is between behavior outside the ethnic community (public) and inside the community (private). For a time at least this
strategy is an acceptable means of avoiding stress. Once children begin the
mate-selection process, however, role separation becomes less viable for it
is at this point that parents demand a tangible commitment to their ethnic
and religious tradition in the form of marriage.

The old adage that one doesn't marry people one marries families
certainly applies to the Middle East, where marriage often has political
and economic implications as well as sociological and psychological ones.
There, property passes through the male line and premarital chastity of
the bride is a requirement. Consequently, relations between adolescents of
the opposite sex are closely supervised. Dating is forbidden, and while
young people are allowed to meet under controlled conditions, the ultimate power over the marriage decision is in the hands of the couples'
parents. Marriages are thus arranged by adults who control the economic
resources of the family. Since children seek to retain access to their patri-
mony and often can find no work outside of the family unit, they generally
acquiesce to their parents decisions. Given these circumstances, love, in

the romantic sense of most Americans, is not an expected part of marriage, and close affective ties are sought outside of marriage with members of the same sex.[3]

Extended kin ties continue to be important among Arab-Americans, and first generation families may persist in arranging the marriages of their children. Usually, however, this occurs only in the cases of the older children. The longer a family remains in the United States, the more resistance there develops to arranged marriage. Indeed, the economic realities of American life, and the availability of wage labor outside of the family offer fewer strictly economic incentives to comply with parental wishes.

In their effort to preserve their cultural and religious heritage, the community has responded to these new circumstances in a variety of ways. As a group they have organized annual conventions of ethnic and religious clubs where young people are brought together so they can get to know one another. Elaborate weddings also provide opportunities for young people to meet. Individually, some parents allow their sons but never their daughters, to continue, at least temporarily, the serial compromise by dating "American" girls, it being understood that when it comes to marriage they will choose from among their own ethnic and religious community. Alternatively, parents will allow their daughters to date their husbands-to-be after they are *maktub*, that is, after the marriage contract is signed but before the marriage is consummated.[4]

Structural devices such as these are coupled with psychological coercion to assure compliance with parental expectations. Principal among the latter are guilt, threats of abandonment, and the individuals' own desires to retain their ethnic identity, though perhaps in a somewhat altered form.

Abdallah provides a good example of the role conflicts encountered by second-generation Arab-Americans. The son of Arab-Muslim immigrants, he was reared in a working-class suburb of a major American city where most of his schoolmates were neither Arabs nor Muslims. After leaving school he entered the military and served for four years. Following his discharge he traveled widely in Asia and Africa and spent a year in a Muslim country were he worked as a teacher. A college graduate, he has completed one graduate degree and is anticipating a second.

Approaching forty, however, Abdallah remains single. It might be argued that his life has left little time for marriage. On the other hand, it may be that he is unwilling to commit himself totally to a role that only partially satisfies him. Nevertheless, the pressure to marry is mounting. Recently, his mother underwent major surgery of a type that does not assure her survival. Her last words to him before entering the operating room were an entreaty to marry and start a family. In retrospect Abdallah is able to see the humor in this situation, but he nonetheless feels enormous pressure.

There can be no question as to his commitment to his ethnic identity. It is manifest both in his travels and his insistent involvement in the activities of the Arab community. Abdallah has visited his parents' country of origin no less than four times in his life and contributes both time and money to community organizations at the local and national levels. As the most active member of his generation in community affairs, he is a logical successor to the leadership of the large extended family of which he is a part. Clearly he derives enormous psychological satisfaction from his ethnicity, and his role performance within the context of the Arab community is more than adequate.

On the other hand, his life outside the community ignores many of the expectations associated with group membership. Abdallah disregards most of the formal prescriptions and proscriptions associated with traditional Islamic practice and is impatient with the petty politics that are characteristic of the ethnic community. At the same time he enjoys a wide range of non-Arab as well as Arab friends including his significant other, Joan, a black woman of similar educational background with whom he has lived intermittently for over three years. About two years ago she began pressing him to marry.

In light of the pervasive racism of American society it should come as no surprise that a black woman is an even less acceptable daughter-in-law than a white non-Muslim. In addition Abdallah has been forced to confront the implications of such a marriage, not only for his relations with his family, but for his future acceptance in the ethnic group to which he is committed. Still, he is in love with Joan and reluctant to leave her.

Some months ago Abdallah made his decision. He broke off with his lover and returned to the Middle East where he betrothed himself to a woman from his parents' village. A peasant girl with scarcely more than a grade-school education, she was to join him in the United States after a few months and consummate the marriage. On returning to the United

States, however, he learned that the woman had, prior to his meeting her, been caught in a moral transgression. As an American this was irrelevant to him, but as an Arab he could not bring her into the community without losing face. Consequently, he dissolved the engagement and has since drifted back into a relationship with Joan, though he is still vacillating as to whether he will marry her or a woman in "the old country."

Meanwhile he complains of a number of psychosomatic ailments including headaches and various gastrointestinal difficulties. Consultation with several physicians turned up no evidence of any physical ailment. Under the circumstances it seems reasonable to conclude that these symptoms represent his somatization of the acute stress associated with this role conflict.

A satisfactory resolution of this dilemma seems impossible. Clearly serial compromise has reached the outer limits of its viability, and while negotiation with his family is a possibility, negotiation with the entire community is impracticable. Barring avoidance or denial, Abdallah must make a choice. Unfortunately, neither of the alternatives available to him is without considerable pain.

Conflicts of this kind are by no means unusual for people of Abdallah's generation, and many elect to delay marriage rather than confront this painful Hobson's choice. In some cases the consequences of such role conflict can be even more severe. Some years ago an adolescent friend of mine turned, first to drugs, and then to suicide as a means avoiding the contradictory expectations that he faced.

One approach to dealing with this problem is to prepare young people for this kind of conflict so that they will be psychologically equipped for the choices they will ultimately have to make. This could be accomplished at school or through community agencies. For individuals like Abdallah, the goal of therapy should be to help him arrive at the solution that is most appropriate for him and to resolve the guilt and grief which must inevitably accompany his choice.

Finally it might be noted that as the first generation fades from the scene, the younger generation will evolve a consensus within the group about what constitutes an acceptable compromise. Such a compromise will permit the group to maintain its ethnic identification but to select, from among the rights and duties associated with that role, those behaviors that are most convenient and conflict least with the expectations of the larger society. It is this kind of role compromise that is the basis for the evolution of our synthetic, hyphenated, American ethnic groups. This synthesis does not come easily, however, especially for second-generation Americans like Abdallah who must suffer painful role conflicts before becoming Arab-Americans.

🕉 References

Barth, Frederik. 1969. "Introduction." In *Ethnic Groups and Boundaries: The Social Organization of Cultural Differences*, ed. Frederik Barth. London: George Allen and Unwin.

Borjas, George J. and Marta Tienda. 1987. "The Economic Consequences of Immigration." *Science* 235 (February): 645–651.

Canino, Ian. 1988. "The Transcultural Child. In *Handbook of Clinical Assessment of Children and Adolescents*, vol. 2, ed. Clarice J. Keslenbaum and Daniel T. Williams. New York: New York University Press.

Cohen, Abner. 1974. "Introduction." In *Urban Ethnicity*, ed. Abner Cohn. London: Tavistock.

Elkholy, Abdu. 1981. "The Arab-American Family." In *Ethnic Families in America: Patterns and Variations*, ed. Charles H. Mindel and Robert Habenstien. New York: Elsevier.

Erikson, Erik H. 1967. "Growth and Crisis of the Healthy Personality." In *Personality in Nature, Society, and Culture*, ed. Clyde Kluckhohn, Harry A. Murray, and David Schneider. New York: Alfred A. Knopf.

McGoldrick, Monica. 1984. "Ethnic Intermarriage: Implications for Therapy." *Family Process* 23: 347–364.

Mindel, Charles H. and Robert W. Habenstein. 1981. *Ethnic Families in America: Patterns and Variations*. New York: Elsevier Science Publishing.

Muus, R. E. 1988. "Erikson's Theory of Identity Development." In *Theories of Adolescence*. New York: Random House.

Rosenthal, D. A. and C. Hrynevich. 1984. "Ethnicity and Ethnic Identity: a Comparative Study of Greek-, Italian-, and Anglo-Australian Adolescents." *International Journal of Psychology* 20, no. 6: 723–742.

Sluzki, Carlos E. 1979. "Migration and Family Conflict." *Family Process* 18, no. 4: 379–390.

Swanson, Jon C. 1988. "Sojourners and Settlers in Yemen and America."

In *Sojourners and Settlers: the Yemeni Immigrant Experience*, ed. Jonathan Friedlander. Salt Lake City: University of Utah Press.

Thomas, Edwin J. 1967. "Concepts of Role Theory" In *Behavioral Science for Social Workers*, ed. E. J. Thomas. New York: Free Press.

VerKuyten, M. 1986. "The Impact of Ethnic and Sex Differences on Happiness of Adolescents in the Netherlands." *Journal on Social Psychology* 126: 259–260.

CHARLENE JOYCE EISENLOHR

Adolescent Arab Girls in an American High School

dolescent behavior cannot be understood apart from the context in
which young people grow up. In a multicultural society like the
United States, cultural conflict may occur when the adolescent is placed in
an environment, a school for example, in which the values and customs are
different from those at home. Some research indicates that high school—
aged youngsters who live in a social environment or go to a school in
which their ethnic or socioeconomic group is a minority are more likely to
have self-image problems than those who are in the majority (Rosenberg
1965).

As a high-school counselor in an Ann Arbor, Michigan, school with a
small Arab population, I became aware of the struggle of adolescent Arab
Muslim girls, particularly with the issue of autonomy. Their effort to
become more independent is validated by the movement of the sexes
toward equality that is occurring in the United States at this time. I then
decided to look at a larger sample of Arab Muslim girls in a high school in
Dearborn, Michigan, with a sizable Arab population. At the time of my
research, 40 percent of the students were from Arab countries and many
more were American-born Arabs. In the city, however, they represent 20
percent of the residents. The customs of the high school such as co-
education are very different from those of their culture.

The Dearborn community is described elsewhere in this book (see
Aswad and Gray),but we may mention here that it includes Muslim immigrants and their descendants from Lebanon, Palestine and Yemen.

Arab parents in America find themselves faced with a dilemma. They want to trust their daughters, but they also believe that they cannot allow them to move about as freely as other female adolescents can and still maintain a good reputation within the Arab community. For female Arab adolescents in America who live in conservative Muslim families, the parameters of independence are well-defined. They are allowed to talk to boys at school, but they are not allowed to date. They are allowed to participate in after school activities if their parents are convinced they will be supervised by school personnel. The usually ride a school bus or are driven by a family member to and from school.

For the female Arab adolescent, the problem is complicated if she does not identify with her parents' values. Like her counterpart raised with American values, she is moving toward maturity and desires more control over her life. Presented with two diverse sets of values, one at school and one at home, she must decide how to behave. Her relationship with her parents is critical to this decision.

It is imperative for those who educate and assist these young Arab women to have a clearer understanding of the impact of cultural conflict on these young women. It is hoped that this chapter will vividly represent the stress and struggle in the lives of these young Arab students.

There is a growing conviction that the ways people cope with stress affect their psychological, physical, and social well-being (Antonovsky 1979; Coelho, Hamburg, and Adams 1974; Cohen and Lazarus 1979; Janis and Mann 1977; Moos 1977). Coping effects serve two main functions: the alteration of the ongoing person-environment relationship (problem-focused coping) and the regulation of stressful emotions (emotion-focused coping). Despite the recent groundswell of interest in coping, little is known about how it plays this mediating role.

Current approaches to measurement are based on three broad perspectives: coping conceptualized in terms of ego processes (Haan 1977; Vaillant 1977), coping conceptualized as traits (Lazarus, Averill, and Opton 1974) and coping conceptualized in terms of the special demands of specific kinds of situations, such as illness (Moos 1977).

In Robert Lazarus's view, coping is a shifting process in which a person must, at certain times, rely more heavily on one form, say, defensive strategies, and at other times on another form, say, problem-solving strategies (1981). This view is supported in a study by Susan Folkman and Robert Lazarus in which they found that both problem- and emotion-focused coping were used in 98 percent of the 1332 episodes analyzed (1980). Intra-individual analyses of these episodes show that people are more variable than they are consistent in their coping patterns. Problem-focused coping is favored in situations in which the person thinks something constructive can be done or thinks more information is required, whereas emotion-focused coping is favored when the situations must be accepted. Work contexts favor problem-focused coping, and health contexts favor emotion-focused coping.

🦏 *Methodology*

The student interviews were intended as a source of enrichment to the study. All the subjects were invited to participate in small-group discussions at their high school. The student interviews were informal, held one or two days after the basic data had been gathered through a questionnaire. These small-group discussions were held in one of the counseling offices and provided the subjects with an opportunity to elaborate on their questionnaire answers. The sessions were tape recorded, and the subjects were told that their identities would be kept secret. Fictional names have been used to ensure this confidentiality, and the material is unedited. Sixty-seven of the 108 students participated in these discussions. The groups ranged in size from five to nine young women. Each discussion group lasted fifty minutes.

Interviews with parents of fourteen of the young women were intended as a supplementary source of enrichment to the study. With the assistance of an Arab interpreter, the subjects' parents were interviewed in their homes. Most of the interviews were held during the day. A random sample (from the subjects in the study) was selected to participate. Ten of the fourteen interviews were conducted with the subjects' mothers, and two interviews were with the subjects' fathers.[1] The researcher took notes instead of using a tape recorder, so as not to appear unduly intrusive.

🦏 *Results: The Daughters' Perspectives*

The student interviews cover several themes, illustrating the common values these young Arab women share with their parents and also showing how these adolescents choose to cope when they find themselves in disagreement with their parents' values. The specific questions asked were: What are some of the good things your parents are doing in raising you? How will you raise your children? What about after-school activities? What if someone wanted to play on a sports team or go out for a play or something like that? Do you have older sisters, and was their life (while at home) different from yours? If you have something really personal that you want to talk about, to whom do you talk? Do you have American (non-Arab) as well as Arab friends? When something does come up that you'd like to do, that you think is okay, but you think your parents would probably not approve, how do you handle it?

VALUES SHARED WITH PARENTS

Q: What are some of the good things your parents are doing in raising you?

INSHAD: Showing us respect.

Q: Your parents are teaching you to be respectful? Is that what you are saying?

INSHAD: No, more people respect you . . . when they look at you and see how you get along with your parents.

LEILA: Encouraging us to do well in school, to get our education.

AIDA: We are taught respect for ourselves and others. And elders . . . we respect our elders more than anything.

FADIA: From the time you are born until the day you die, you always respect your parents. No matter what. If you take a beating from them, you take a beating. My grandma when she had four kids, she took beatings from her four uncles. You know, you respect your elders no matter what.

HANAA: You see I don't know (laughter). If I feel I'm right, I stick up for myself. If they yell, I yell right back. I'm stubborn.

Q: You say that's sort of a common belief that people should respect their elders but not necessarily one that you . . .

HANAA: No matter what (to another girl), I know you believe that. You've been brought up in a good family. But you've always respected your elders, haven't you?

AIDA: Yes.

SALWA: They're protecting us.

Q: So when your parents say whatever.

SALWA: They are doing it because they want things to go well for us.

RANA: I have a lot of respect for my father. If I go out with some friends, he wants to know what time I'll be back. He told me if I'm in any trouble to call him.

Q: A big part of this is trust, isn't it?

LEILA: Yes

AIDA: I don't know any good things.

FADIA: It's hard.

LUBNA: Responsibility, my parents have total trust in me, but also they put a lot of responsibility on me. I am the oldest. I have to take care of this and take care of that, my little brothers and sisters, I have to take care of them. And that sort of helps you when you get older, you sort of know what's going to happen.

Q: Helps you mature, you think?

LUBNA: Uh-huh. I think most of the Arabic girls mature more fast than the other girls. (Several girls agreed with this.)

THE GENERATION GAP

The conversation turned to some differences they had with their parents.

Q: How will you raise your children?

INSHAD: Not the way I was raised. I would give them more freedom.

LEILA: I'd give them a curfew.

AIDA: I'd give them more freedom. If they want to go out with their friends, if they like someone, a guy, I would want them to bring him over so I could meet him.

Q: So you're talking about going places with your girl friends if they wanted to and if you knew the guy they were going to go out with, they could date if they wanted to?

AIDA: Uh-huh.

FAIDA: If I could change one thing, I'd change how the Muslim guys get more freedom than the girls.

LUBNA: It's not fair.

HANAA: I tell my mother that I would let my daughter have more freedom.

Q: And what does she say?

HANAA: She says, "I don't care what you say just as long as you don't ruin your reputation by doing something."

LUBNA: They think like if you go out you are going to right away go with a guy or do something. A lot of Arab girls aren't allowed out at night.

SALWA: I'd raise my daughters the same as my sons. It seems like right now the guys get more freedom. They get to do more, I mean, I don't think it's trusting their kids, I mean the trust they have for the outside world, I mean a guy is a guy, some girl is not going to come out and attack him or something. I'd show a little more freedom toward my daughters than I have right now.

RANA: I'd let my daughter go out more but in the daytime. She can go to other friends' houses or she'll tell me like where, talk to her, be honest with her, you know, and she'll be honest with me and she'll do anything she says. Just let her go out just a little bit more.

SALMA: I'd make sure they don't do anything wrong but I'd make sure they get to go out because I know how I feel right now. I mean . . .

IBTISAM: Instead of these threats, "If you do this, I'm going to beat you up."

SALMA: I will be so understanding. Have a talk with your kids. There's so much, "I'm going to give you a beating if you do this." If that's what you want to do, fine, go ahead. I'll let them do what they want as long as their name is kept good.

SINA: I go to my room and cry.

Q: You cry?

SINA: Yes, I go to my room and cry because my parents are too strict on me and I'm pretty much limited to things like I don't get to go out at all.

BAHIYA: Like cause she had a party.

MAY: I agree with my parents about 50 percent because it's the culture, but they have to understand that I was practically raised here and have a different way of looking at things than they do, but they never take how I feel and how I am into consideration. Like what they want is the way it's gotta be because that's the Arabic culture and that causes problems.

PARENTS' RESTRICTIONS ON DAUGHTERS

One area of disagreement is the parents' reluctance to let their daughters participate in after-school activities.

Q: What about after-school activities? What if someone wanted to play on a sports team or go out for a play or something like that?

FERYAL: I play soccer now. I like it so much. I usually use it as an excuse to get in better shape, to lose weight.

Q: Not all parents will let their daughters stay for after-school activities. What would the school have to do? Is there a concern about boys being present after school? Is that the main concern?

FATMEH: That's always the concern with them.

Q: What would the school have to do to help?

FATMEH: The school could call them up and assure them that nothing's going to happen, that I have transportation home.

Q: Then they might consider it?

AMINA: I asked my father if I could go out for tennis. You know he thinks tennis, mini-skirts. Shorts are out. You know the uniform with the guys watching. He doesn't want anyone looking at me. If I go someplace with him, I have to stay in the car.

RAEDA: I can wear shorts so long as it's around the house.

AMET: If we're away, and there are no Arabic people there, it's different. It depends on who's there to see you.

RAEDA: People talk. That's the main thing, because people talk.

AMET: What parents are really concerned about is what people have to say about you. If people start talking about you, that's it, no more school, no more nothing. I got caught skipping once. My father hit the ceiling. I can't talk on the phone. I had to come straight home from school for three weeks. So they are really strict on me.

NAJLA: My parents care a lot about what other people say. They compare me to their best friend's daughter. I want to do sports, and I want to do all these things, and they just tell my parents, "Why do you let her do all this stuff? She's so skinny." I hate that. It's not that I want to be skinny, I want to be healthy.

SAMAR: You're healthy. What's healthy?

NAJLA: Right.

SAMAR: They eat healthy. Just eat and that's it. Eat, get married, have kids.

NAJLA: I mean how can you be active when all you do is sit around all day an watch TV, you're going to get restless.

MOUSSA: My mother doesn't get involved in what I do. I say to her, "You just sit back and criticize me. And, I wish you'd come to one of my games." She says, "You play a boy's sport—basketball." It's a trip.

FANDA: My dad, like my sister, was really into sports. He liked that a lot. He went. I wanted to join track and my dad said, fine, he wanted me to. He really likes us to get into things, to do something instead of staying home all the time, but my mother wouldn't let me join. I don't know it's because she went to school here in America and she knows how it is, but she says, "No, I need you at home." I say, "Don't you trust me?" Then she says, "Of course I trust you. It's just that I don't trust anybody else." I mean, come on now.

Q: She worries that someone will take advantage of you?

FANDA: Yeah, and reputation. "What if your uncle comes?" He came back here for college, then he's back there right now like for a vacation, he's coming back next week. My mother says, "When your uncle comes back what is he going to say?" I said, "Who cares? Daddy said it's okay."

SALEH: They're going to put the relatives in there.

RAFAA: Uh-huh.

SALEH: Who cares? I mean, what could they say about running track.

RAFAA: It's the running shorts.

SALEH: I hate to tell my mom, "Well, Mom, I won't even wear the shorts. I'll just wear the shorts for meets." She doesn't mind me running out in the shorts, but she minds what people are going to say if they see me running in the shorts.

RAFAA: Yeah.

JAMELEH: Here's the situation. When I first started tenth grade, I wanted to join track and basketball. My mother said, "I want you home to do this and that." She came up with all these problems. My sister comes into the tenth grade, and she wants to go out for track, and my mother says, "Go ahead." I looked at her and said, "When I asked you I wanted to join everything you said no." She says, "Well, if you want to join go ahead and go." I'm a senior right now. I wanted to join from the beginning. She goes, "Well," she brings up another thing.

RAFAA: Sometimes they say no out of their minds just because they want to say no.

JAMELEH: Because I'm the oldest, I get, "No."

MINET: When I came to high school, I was allowed to go out for basketball. I thought I was pretty good. I was late after one practice and that was it. I haven't been on anything since.

Q: Because you were late getting home from one practice?

MINET: They didn't trust me no more.

Parental Treatment of Older and Younger Daughters

In some families there is a difference between the treatment of older and younger sisters. Usually this is attributed to an adjustment to American culture on the part of the parents.

Q: Do you have older sisters?

BALOUL: Yes.

Q: Was their life different from yours?

BALOUL: Yes, very much. We were just talking about that.

Q: How was it different?

HALA: We have a lot more freedom.

Q: Like in what ways?

BALOUL: My older sister has two small babies, and she's pregnant again. She tells my parents, "Don't keep them home because you'll regret it."

Q: She stays home because of the responsibility to her children, not because she couldn't go if she wanted to?

BALOUL: Yes, she could go if she wanted to.

AMAL: My sister, my parents learned from my sister's experiences. One of my sisters was married when she was fourteen. When my parents came to America, people who were Arabs in America started to say, "Rush off your daughter and get her married because she's going to become Americanized. She'll start smoking," and they brought up the bad side of the American culture. So my parents, they believe it, because they didn't know what was going on in America. So they sent her back to Lebanon and had her married and brought her back here. Now she never got to go to school or got her education or anything, she was a housewife with four kids.

FADUA: I think my mother started putting responsibility on me. I think that was a mistake, when I was seven or eight, that's what I remember. I couldn't go out as much as other kids. She taught me things. She thought she was doing good, and I think that is good, but now I feel that I've missed a lot of my childhood.

Q: Because you didn't get to play as much?

FADUA: Yes, I didn't play as much. I didn't get to run around and jump up and down like kids do. She thought she was doing good. She taught me everything, the housework, everything, because I'm the oldest. Now my little sister is nine, and she is given the freedom to do anything she wants, to go over to her friend's house, have her friends over.

BROTHERS AND SISTERS

There are also differences between families in the influence and responsibility given to brothers in regard to their sisters' behavior.

Q: How many of you have brothers? Everybody has brothers?

SAMAR: I don't think they stop until they get one. (laughter).

Q: It's important to have a boy?

RASHIDA: My mother is pregnant now. She's hoping for a boy.

SAMAR: They have to get the boy, no matter how many kids it takes. They name the father and mother after the oldest son.

Q: Yes, I know a family whose oldest son is Hasham. The mother is called Um-Hasham and the father is called Abu-Hasham. How do you feel about your brothers and their freedom compared to yours?

RASHIDA: There are a lot of girls whose brothers tell them what to do, but my mother and father have said to my brothers that what we do does not concern them. Sometimes my older brother will say, "Why are you going there?" And I'll say, "Does that concern you? I'm doing it, not you." But he'll try to tell me because he's protective.

MONA: They're very protective of their sisters.

HANAN: My parents think I shouldn't have girl friends four or five years older than I because they just might be only interested in getting to know my older brother.

NEHMEH: My parents don't care about age.

FARIDE: If my parents say I can go someplace but I can't go by myself, I have to ask my brother to go with me, and he'll usually say no. (laughter)

RASHIDA: We love them a lot. I don't know why. (laughter)

NEHMEH: I have three brothers who don't live at home, but I see them just as much as if they did live at home. One gives his opinion. He really can't do anything because he knows that if I feel a certain way, I don't care what he says or what he does unless he talks to my parents. He gives his opinion and that's about it. He might say, "That's not right. Think about what you're doing. If I find out what you're doing and I don't like it, then you're in trouble." But as long as all that he is doing is assuming things, he can't do anything. I have one brother that's two years older than me. We hardly ever get along because I hardly ever see him anyway. When we do get along, I can tell him. I can't tell him everything, but can tell him most things. He lets me talk to guys, guys can call. All that's okay, but going out with them, he's gotta really know because he's not much older than me and he thinks, well, I know how guys act and I can't let you do that because they might try something on you. I know how they are. I do it.

Q: So he could say, you can do this or that and this would be okay with your parents?

NEHMEH: Yes, because he's so close to my age that my parents think what he says, he must be right. If he says, don't let her go to this party, well my parents think, well he's been there, and it must not be good, so you can't go. So that's why I never let him know where I'm going.

Q: (to another girl in the group) Do you have any brothers?

FARIDE: Yes, one older.

Q: Does your brother feel any responsibility for you?

FARIDE: Sometimes he does.

Q: How do you feel about that?

FARIDE: My mother says he should and my dad says he shouldn't.

Q: So who decides?

FARIDE: I go to my dad. (laughter)

Q: If your brother doesn't think you should go where you want to go.

FARIDE: If I want to go somewhere, I just ask my dad, if my brother sees me talking to some guy in school he usually won't say anything, but, one time, he saw me and this one guy walking and talking in the halls every day because there was something going on between us. My brother asked me why I kept hanging around with him. I told him, "Don't think we're going out because we're not," and he said, "I just don't want people talking about you. I'm doing this for your own good."

Q: You're saying you know what you're doing?

FARIDE: Yes, I can take care of myself.

ZOBEIDA: My brother helps me. When my parents say no, he says, "Why are you doing this? Let her do this. She's telling you what she's going to do. She's not going to do something else."

CONFIDANTS

When it comes to discussing personal problems, these adolescents turn to a variety of people, relatives as well as school friends.

Q: If you have something really personal that you want to talk about, who do you talk to?

SAMAR: I talk to my sister.

RASHIDA: My mother.

MONA: I talk to my cousin.

Q: Do you feel all those people will keep a confidence?

SAMAR: That's why it's better to tell your sister or someone in the family. Your best friend and you could become enemies.

RASHIDA: Sometimes my sister can keep a secret, and sometimes she can't. I go and tell her who I like, and she tells my mother, and I get mad, but when I talk to my mother she doesn't go and tell my father if I tell her not to. But if I tell her to talk it over with my father because I don't like talking to them face to face, then she would tell him.

HANAN: I'd like my parents to be able to talk to me. Right now I'm too embarrassed to talk to them. I talk to my mother some but I'm still embarrassed.

Q: It's difficult to talk with your mother about certain issues? What issues.

HANAN: Well, I ask my mother any questions I have to know, we talk it over together.

Q: But you wish you felt more comfortable?

HANAN: Yes.

NEHMEH: I talk to my sisters usually, or my best friend. If it's school-related, my best friend; or if it's something I can't talk to my sisters about. But if it's something I think my sisters went through, then I'll talk to them about it. Sometimes they talk to my mom for me because they're older.

Q: Are they married?

HANAN: Yes.

FARIDE: There's no one I can talk to.

Q: No one?

FARIDE: It depends on what kind of problem. Because you can't trust anybody. You can trust friends, but when friends they get mad at you, that's it.

RASHIDA: You can trust your parents.

ZOBEIDA: I can't talk to my parents. They don't understand.

MAGGIE: When I have a problem I go talk to my uncle, he understands. He tells me what to do, but he won't tell my parents.

MIRVAT: The only one I talk to is her (another girl in the group).

Q: Do you have American as well as Arab friends?

SAMAR: That was one of your questions on the questionnaire. I enjoy being with the American people because you can get closer, but in the long run, Arabic friends understand you more.

Q: Because you have the same background?

SAMAR: Yes, because we have the same background so that's why I sort of stick with them. Sometimes there is pressure from friends and parents to pick Arab girls as friends.

LINA: When I was in the ninth grade it was like none of the Arabic girls liked me because, basically, all of my friends were non-Arab, and all of the Arabic girls resented that. They thought that I was trying to be cool or that I was stuck-up. It finally got so bad that about fifteen of them jumped me and the whole school got into a fight over it. Ever since then, I really don't hang around with Arabic girls, maybe just a few. I didn't do anything to these girls, so I can't understand why the hate me so much.

SAMIH: This is a problem which has occurred in more than one instance, a problem which really does upset me. The thing is that at times, I will have a person of the Arabic race who will question me on whether or not I am Arabic. Though this may seem as not a true tragedy, I do. I become furious when this occurs because I am being put down by people because I don't act in the exact way they do. I must behave according to their so-called "Arabic-culture," or be classified as an "out-cast."

PARENTAL CONTROL AND DAUGHTERS' COPING STRATEGIES

These adolescents appear to be similar to typical American teenagers, trying to convince their parents to let them go to certain places, but doing some things on their own if they think their parents won't approve, while keeping in mind the importance of their reputation.

Q: When something does come up that you'd like to do, that you think is okay but you think your parents would probably not approve, how do you handle that?

MARIAM: You be very careful if you do it.

ROSE: I try to build up to a thing. I just don't come out and say I'm going to do this, because as soon as you do that they come right out and say no.

FATME: They don't even bother to think.

ROSE: I asked if I could have a job. "No." But I got one. I said to my mother, "Hear me out, and then say no if you want to."

NAYLA: I try to get them to look at the things possible. My parents are extremely strict. I don't get to do some of the things most Arabic girls do.

NADIA: All of us sneak behind their backs. Some of my American friends do the same thing. Everybody does that. In America that's not so different.

HANA: Sure, any child, American, Chinese, or whatever. Most of the time we don't bother to ask, because we know they're going to say no.

NADIA: It's not that we're out doing bad things. It's because we want a little more freedom. We're not doing anything bad, but if other people see us going out there, they'll say, "Oh, she's a

HANA: Prostitute.

NADIA: Uh-huh.

Q: In other words, you just decide yourself that, according to you, it's probably okay?

FAIROUZ: I have an Italian friend and her mother is more strict than mine.

NOLL: I have a Greek friend, and her mother is more strict than mine. That's why my mother likes her so much.

FAY: Yeah, sometimes you can't do too much and you just sit there and look at the four walls every day at home, you get bored with it. You have to do something. You're not going to do anything to hurt yourself.

CHADIA: My uncle, he pulled his daughters out of high school before they started their sophomore year. He said, "No, you're not going to high school." I found that really sad because one is twenty-one and the other one is nineteen, and now they have to go to night school. The father said, "Okay, I'll let you go," but all these years they got gypped of their education. Now they go to night school and they're learning what I already know, and I think that's a real bad situation. It's a gyp for them because they're learning algebra, and I'm past algebra. Night school . . . if he was so worried about their reputation . . . so okay the girl is going at night to a school. My father told him, "I don't know what you're doing."

Q: Did they marry?

CHADIA: No, I guess that's why he changed his mind, because they got offers but they wouldn't get married. They said, "No we want a job. We want to go to school." They kept persisting and persisting. Finally their father said, "Okay, go." But I mean, look at all these years their father has wasted for his daughters and I thought that was pretty sad.

The two mutually supportive sisters described by Chadia coped by remaining doggedly determined to attend school and resisting pressure from their father to marry. Without knowing more of the dynamics of this situation, one has to wonder how long one of them would have been able to resist the pressure without the other's support.

ARIBA: I want to say something. A lot of parents . . . I think . . . if a girl falls in love with a guy and she's not forced to do anything like sleep with him or anything . . . okay they love each other and they understand each other, and he comes to ask for her, I think the parents should accept . . . not get so hyper.

NAHIA: Yeah.

KAMLEH: See, that's how my parents are. Okay and everybody knows this. I was in love with a guy before I got engaged, and my parents would not agree because my parents did not think he had a future. He quit high school, see he came three times for me, to ask me. I got beatings from my parents. I was going to be out of school. They were so strict with me. I used to be able to go anywhere because they trusted me, then they untrusted because, if I go somewhere they think I'm going to see him, if I go there he's going to be there. My brother used to come to school to see if I was seeing him. When I got home I got the biggest beating, I got wounds all over my body. Somebody called the school and told them about it. I had to see the nurse. I said, "No, no." She saw all these red spots. She said, "I have to call." (Kamleh started crying and could not talk; the group became very quiet.)

Q: You certainly didn't feel good about that, but you didn't want to have your parents . . .

KAMLEH: I got more than one beating. I got lots of beatings. But see, we wanted each other. I wasn't doing nothing wrong. It's just that we wanted each oth er. They won't get that through their head. A girl, when a guy wants her, he comes here, not to see you outside, you know, it's hard to explain that to them, we understand each other, I'm not going to marry somebody that I don't know. I can't get that through their head. My brothers, they all used to beat me up. I got six brothers and no sisters, nobody. My fiancé now knows everything about me. I told him a lot of stuff, all the stuff really, how I got beatings, where I used to see him, who he is, he knows him, and well, he just understands. I told him just like I said to you. If he understands . . . I told him if you want to , . . I'm being honest with you, if you want to trust me, I didn't do nothing wrong, I didn't even sleep with the guy, if you want to be honest, I was with the guy for a year and a half, if you want to trust me, you're welcome, you know, and if you don't, well, then that's your problem. I can't do nothing about it, because I'm being honest with you.

Q: It sounds as though he understood.

KAMLEH: Yes, he understood.

ADIBA: Some guys do understand.

In Kamleh we see an adolescent in open rebellion against her culture's taboo on dating and being severely punished for it; eventually protective services became involved through the school. This is an example of the significant amount of abuse that many American children in the mainstream culture also suffer. As in any identified case of abuse, school personnel must enforce the law. Abuse is an extremely difficult and touchy problem whenever it occurs in our society.

CHADA: Most girls who are Arab, if they're not married by the time they're seventeen, most people start to wonder if something is wrong with them. And then, when you tell them you're going overseas, they think she can't marry anyone here, so she's going over there. Most of the girls who get married are the ones who stay home and do not leave the front porch.

YOLET: No one sees them. These type of girls love to come to school.

SAMIRA: You know what I think? The people she's talking about, the ones that stay home, are the ones that have the most problems in marriage, but you know they're so much into the culture that they don't argue about it. Like no matter what happens, you're supposed to stay with your husband. You're not supposed to divorce him, no matter how badly he treats you. At the end it's always going to work out. But those are the kind of people that get into a lot of problems because they don't know what life's about.

Q: What about when they're here at school, those girls?

SAMIRA: They go wild.

YOLET: Okay, we parked our car. This girl's dad brought her to school. She had a scarf on. As soon as she walked into school she took it off and put it in her pocket. She was just setting up for something.

SAMIRA: They are so wild and it's the parents' fault because they won't let them go anywhere. When they do go out for just an hour, a half hour, they could do enough damage to themselves then. They just go crazy. They're not used to it. They don't know how to act in front of people.

Q: What are the consequences if their parents find out?

SAMIRA: Good-bye.

Q: The consequences are so . . . they could beaten or . . .

SAMIRA: Some of them, if they are old enough, they will send them overseas as soon as they think their reputation is getting bad enough, get them married, and people will stop talking. When they come back, the people over there are looking for a ticket here, and they divorce them. It's stupid.

Q: Really. When they go over there the guy who would marry them . . .

SAMIRA: When an American citizen goes to Lebanon, everybody wants her. She could be the dirtiest girl with the worst reputation, and any guy would marry her just to get here. To get his citizenship, and that's it.

Q: Why is that so important?

SAMIRA: Because they want to come here.

CHADA: I don't think it would be as bad if there wasn't a war. Over there, it's not like it's expensive or anything. It is just bad because of the war. If it wasn't for the war, there wouldn't be such a problem with that.

Q: That makes it more important right now?

YOLET: Yeah. Everyone who comes here stays for a year, can't wait to get back. While the people who have lived here all their lives can't wait to get over there to see what it's all about. So it can't be all bad.

The girls from conservative homes, who find their personal freedom within the school day, are at risk because of the difficulty they have handling their freedom in a culturally acceptable way. Their lives can be extremely stressful, as presented in the case of Kamleh.

✿ *Results: The Parents' Perspectives*

In the parent interviews, the following questions were asked: What advice did you give your daughter on what to expect, or how she should behave in high school? Would you permit your daughter to participate in after-school activities? How does your daughter spend her leisure time? What does she worry about? What are her future plans?

Basically, these parents trusted their daughters to behave in a manner acceptable to their Arab heritage. "She knows what is expected of her," "She uses her own mind," "She isn't a follower," and, "She respects herself," were among their responses. However, they had some advice for their daughters, "Don't get involved with boys, only business. Follow what we do and how we've raised you," "Don't use drugs or drink, and avoid girls who do," "Pick good friends and be friendly," and "Tell your mother first if anything bothers you."

The parents were about evenly divided as to whether they would permit their daughters to participate in after-school activities. If the parents agreed to their participation, the major concern was that there be adult supervision and no boys present.

Participating in after school activities usually meant being on a sport's team. The girls would not be allowed to be part of a swimming team as the religious restriction against exposing too much of the female body in front of men would be violated. Subjects who were allowed to participate in sports activities were also allowed to go shopping with girl friends and, in one case, to hold an after school job at a fast-food chain. Parents or other family members usually provided transportation home.

Those parents who did not allow their daughters to stay after school were principally concerned about the amount of freedom they would have then and the fact that boys would be present. "If her whole body is covered and there are no boys around, we would reconsider." Transportation home was a problem for a couple of parents, and one parent, who worked until 7:00 P.M. needed her daughter at home after school to help with younger children. One mother bought her daughter a basketball backboard to use at home rather than have her participate on the school team. "At school there is a safety concern. The doors are open and drugs are around. At a basketball game, the kids are not normal there." With some assurances about these things, she would reconsider. "It's not my daughter who concerns me. It's the environment."

The parents indicated that their daughters spent their spare time listening to music, watching television, shopping and spending time with their girl friends. One daughter who didn't care for Arab movies on the family VCR had access to cable television.

Several mothers mentioned their daughters' concern about weighing too much, a concern not shared by the mother. One mother said, "All my daughters are too skinny." Another mentioned that her daughter worried about clothes, that she wouldn't have the right ones, or sufficient clothes to be fashionable. Another worry shared by a daughter with her mother was one of wanting only one or two children when she married. Another fear a daughter had was the fighting that had occurred between Arab and non-Arabs in school.

The decision as to whether the daughter would attend college seemed to be hers to make for this group of parents. "College is okay. Whatever she wants. She should be at least twenty-one or twenty-two before she married. "We would like to see her go to college. It's up to her. She would stay at home and go. She will drive or her father will take her. She doesn't know yet. College or marriage, its up to her." One mother mentioned, "My daughter wants to be a secretary. I would like to see her aim higher."

The number of parents interviewed (14) was too small to allow for any significant conclusions. However, this group of parents trusted their daughters and were supportive of their educations.

ᛤ Discussion

Historically, the United States has been thought of as a melting pot, a place for the amalgamation of cultures. However, the single melting pot vision of America now seems to be something of an illusion. Arabs, as well as other immigrants, maintain their cultural heritage for several reasons; these ties provide a source of identity and a network of relationships (Kallen 1964).

In reality schools need to respect the individual cultures that are represented in their populations. In this regard, the administration and staff of the high school referred to in this article have a difficult and challenging task. As the principal says, "When I walk in the halls, I think we look like the United Nations." Forty percent of the population of eighteen hundred and fifty are Arab students. However, not included in this percentage are those Arab students who were born in America. The number of Arab immigrants to the United States is expected to continue to rise because of the unrest in the Middle East. High inflation in the Middle East is another contributing factor to the present levels of immigration.

According to the high-school principal, as of September 1987, there were ninety-two students in the English-as-a-second-language program. Some Polish and Rumanian students are included in this group, but the majority are Arab students. Of this number, forty-four were new to the country, and twenty-eight of them were illiterate in their own language.

The co-ed nature of the school may add stress to these adolescents' lives if their parents have expectations of little interaction with boys. An Arab girl may also feel deprived if she is denied the opportunity to participate in the rich and varied extracurricular program of the school. School personnel, working with the parents of individual adolescents, may be able to provide adequate assurances so their daughters may participate in the after-school programs. There also may be dissonance between the school and the parents, or between the parents and daughters in terms of academic expectations for these students.

The professional literature tells us that the clearer the values, the clearer the limits, the easier the adolescence. Although this sample of Arab Muslim students may be biased on the liberal side, there appears to be a security, for these adolescents, in having an understanding of their cultural values and limits, which contributes to high self-esteem. It is especially important for the parents to communicate to their children why the cultural customs and values are so important to their well-being. If school personnel are familiar with important Arab values, such as the significance of reputation, the female Arab adolescent may feel validated, and this may also contribute to her positive feelings about herself.

ﷺ *References*

Antonovsky, Aaron. *Health, Stress and Coping.* San Francisco: Jossey-Bass, 1979.

Coelho, George V.; David A. Hamburg; and John E. Adams, eds. 1974. *Coping and Adaptation.* New York: Basic Books.

Cohen, F. and R. S. Lazarus. 1979. "Coping with the Stresses of Illness." Pp. 217–254 in *Health Psychology,* ed. George C. Stone, Francis Cohen, and Nancy E. Adler. San Francisco: Jossey-Bass.

Cohen, Yehudi A. 1964. *The Transition from Childhood to Adolescence: Legal Systems and Incest Taboos.* Chicago: Aldine Publishing.

Eisenlohr, Charlene J. 1988. *The Dilemma of Adolescent Arab Girls in an American High School.* Ph.D. diss., Department of Education, University of Michigan, Ann Arbor.

Folkman, Susan, and Robert Lazarus. 1980. "An Analysis of Coping in a Middle-Aged Community Sample." *Journal of Health and Social Behavior*, 21: 219–239.

Haan, Norma. 1977. *Coping and Defending.* New York: Academic Press.

Janis, Irving and Leon Mann. 1977. *Decision Making.* New York: Free Press.

Kallen, H. 1964 "Theories of Assimilation: Part III." Pp. 132–159 in, *Assimilation in American Life: The Role of Race, Religion and National Origins*, ed. Milton Gordon. New York: Oxford University Press.

Lazarus, Richard S. 1981. "The Stress and Coping Paradigm." Pp. 174–214 in *Models for Clinical Psychopathology.* ed. C. Eisdorfer, D. Cohen, A. Kleinman, and P. Maxium. New York: Spectrum.

Lazarus, Richard S.; J. R. Averill; and E. M. Opton, Jr. 1974. "The Psychology of Coping: Issues of Research and Assessment." Pp. 248–315 in *Coping and Adaptation* ed. George V. Coelho, David A. Hamburg, and John E. Adams. New York: Basic Books.

Moos, Rudolf. 1977. *Coping with Physical Illness.* New York: Plenum Press.

Rosenberg, Morris. 1965. *Society and the Adolescent Self-Image* Princeton: Princeton University Press.

Vaillant, George. 1977. *Adaptation to Life.* Boston: Little and Brown.

MARY C. SENGSTOCK

Care of the Elderly within Muslim Families

Meeting the Service Needs of American Muslim Elderly

A major problem in the health and social-service professions in recent years has been the provision of services to communities that are dramatically different in culture and outlook from those of most of the practitioners of those professions in U.S. society. When the family structure, religious values, and other cultural patterns of the group vary considerably from those of the professional provider, problems of providing care are exacerbated (McGoldrick 1982).

This is particularly true of groups that are relatively new in this country and that present cultural values and patterns of needs that have been little seen in previous cultural groups. Many professionals are not only unaware of their needs, but are also unaware of what issues may be sensitive, impeding the provision of professional care. In such instances it

The author wishes to acknowledge the Michigan State Office of Services to the Aging, which provided the financial support for this research. Mary Lindeman, M.A., of the Michigan State Office of Services to the Aging, was particularly helpful. The two project research assistants, Salim Alqaisi, Ph.D., and Rifaat Dika, Ph.D., both Arab-speaking members of the Dearborn Muslim community, were indispensable as translators, interviewers, and contacts with the Muslim community. Ms. Ferial Seblani, an Arab-speaking graduate student at Wayne State University, also provided critical assistance with the interviewing.

271

is imperative that research be conducted to provide insight into the needs of the group, so that professionals may provide appropriate services on a more knowledgeable basis.

American Muslims represent such a new cultural group. Immigration of Muslims into the United States is relatively of recent origin, substantial numbers arriving during the second half of the twentieth century (Aswad 1974b: 53, 63; Elkholy 1988: 440–441). Consequently, few in the health and social-service professions understand much about either the Muslim religion or the needs of its adherents.

Elderly residents of these communities are especially likely to present problems to service providers. An obvious reason for this is the fact that the elderly in most communities are likely to exhibit traditional values that conflict with many professional service standards. In the past, foreign cultural groups did not have many elderly members until the earliest immigrants grew old and the community was relatively well established. Immigrants did not come in old age, since they could not withstand the rigor of travel. With modern jet travel, however, older immigrants are more common, as adult offspring are able to bring their aged parents to this country to join the family. Consequently, elderly Muslims are becoming more frequent, as the earliest Muslim immigrants reach old age and elderly parents come to join their children and friends. Providing services to the Muslim aged population thus becomes a special need.

The lack of knowledge about the needs of the aged Muslim population has major consequences for professional services on both the individual and the institutional levels. On the level of the individual service provider, doctors, nurses, social workers, and other professionals may be insensitive, albeit unintentionally, to the needs of their Muslim clients. They may, for example, suggest treatment programs that unnecessarily interfere with religious restrictions, or require that male professionals interact with female Muslims in ways that Muslim tradition considers inappropriate. As Aswad (1974b: 64) has noted, when professionals, such as teachers, accommodate the requirements of the ethnic culture, community members can be highly supportive. In many instances, however, such sensitivity does not exist.

On the institutional level the interference may be even more serious. A lack of sensitivity to Muslim cultural traditions may establish continuing patterns or service criteria, such as those mentioned above, that inhibit service provision in accordance with a Muslim cultural tradition. Such institutional provisions may make it impossible for even the most sensitive individual to minister appropriately. Knowledge of the health and social service needs of American Muslims, as well as of the sociocultural traditions that may place limitations on serving these needs, is essential if this population is to be adequately served.

⚗ Problems of Determining Appropriate Services

New and unfamiliar cultural groups also present problems in using the major techniques that health and social service professionals, as well as social researchers, have used in uncovering the needs of clients or patients. The structure of professional assistance in the United States largely assumes that people recognize their need for assistance and seek out professional help. General health-screening programs do not play a major part in the American health-care system. Needs assessment surveys also tend to ask people to assess their own needs (Dluhy 1987). This focus has been found to be inappropriate for some populations. For example, research on family violence has shown that case workers must identify this type of problem without depending on the client to provide the information. Victims of child, spouse, or elder abuse are unlikely to provide this information without prompting (Sengstock and Barrett 1984: 168; Burr, Day, and Bahr 1993: 413). Agencies serving the homeless have also found them to be unable or unwilling to recognize their health and social-service needs (Padgett, Struening, and Andrews 1990). For a variety of reasons, immigrant populations frequently exhibit the same reluctance or inability to provide accurate and functional information about their health and social-service needs. Such groups require special understanding on the part of professionals to provide appropriate services (Davis 1993: 102).

This is true of Muslim immigrants as well. The problems of determining the health and social-service needs and of providing assistance to a Muslim immigrant community will be the major focus of this chapter, which will focus on two major issues. Not only will the reported needs of the elderly Muslim respondents be discussed, but the similarity or discrepancy between the respondents' assessments and those of the interviewers will also be analyzed. Finally, some reasons for the observed patterns will be presented, in the hope that these may help to improve service providers' ability to serve this population more effectively.

🕱 *Methodology*

The analysis will be based on data collected as part of a survey of elderly Arab and Chaldean residents of southeastern Michigan. This region, comprising the city of Detroit and its suburbs, has one of the largest concentrations of Arabic-speaking people in the United States (Aswad 1974a: 10; Parrillo 1990: 322). The Arabic population consists of several subgroups; two of the largest are Chaldean Christian Iraqis (Sengstock 1975; 1982) and Muslim residents of Dearborn (Aswad 1974a; 1974b).

In June 1990 the Michigan State Office of Services to the Aging contracted for a study of two hundred people in these two communities aged sixty and over. The purpose of the study was to assess the health and social-service needs of this population, employing a survey instrument developed for the analysis of service needs of a general sample of elderly Michigan residents in 1985 (Dluhy 1987). The instrument was designed to collect data on the respondents' perceptions of their own needs in a variety of areas including economic and housing needs, health status and medical needs, mental-health status and social support, need for assistance with the activities of daily living, and so on. In addition to the respondents' assessments of their own needs; each interviewer was asked to provide an independent assessment of the respondents' needs in these areas.

The questionnaire was translated into Arabic, no small task in view of the fact that some services mentioned in the questionnaire, such as Meals on Wheels, are not translatable. Five Arabic-speaking interviewers, all Muslims from the Dearborn community, conducted the interviews, with the vast majority (88.8%) conducted by two graduate students from Wayne State University. Interviewers were trained by the author and by representatives from the Michigan State Office of Services to the Aging, which provided the interview staff with a general background in the types of services that were accessible to the older residents of the state. Because of the difficulty in finding respondents in most immigrant groups, no attempt was made to develop a random sample; rather a convenient sample was undertaken. Data collection took place from November 1990 through June 1991. The final report was submitted in January 1992 (Sengstock 1992).

ä Demographic Characteristics of the Respondents

This chapter discusses the ninety-eight respondents to this survey who reside in the Dearborn Muslim community. Tables 1–9 list a number of key demographic characteristics of the sample. The sample consists primarily of a "young-old" population, with a mean age of 66.8 years and a median age of 65. Over half of the sample was under 65, with another 30 percent between the ages of 65 and 69. Less than 20 percent was 70 or over (see Table 1). Respondents were rather evenly divided between men and women, with 48 percent male and 52 percent female (see Table 2).

The respondents had large families (between one and eighteen children),

TABLE 1
RESPONDENTS' AGE

AGE	FREQUENCY	PERCENT
60-64	50	51.0
65-69	29	29.6
70-74	5	5.1
75-79	7	7.1
80-84	3	3.1
85+	2	2.0
MISSING	2	2.0
TOTAL	98	99.9

MEAN	66.781	STANDARD DEVIATION	6.248
MEDIAN	65.000	MODE	61.000
VALID CASES	96	MISSING CASES	2

TABLE 2
RESPONDENTS' GENDER

GENDER	FREQUENCY	PERCENT
Male	47	48.0
Female	51	52.0
TOTAL	98	100.0

not a surprising finding in view of traditional Muslim family patterns (Aswad 1974b; Elkholy 1988; Wigle 1974: 156–162). Only one respondent never married and 94 percent have children. The average number of children is 7.2. Four respondents did not provide information about their family size.

This community is primarily a Lebanese Muslim community. Over three-fourths of those in the sample were born in Lebanon, 8 percent in Palestine, and 6 percent in Yemen; 5 percent were born in other Middle Eastern countries while 3 percent were born in the United States (see Table 3). All were Muslims, which was a criterion of their being considered for this analysis. Slightly over half did not indicate to which sect they belonged; 38 percent were Shi'ites; and 11 percent were Sunni Muslims (see Table 4).

Respondents had relatively little education: over half had none; 37 percent had some elementary schooling; 5 percent completed the equivalent of eighth grade; and only 4 percent had any education beyond grade school (see Table 5). Most (33%) of those who attended school did so in Lebanon. The others were educated in a variety of Middle Eastern nations, with 2 percent having some schooling in the United States (see Table 6). The survey did not ask whether respondents were from urban or rural background; however, earlier research suggests that this community consists of people largely from agricultural or village backgrounds (Aswad 1974a: 2; 1974b: 64).

Income levels in the community are low, with a median household income of $7,499.50 and a mean of $10,564.43. Since these families tend to be large, the households also included a variety of other people. Most respondents (59%) lived with a spouse. One-fourth live with a child under eighteen years of age, more than half (54%) lived with a child over eighteen, and 8 percent lived with other relatives. Only 13 percent of the sample lives alone (see Table 7). Since multiple responses are possible, these data may represent a multiplicity of household composition. The average household had 3 residents and 9 percent had 5 or more. Thirty percent of the sample had 1 child in the household, 18 percent had 2, 9 percent had 3, and 7 percent live in households with 4 or more children (see Table 8). Compared with other elderly households in the United States these are relatively large.

At the time of this study (1991) the poverty-level income as determined by the federal government was $8,880 for a two-person family. Considering that their median household income was $7,499.50, and that many of them live in

TABLE 3
Respondents' Place of Birth

Birth Place	Frequency	Percent
Lebanon	76	77.6
Palestine	8	8.2
Yemen	6	6.1
Other Mid-East	5	5.0
United States	3	3.1
TOTAL	98	100.0

TABLE 4
Respondents' Religion

Religion	Frequency	Percent
Muslim (unspecif.)	50	51.0
Shi'ite Muslim	37	37.8
Sunni Muslim	11	11.2
TOTAL	98	100.0

TABLE 5
Respondents' Education

Level of Education	Frequency	Percent
None	52	53.1
Some elementary school	36	36.7
Completed grade school	5	5.1
Some high school	1	1.0
Graduated high school	2	2.0
College plus	1	1.0
MISSING	1	1.0
TOTAL	98	99.9

VALID CASES	97	MISSING CASES 1

TABLE 6
Where Respondent Attended School

Country	Frequency	Percent
Lebanon	32	32.7
Yemen	3	3.1
Palestine	3	3.1
Syria	2	2.0
Other Midddle East	2	2.0
United States	2	2.0
Other	1	1.0

TABLE 7

PERSONS IN RESPONDENTS' HOUSEHOLD

(MULTIPLE RESPONSES POSSIBLE)

PERSONS INCLUDED	FREQUENCY	PERCENT
Spouse	58	59.2
Child under 18	25	25.5
Child over 18	53	54.1
Other relatives	8	8.5
Lives alone	13	13.3

households with more than two residents, it is clear that these older Muslim respondents were likely to have serious economic problems.

The community is a fairly stable one. The length of time the respondents had lived in the area ranged from 1 to 22 years, the average being 6.8 years (see Table 9). There were also a fair number of newcomers, however, who had only lived in the community for 1 year.

To summarize the nature of the sample, these were older Muslims, nearly all immigrants, living in the city of Dearborn, Michigan. They were largely a "young-old" population, most in their early sixties and almost equally divided between males and females. The majority of the respondents were immigrants from Lebanon, with others from other nations of the Middle East. A few were born in the United States. They were relatively uneducated, and what education they may have had was obtained prior to coming to this country. They lived in fairly large households when compared with other elderly in the United States, and had a relatively low household income.

🐚 Data Analysis

The respondents' health and social-service needs will be discussed in each of the six areas covered by the needs-assessment survey. As noted earlier, the respondents' own perception of their needs in each area will be compared with those of the interviewers, who had been provided with a background in the types of services and assistance that can be obtained by elderly residents of the state. The six areas of service covered are: housing conditions; adequacy of social support; mental-health needs; physical-health status, including medical and dental needs; transportation requirements; and economic needs.

TABLE 8
SIZE OF RESPONDENTS' HOUSEHOLD

A: TOTAL NUMBER OF PERSONS

TOTAL NUMBER	FREQUENCY	PERCENT
One	13	13.3
Two	17	17.3
Three	14	14.3
Four	12	12.2
Five or more	9	9.2
MISSING	33	33.7
TOTAL	98	100.0

MEAN	3.077	STANDARD DEVIATION	1.873
MEDIAN	3.000	MODE	2.000
VALID CASES	65	MISSING CASES	33

B: TOTAL NUMBER OF CHILDREN

TOTAL NUMBER	FREQUENCY	PERCENT
One	29	29.6
Two	18	18.4
Three	9	9.2
Four	4	4.1
Five or more	3	3.1
MISSING	35	35.7
TOTAL	98	100.1

MEAN	2.048	STANDARD DEVIATION	1.442
MEDIAN	2.000	MODE	1.000
VALID CASES	63	MISSING CASES	35

TABLE 9
LENGTH OF RESIDENCE IN PRESENT HOME

MEAN	6.794 years
STANDARD DEVIATION	5.710
MEDIAN	5.000 years
MODE	1.000 year
RANGE	1 to 22 years
VALID CASES	97
MISSING CASES	1

Housing Conditions

Respondents appeared to be relatively uncritical of their housing (see Table 10A). Nearly three-fourths (70.4%) said they were "very satisfied" with their housing, 21.4 percent said they were "somewhat satisfied," and only 7.1 percent expressed any dissatisfaction at all with their housing.

There is a wide discrepancy between the perceived needs of these elderly Muslims as viewed by the interviewers, and the interviewees. Interviewers generally considered the elders' housing to be of average quality. Only 4 percent of the housing was rated as "very poor," with 14 percent rated "poor." However, interviewers also noted that nearly one-third (30.6%) of the elders' homes needed repairs (see Table 10B).

If we assume that respondents would be expected to be "very satisfied" with "good" or "very good" housing, not in need of repairs, "somewhat satisfied" with housing that is "average," and "dissatisfied" or "somewhat dissatisfied" with housing that is "poor" or "very poor" and needs repairs, then these elders seem far more satisfied with their housing than the interviewers' assessment would consider justified.

Adequacy of Social Support

In the area of social support, a similar discrepancy appeared. The respondents' own ratings of satisfaction with their social support are quite high (see Table 11A). Nearly nine out of ten (88.8%) expressed satisfaction with their relationships with children and friends, while another 81.6 percent were satisfied with their relationship with siblings. The lowest level of satisfaction was with spousal relationships, with which 64.3 percent were satisfied.

Although interviewers generally rated the respondents as "not needy" in the area of social support, their views were somewhat less optimistic than those of the respondents (see Table 11B). On a scale on which 3 equals "not needy," the average was 2.50 indicating a low rate of need in this area. More than half (58.2%) were rated as "not needy"; 24.5 percent were ranked "somewhat needy"; and only 11.2 percent were listed as "very needy." While the scales are admittedly quite different, 80–90 percent of respondents expressing satisfaction with most relationships seemed considerably more optimistic than were the interviewers, who considered one in four to be "somewhat needy," and one in ten to be "very needy" in the area of social support.

TABLE 10
RESPONDENTS' HOUSING CONDITIONS

A: RESPONDENTS' SATISFACTION (ON A SCALE OF 1 TO 4)

LEVEL OF SATISFACTION	FREQUENCY	PERCENT
Very dissatisfied (4)	1	1.0
Somewhat dissatisfied (3)	6	6.1
Somewhat satisfied (2)	21	21.4
Very satisfied (1)	69	70.4
MISSING	1	1.0
TOTAL	98	100.0

MEAN	1.371	STANDARD DEVIATION	.651
MEDIAN	1.000	MODE	1.000
VALID CASES	97	MISSING CASES	1

B: INTERVIEWER'S ASSESSMENT (ON A SCALE OF 1 TO 5)

HOUSING CONDITION	FREQUENCY	PERCENT
Very poor (1)	4	4.1
Poor (2)	14	14.3
Average (3)	20	20.4
Good (4)	25	25.5
Very good (5)	23	23.5
MISSING	12	12.2
TOTAL	98	100.0

MEAN	3.570	STANDARD DEVIATION	1.184
MEDIAN	4.000	MODE	4.000
VALID CASES	86	MISSING CASES	12

C: INTERVIEWER'S ASSESSMENT OF REPAIR NEEDS

NEEDS REPAIRS	FREQUENCY	PERCENT
Yes	30	30.6
No	56	57.1
TOTAL	98	100.0

VALID CASES	86	MISSING CASES	12

MENTAL-HEALTH NEEDS

Slightly over one-third of the respondents (36.7%) rated their own mental health as either "fair" or "poor" (see Table 12A). When respondents were questioned about their "satisfaction with life," 6.1 percent said they were dissatisfied, while 38.8 percent had "mixed" sentiments (see Table 12B).

TABLE 11
RESPONDENTS' SOCIAL SUPPORT NEEDS

A: RESPONDENTS' SATISFACTION WITH SOCIAL RELATIONSHIPS
("SATISFIED" AS OPPOSED TO "MIXED" OR "DISSATISFIED")

RELATIONSHIP	FREQUENCY	N	PERCENT
Children	87	93	88.8
Friends	87	94	88.8
Siblings	80	87	81.6
Spouse	63	71	64.3

B: INTERVIEWER'S ASSESSMENT

SOCIAL-SUPPORT NEEDS	FREQUENCY	N	PERCENT
Very needy	11	1	11.2
Somewhat needy	24	2	24.5
Not needy	57	3	58.2
MISSING	6		6.1
TOTAL	98		100.0

MEAN	2.500	STANDARD DEVIATION		.703
MEDIAN	3.000	MODE		3.000
VALID CASES	92	MISSING CASES		6

Consequently, about 45 percent of respondents rated their mental health or life satisfaction as lacking in some manner.

Mental health appears to be one of the few areas in which the respondents thought their needs to be greater than the interviewers did. Interviewers assessed slightly more than one in five (21.5%) of the respondents to be either "very needy" or at least "somewhat needy" (see Table 12c). This stands in dramatic contrast to the one in three respondents whose self-reports indicated problems in this area. The discrepancy between interviewer rating and self report is probably one of definition, with interviewers using, perhaps, a more clinical definition of "mental health," while respondents were expressing a feeling of dissatisfaction with life.

PHYSICAL-HEALTH STATUS: MEDICAL AND DENTAL NEEDS

In contrast to mental health, the area of physical health is one in which the respondents appear more satisfied than the interviewers believe justified.

Three-fourths of the respondents indicated a belief that it was "very

TABLE 12
RESPONDENTS' MENTAL-HEALTH NEEDS

A: RESPONDENTS' RATING

SELF RATING	FREQUENCY	N	PERCENT
Poor	6	4	6.1
Fair	30	3	30.6
Good	41	2	41.8
Excellent	18	1	18.4
MISSING	3		3.1
TOTAL	98		100.0

MEAN	2.253	STANDARD DEVIATION	.838
MEDIAN	2.000	MODE	2.000
VALID CASES	95	MISSING CASES	3

B: RESPONDENTS' EXPRESSED SATISFACTION WITH LIFE (ON A SCALE OF 1 TO 3)

LEVEL OF SATISFACTION	FREQUENCY	PERCENT
Dissatisfied (3)	6	6.1
Mixed (2)	38	38.8
Satisfied (1)	51	52.0
MISSING	3	3.1
TOTAL	98	100.0

MEAN	1.526	STANDARD DEVIATION	.616
MEDIAN	1.000	MODE	1.000
VALID CASES	95	MISSING CASES	3

C: INTERVIEWER'S ASSESSMENT (ON A SCALE OF 1 TO 3)

MENTAL-HEALTH NEEDS	FREQUENCY	PERCENT
Very needy (1)	3	3.1
Somewhat needy (2)	18	18.4
Not needy (3)	74	75.5
MISSING	3	3.1
TOTAL	98	100.0

MEAN	2.747	STANDARD DEVIATION	.505
MEDIAN	3.000	MODE	3.000
VALID CASES	95	MISSING CASES	3

likely" that they would get good medical care when they need it (see Table 13A). Another 19.4 percent thought this was a "somewhat likely" possibility. Only 4.1 percent thought it was "not likely at all."

Furthermore, when asked to rate various aspects of American health care, more than two-thirds of the respondents expressed satisfaction with most factors mentioned (see Table 13B). Over seventy percent of respondents were "very satisfied" with five aspects of their medical care: the time the doctor spends with the patient; the ability to get care in an emergency; the doctor's office hours; ease of getting in touch with their doctor; and the length of time they had to wait to get an appointment. Two-thirds were "very satisfied" with the length of waiting time in the office, and nearly sixty percent (59.2%) were "very satisfied" with their health insurance. Satisfaction dropped considerably, however, when financial issues related to health care were raised. Only about one respondent in three is "very satisfied" with the doctor's prices (34.7%) or with how soon the bill needed to be paid (32.7%).

The respondents' generally high level of satisfaction is not shared by the interviewers. They rated over half of the respondents as being at least "somewhat needy" of medical care (see Table 13C). Over one-third (34.7%) were rated as "somewhat needy" with almost one in five (19.4%) ranked as "very needy." Slightly less than half (42.9%) were thought to be "not needy." Hence, we see a picture of a population generally quite satisfied with their health care, except for its cost; but an outside opinion would question whether this satisfaction were justified.

That the interviewers' opinions may have some validity is illustrated by the respondents' dental-care problems. Nearly half (46.9%) report that they have some problems with their teeth (see Table 14A). Yet, only slightly over one-third had been to the dentist within the year (see Table 14B). Just under one in five (17.3%) had gone to the dentist within the last three years. For over one-third (36.7%), their last visit to the dentist was three or more years before. Five percent chose "other"; it should be noted that some of these respondents reported that they had never been to a dentist. One-fourth reported that there have been times when they needed to go to a dentist but did not go (see Table 14C). The reasons for their not going varied, but most frequently involve the lack of money or dental insurance.

TRANSPORTATION REQUIREMENTS

One area in which respondents and interviewers appear to agree is that of transportation. Sixty percent of the respondents reported that they had difficulty getting where they need to go (see Table 15A). Interviewers rated 44.9 percent of the respondents as "not needy," nearly one fourth (22.4%) as "very needy," and nearly one-third (29.6%) as "somewhat

TABLE 13
RESPONDENTS' MEDICAL NEEDS

A: RESPONDENTS' ESTIMATE OF THE LIKELIHOOD OF GETTING GOOD MEDICAL CARE WHEN NEEDED (ON A SCALE OF 1 TO 3)

LEVEL OF LIKELIHOOD	FREQUENCY	PERCENT
Not likely at all (3)	4	4.1
Somewhat likely (2)	19	19.4
Very likely (1)	74	75.5
MISSING	1	1.0
TOTAL	98	100.0

MEAN	1.278	STANDARD DEVIATION	.535
MEDIAN	1.000	MODE	1.000
VALID CASES	97	MISSING CASES	1

B: RESPONDENTS' LEVEL OF SATISFACTION WITH HEALTH CARE (RESPONDENTS STATING THEY ARE "VERY SATISFIED")

AREA OF SATISFACTION	FREQUENCY	N	PERCENT
Time doctor spends with patient	78	88	79.6
Ability to get care in emergency	74	90	75.5
Doctor's office hours	73	85	74.5
Ease of getting in touch with doctor	72	85	73.5
Time waiting to get an appointment	69	89	70.4
Waiting time in office	65	88	66.3
Health insurance	58	74	59.2
Doctor's prices	34	59	34.7
How soon bill must be paid	32		32.7

C: INTERVIEWER'S ASSESSMENT (ON A SCALE OF 1 TO 3)

LEVEL OF MEDICAL NEEDS	FREQUENCY	PERCENT
Very needy (1)	19	19.4
Somewhat needy (2)	34	34.7
Not needy (3)	42	42.9
MISSING	3	3.1
TOTAL	98	100.0

MEAN	2.242	STANDARD DEVIATION	.768
MEDIAN	2.000	MODE	3.000
VALID CASES	95	MISSING CASES	3

needy" (see Table 15B). This amounts to over half (52.0%) with some transportation needs. The difference between the respondents' and interviewers' rating in this area could easily be due to sample error or the difference in the way the questions were worded.

TABLE 14
RESPONDENTS' DENTAL CARE

A: PROBLEMS WITH TEETH

RESPONSES	FREQUENCY	PERCENT
Had problems	46	46.9
Had no problems	49	50.0
MISSING	3	3.1
TOTAL	98	100.0

VALID CASES	95	MISSING CASES	3

B: VISIT TO DENTIST (ON A SCALE OF 1 TO 4)

LAST DENTIST VISIT	FREQUENCY	PERCENT
Less than 1 year (1)	36	36.7
1 to 3 years (2)	17	17.3
3 or more years (3)	36	36.7
Other* (4)	5	5.1
MISSING	4	4.1
TOTAL	98	100.0

MEAN	2.106	STANDARD DEVIATION	.989
MEDIAN	2.000	MODE	1.000, 3.000
VALID CASES	94	MISSING CASES	4

* "Other" may include "Never"

C: DENTAL NEEDS (HAVE YOU EVER NEEDED TO GO TO THE DENTIST BUT DID NOT GO?)

RESPONSE	FREQUENCY	PERCENT
Yes	24	24.5
No	69	70.4
MISSING	5	5.1
TOTAL	98	100.0

VALID CASES	93	MISSING CASES	5

ECONOMIC NEEDS

The final area of concern relates to the respondents' economic needs. Do they have sufficient resources to cover their daily needs? Half of the respondents said that they have sufficient economic resources and that

TABLE 15
RESPONDENTS' TRANSPORTATION NEEDS

A: RESPONDENTS' TRANSPORTATION NEEDS (DO YOU HAVE PROBLEMS GETTING WHERE YOU NEED TO GO?)

RESPONSE	FREQUENCY	PERCENT
Yes	59	60.2
No	39	39.8
TOTAL	98	100.0

VALID CASES   98   MISSING CASES   0

B: INTERVIEWER'S ASSESSMENT (ON A SCALE OF 1 TO 3)

TRANSPORTATION NEEDS	FREQUENCY	PERCENT
Very needy (1)	22	22.4
Somewhat needy (2)	29	29.6
Not needy (3)	44	44.9
MISSING	3	3.1
TOTAL	98	100.0

MEAN	2.232	STANDARD DEVIATION	.805
MEDIAN	2.000	MODE	3.000
VALID CASES	95	MISSING CASES	3

money was "not a problem." Another 28.6 percent said that they had serious economic problems but could "manage." Nearly one respondent in five (18.4%) reported that obtaining adequate economic resources was a "very serious" problem (see Table 16A).

When asked about their satisfaction with their economic situation 18.4 percent said that they were "dissatisfied," while 44.9 percent were "satisfied," and 33.7 percent had "mixed" feelings (see Table 16B). When respondents were asked whether or not they ever have difficulty paying their bills 61.2 percent reported "never" having had this problem, while 21.4 percent had difficulty "sometimes," and 4 percent had difficulty "frequently" (see Table 16c).

The interviewers' views of the respondents' economic status bear some similarities and some differences to the views of the respondents themselves. Like the respondents, interviewers believed that under 20 percent were "very needy." However, interviewers rated about half of the respondents as "somewhat needy," in contrast to the respondents themselves, only about one-third of whom rated themselves as having some

TABLE 16
RESPONDENTS' ECONOMIC NEEDS

A: RESPONDENTS' ASSESSMENT (ON A SCALE OF 1 TO 3) (Do you have enough money to live on? How serious a problem do you have?)

SERIOUSNESS	FREQUENCY	PERCENT
Very serious (1)	18	18.4
Serious but can manage (2)	28	28.6
Not a problem (3)	49	50.0
MISSING	3	3.1
TOTAL	98	100.0

MEAN	2.326	STANDARD DEVIATION	.778
MEDIAN	3.000	MODE	3.000
VALID CASES	95	MISSING CASES	3

B: RESPONDENTS' SATISFACTION WITH FINANCIAL STATUS (ON A SCALE OF 1 TO 3)

SATISFACTION	FREQUENCY	PERCENT
Dissatisfied (3)	18	18.4
Mixed (2)	33	33.7
Satisfied (1)	44	44.9
MISSING	3	3.1
TOTAL	98	100.0

	MEAN	1.726 STANDARD DEVIATION	.764
MEDIAN	2.000	MODE	1.000
	VALID CASES	95 MISSING CASES	3

C: RESPONDENTS' DIFFICULTY PAYING BILLS (ON A SCALE OF 1 TO 3)

HAS DIFFICULTY	FREQUENCY	PERCENT
Frequently (3)	4	4.1
Sometimes (2)	21	21.4
Never (1)	60	61.2
MISSING	13	13.3
TOTAL	98	100.0

MEAN	1.341	STANDARD DEVIATION	.568
MEDIAN	1.000	MODE	1.000
VALID CASES	85	MISSING CASES	13

economic need. In contrast, interviewers thought that one-third were "not needy," while the respondents indicated that about half were not in economic need (see Table 17).

Consequently, there appears to be agreement between interviewers and respondents when the issue is one of clear economic need. With the

TABLE 17

INTERVIEWER'S ASSESSMENT OF RESPONDENTS' ECONOMIC NEEDS

(ON A SCALE OF 1 TO 3)

LEVEL OF ECONOMIC NEED	FREQUENCY	PERCENT
Very needy (1)	15	15.3
Somewhat needy (2)	46	46.9
Not needy (3)	33	33.7
MISSING	4	4.1
TOTAL	98	100.0

MEAN	2.191	STANDARD DEVIATION	.692
MEDIAN	2.000	MODE	2.000
VALID CASES	94	MISSING CASES	4

middle economic level, where the issue is less clear, respondents and interviewers draw the line of "economic need" differently, with interviewers more inclined to define the respondents as somewhat needy, the respondents more likely to define themselves as not being in need.

🗟 Discussion and Analysis

The data suggest a considerable discrepancy between respondents' recognized needs and those observed by the interviewers in most areas. In only one area, transportation, was there considerable agreement between the two groups. It should be noted that this is probably the most objectively quantifiable of the areas: either the respondents had transportation available or not. There is little room for disagreement or for differing standards.

In the other areas, however, there is considerable room for disagreement. What constitutes "adequate" housing or social support or health care largely depends upon how one defines "adequacy." In these areas, it is very likely that the definitions of professionals from other cultural backgrounds might be very different from those of the respondents for a variety of reasons. Such variation in definition could easily form the basis for problems in providing services, with clients having one set of expectations and the professionals having another.

In many respects the project interviewers are representative of professional service providers. Although they were Arabic-speaking Muslims who had lived in the community, they were graduate students from urban backgrounds, with professional training. Furthermore, they had received training as interviewers, during which they learned what services were available to elderly Michigan residents. Consequently, the interviewers and their elderly respondents articulate the contrast among American Muslims as the twentieth century draws to a close. Many, if not most, of the elderly members of the community are likely to be poor, relatively uneducated, from rural origins, and with little knowledge of the patterns of services available in an urban environment (Aswad 1974b). This is particularly true in view of the fact that in their villages of origin, the extended family provided all such services (Elkholy 1988: 448, 451–452).

Younger members of the community, on the other hand, both immigrants and those born in the United States, are likely to be from urban backgrounds, more educated, and highly sophisticated in their knowledge of urban culture and services. In the future, as the urban educated professionals now in their forties and fifties join the category of "elderly," many of the discrepancies found here will likely disappear.

In the meantime the views of the professional interviewers in our study are likely to be indicative of the views of educated professionals in an industrialized urban society. An analysis of the reasons why their assumptions might differ from those of the respondents could suggest ways to improve professionals' understanding of the needs of their clients, and indeed, of elderly Muslims in general.

The reasons these aged respondents did not recognize some of their problems are: differing cultural standards for problems and services between the country of origin and the United States; the importance of avoiding embarrassment in the community should one's problems become known; the desire to avoid embarrassment for the community as a whole before outsiders; discomfort in asking outsiders for help; and the presence of relatives and friends in the interview as well as in most professional situations.

DIFFERING CULTURAL STANDARDS

Perhaps the most obvious reason for differences in standards between these elderly Muslims and the interviewers is the reality of their differing cultures. Like most educated professionals, the interviewers recognize a standard of service that has largely become accepted in an urban industrialized society. The elderly Muslims, on the other hand, mostly came from areas that have been industrialized only recently. They have grown up and perhaps spent most of their lives in a society dependent upon the family for most needs, a society in which community services are largely nonexistent (Elkholy 1988: 451–452). Consequently, their views about what constitutes a "need," or whether their problems require outside assistance, will differ considerably from those of the interviewers, as well as of any other professionals with whom they come into contact.

Their homes may be in need of repair, might even merit condemnation by U.S. housing standards. But if the home is substantially better than the one in which they grew up, they are likely to be quite satisfied. For those who have never been to a dentist, the knowledge that one is available to them marks a substantial improvement in their health care. Similarly, waiting many weeks for a doctor's appointment, or long hours in the waiting room, is not considered a problem to one who has never had physician's services available at all.

Recognizing that such cultural differences exist, it is clear that professionals serving such populations cannot depend upon their clients to recognize their own needs or the adequacy of services. Service providers have found that victims of abuse or neglect, or the homeless are often unable or unwilling to recognize their health and social service needs. In such instances, professionals must make special efforts to identify clients and their needs, independent of effort on the part of clients to seek help for themselves.

Elderly Muslims appear to comprise a population in need of assistance identifying their problems and the professional services that can help. By extension, one might infer that other immigrant populations, particularly those from nonindustrial or rural backgrounds, might have similar needs.

Avoiding Embarrassment in the Community

Personal and family status is of extreme importance in the Muslim community. It is highly critical that the family be viewed as capable of taking care of its own problems and needs (Elkholy 1988: 451–452; Wigle 1974: 158). Expecting others to care for one's family can be seen as an embarrassment. In this regard these Muslims are not unlike many other groups that have come upon the American scene. Polish-Americans have been known to exhibit this trait (Lopata 1976), as have Hispanics (Saenz 1984; Hispanic Task Force 1986).

Consequently, it is critical for professionals to be especially discrete in dealing with people from backgrounds in which personal and family pride is an important factor. Unless clients can be absolutely assured that their concerns will be kept confidential, they will not be shared. This is particularly true of members of the clients' families or their close friends. The assumptions of many professionals that family members share their problems with each other is not a valid one for many cultural groups.

Avoiding Embarrassment of the Community before Outsiders

Members of many ethnic communities, including Muslims, are extremely concerned about the reputation of their people in the population at large. They are anxious to be known as good citizens and respectable people. They have often seen other groups victimized who are believed to create problems for others, and may have experienced such victimization themselves. Consequently, they try to keep their problems and needs to themselves so as not to have others view them as creating difficulty for the larger community. Professionals who serve an ethnic population must be sensitive to this concern and reassure their clients that their needs will be kept confidential and that the services they receive are appropriate and within their rights.

Discomfort in Asking Outsiders for Help

Closely related to the community's desire to avoid embarrassment is their sense of discomfort in seeking help from outsiders. Because of their long-term cultural convictions that "good families" take care of their own problems (Elkholy 1988: 451; Wigle 1974: 158), many Muslims, like members of other ethnic communities, are embarrassed to admit that there are situations in which they cannot meet their own needs. This stems, at least in part, from a fear that requests for outside help may be held against them or bring embarrassment. They may also feel that outsiders may not understand them, or may blame them for their problems or consider them inadequate.

This reluctance exemplifies the importance of professionals going to the community, rather than expecting members of the group to identify their own needs and seek assistance. Whether from embarrassment, lack of knowledge, or a reluctance to admit their problems to strangers, elderly Muslims, like members of other immigrant groups, are disinclined to seek help from outsiders. Only extreme sensitivity on the part of the professional will overcome this hesitancy.

PRESENCE OF RELATIVES AND FRIENDS IN PROFESSIONAL SITUATIONS

A final factor that may contribute to the discrepancy between the needs assessment of the elderly Muslim respondents and those of the professionals who work with them stems from the extreme family and group orientation of this community. I have said that these are people very concerned with the opinion of their peers, and that professionals must take extreme care to assure that their concerns will remain confidential. At the same time, the nature of the community is such that such confidentiality is well nigh impossible.

This community is extremely social in character. Everyone is concerned about others' activities and expects to be involved in them. Even social-research interviewing in this community is rarely an individual activity. Visiting is almost constant, so that the interviewer rarely finds the respondent alone. In the rare instance when respondents are alone, they rarely remain so. Neighbors note the presence of someone new and drop over to see what is going on.

This situation is illustrated by the data in Table 18, which describes the characteristics of the interview setting in this study. Most common situation, found in over one-third of the interviews, was for other people not only to be present during the interview, but to participate in the interview as well by providing their own comments and responses to the questions.

The characteristics of the interview situation in this study can be used as an illustration of the type of situation professionals can expect to occur in many encounters with a similar population. While it is extremely important for the professional to ensure confidentiality of the client's concerns, the family and other community members make it very difficult for this confidentiality to be maintained.

Since everything is seen to be the family's business, family members, including extended family, may often accompany a person to the office of

TABLE 18
CHARACTERISTICS OF THE INTERVIEW SETTING

INTERVIEW CHARACTERISTICS	FREQUENCY	PERCENT
Others present and responding	35	35.7
Smooth, no interruption	12	12.2
No one else present	11	11.2
Others present but not responding	9	9.2
Several interruptions	7	7.1
Respondent tired, uncomfortable	5	5.1
Not specified	19	19.4
TOTAL	98	100.0

VALID CASES	98	MISSING CASES	0

a doctor or other professional. They will expect to be included in the conversation, and may even answer for the client or patient. In some instances, such as a situation in which a female patient is seeing a male professional, it would be an extreme violation of community values for client and professional to be left alone. Only drastic efforts on the part of the professional will ensure confidentiality. Such efforts might include finding a female professional who can conduct the interview or perform the required procedures. Family members can also be assigned different, but equally important tasks, such as providing additional information to another professional. Indeed, there may be instances in which efforts to maintain confidentiality may be so disruptive of family and community structure that they may be counterproductive and will have to be abandoned.

Finally, it is important that professional workers see the family and community as an aid, not a hindrance, to their attempt to provide services. In the close-knit Muslim extended family, members feel a strong sense of responsibility for each other and have a strong tradition of providing assistance in numerous ways. This can be a great asset to professional workers. As Bruhn has pointed out, members of the family or community can be of considerable assistance in the role of "natural helpers"—a network of persons who are part of the client's social group and who can provide ongoing assistance as well as support for the aid provided by the professional (1991: 212).

🕌 *Conclusion and Recommendations*

Providing health and social services is a difficult task at best. Even when workers serve a population similar to themselves problems arise. There is always a difficulty in gaining the confidence and trust of the client. Even under the best of circumstances, clients often feel uncomfortable, ill at ease, and reluctant to address their most intimate personal health and family difficulties with strangers. When such uncertainty is complicated by any differences in background or viewpoint, the problems of establishing rapport with clients is greatly exacerbated.

Working with clients of different ethnic, racial, or cultural background is clearly an example of such a setting. Obviously, clients who speak different languages or exhibit other outward differences in culture require special skills and attention on the part of a worker, and most professionals are aware of the need to accommodate to the needs of clients in these areas. More obscure sources of cultural differences are less likely to be recognized or considered by workers. Hence the agency providing family services to a family may easily recognize the need for an Arabic-speaking worker or translator. Agency personnel may find it difficult, however, to recognize the family or educational patterns that complicate the provision of services to such clients.

The Muslim elderly described here are a group requiring special attention in a variety of areas if their needs are to be adequately met. These special needs stem, however, not merely from their language or religious differences. While these surely cannot be ignored, other characteristics also require sensitive management if this group is to be served appropriately.

Chief among these characteristics are their long tradition of dependence upon a close-knit extended-family structure; a strong commitment to maintaining family and community solidarity and confidentiality; and a corresponding absence of the independence and individualism that is valued in American society. Effective service to such clients must include the family and community in ways unfamiliar to most American professionals. These characteristics are particularly heightened in the present generation of Muslim elders, who are largely uneducated and have their origins in villages and rural areas. With limited knowledge and understanding of the assistance available from professional workers in an urban, industrial environment, they can enjoy these benefits only if agencies and workers exhibit sensitivity, understanding, and an appreciation for their culture and its traditions.

※ References

Abraham, Sameer Y. 1983. "Detroit's Arab American Community: A Survey of Diversity and Commonality." In *Arabs in the New World*, ed. Sameer Y. Abraham and Nabeel Abraham. Detroit: Wayne State University Center for Urban Studies.

Aswad, Barbara C. 1974a. "Introduction and Overview." Pp. 1–20 in *Arabic Speaking Communities in American Cities*, ed. Barbara C. Aswad. Staten Island, N.Y.: Center for Migration Studies.

———. 1974b. "The Southern Dearborn Arab Community Struggles for Survival against Urban 'Renewal'." Pp. 53–83 in *Arabic Speaking Communities in American Cities*, ed. Barbara C. Aswad. Staten Island, N.Y.: Center for Migration Studies.

Bruhn, John G. 1991. "Health Promotion and Clinical Sociology." Pp. 197–216 in *Handbook of Clinical Sociology*, ed. Howard M. Rebach and John G. Bruhn. New York: Plenum Press.

Burr, Wesley R.; Randal D. Day; and Kathleen S. Bahr. 1993. *Family Science*. Pacific Grove, Calif: Brooks/Cole Publishing.

Davis, Eddie. 1993. "Social Policy, Psychosocial Development, and Minorities." In *American Mosaic*, ed. Young I. Song and Eugene C. Kim. Englewood Cliffs, N.J.: Prentice-Hall.

Dluhy, Milan J. 1987. *Michigan Needs Assessment of the Sixty and over Population: Executive Summary and Independent Variable Analysis*. Lansing: Michigan Office of Services to the Aging.

Elkholy, Abdo A. 1988. "The Arab American Family." Pp. 438–455 in *Ethnic Families in America*, ed. Charles H. Mindel, Robert W. Habenstein, and Roosevelt Wright. New York: Elsevier.

Hispanic Task Force. 1986. *A Study of the Hispanic Community in the Detroit Metropolitan Area*. Detroit: United Community Services of Metropolitan Detroit.

Lopata, Helena Znaniecki. 1976. *Polish Americans*. Englewood Cliffs, N.J.: Prentice-Hall.

McGoldrick, Monica. 1982. "Ethnicity and Family Therapy: An Overview." Pp. 1–30 in *Ethnicity and Family Therapy*, ed. Monica McGoldrick, John K. Pearce, and Joseph Giordano. New York: Guilford Press.

Padgett, Deborah; Elmer L. Struening; and Howard Andrews. 1990. "Factors Affecting the Use of Medical, Mental Health, Alcohol, and Drug Treatment Services by Homeless Adults." *Medical Care* 28, no. 9 (Sept.): 805–821.

Parrillo, Vincent N. 1990. *Stranger to These Shores*. New York: Macmillan.

Saenz, Sigifredo. 1984. *An Assessment of the Mental Health Needs of Hispanics in Michigan*. Lansing: Report to the Michigan Department of Mental Health.

Sengstock, Mary C. 1975. "Kinship in a Roman Catholic Ethnic Group." *Ethnicity* 2: 134–152.

———. 1982. *Chaldean-Americans*. Staten Island, N.Y.: Center for Migration Studies.

———. 1992. *1991 Needs Assessment of the Arab and Chaldean Sixty and over Population in the State of Michigan*. Lansing: Michigan Office of Services to the Aging.

Sengstock, Mary C. and Sara Barrett. 1984. "Abuse of the Elderly." Pp. 245–188 in *Nursing Care of Victims of Family Violence*, ed. Janice Humphreys and Jacqueline Campbell. Reston, Va.: Reston.

Wigle, Laurel D. 1974. "An Arab Muslim Community in Michigan." Pp. 155–167 in *Arabic Speaking Communities in American Cities*, ed. Barbara C. Aswad. Staten Island, N.Y.: Center for Migration Studies.

PART THREE

Immigrants' Life Stories

LINDA S. WALBRIDGE

Five Immigrants

The material for these vignettes has generally been gathered during interviews arranged in advance, either in people's homes or in the workplace. Some were eager to tell their stories, knowing that their life experiences were rich and unusual and should be shared. At least one of the individuals interviewed was initially hesitant, yet very quickly overcame her reluctance and confided a very personal account of her girlhood. At the conclusion of our meeting, however, she expressed concern that her identity not be disclosed. I assured her that neither her name nor any other identifying information would be used. In any case, unless given specific permission to the contrary, I followed this same policy. In one case, that of the person I have named Abu Hassan, an interview per se was not required since I have been closely acquainted with this family for quite some time.

Memories

Nadia comes from a large Palestinian town near Ramallah on the West Bank of the Jordan River. Twenty years ago, though, it was a tiny Arab village where people such as Nadia bint Ahmad's family worked the land, growing olives and grapes.

Nadia's father did not own much land, and what land he had was shared with his sister and brothers.

The whole family worked the land. It was so beautiful, so beautiful. You can't believe it.

When I was a child I only wanted to play—basketball, hopscotch, everything. Just play. I would forget about eating. My mother would have to call me inside to tell me to eat. I was a flower girl—no like a girl scout, like you have here, and I remember one time King Hussein came and I carried the flag.

The flag. It is thick stripes of black, white, and green. The flag of Palestine. It hangs on the living room wall in her meticulously clean house in East Dearborn. It is there with the pictures of her many children.

I played a lot, and I had lots of friends, but I was good in school. I only went to the sixth grade. I would have had to leave the village to continue my schooling, and my father would not allow that.

The principal always asked me to do things. I was a good student. Once there was a school trip that was planned, but my mother did not have the money to give me for the bus ride. She said, "If you are lucky, your father will come home, and give you some money." He came home and he happily gave me the money. The next day I gave the money to my teacher for the trip. It was wonderful. We went to Bethlehem and to Khalil (Hebron). I will always remember that. That is a good thing I remember about my father.

Her father.

My father was the boss. One day he came to me and told me I was going to marry Mohammad. He came from a village far away. His family heard about me and my family, and they came to my father to ask for me to marry Mohammad. I never saw him before. He was not a relative. His family had a lot of land, and my father liked money. They paid a big *mahr* (bride wealth, money given the bride's family by the groom's to compensate for the loss of their daughter) for me—$3,000. It was a lot of money in those days. They bought gold jewelry for me, but gold meant nothing to me.

I didn't like the idea but I married. I will never forgive my father, never.

I cried a lot. Others wanted to marry me, but my father wanted Mohammad. My mother did not want me to marry him. She saw I was unhappy, but she had nothing to say. She was angry, but what could she do? My father was boss.

Mohammad's family came and took me from my village. There were many people, many cars. It was very scary. It was a happy night for him, but not for me. My oldest brother cried when I married. He was so angry with my father.

Other girls in the village could say no to their fathers and get away with it. Their parents would come to them and tell them about a boy, and she could say yes or no. But not me.

I will never forgive my father, but both my parents loved me so much.

Nadia and her husband lived in the West Bank until the 1967 war. Then, they fled to Jordan where Mohammad worked in construction, as did so many other Palestinians. Housing was needed for the ever–burgeoning Jordanian population, growing from a high birth rate and the influx of refugees.

But Jordan was not to be their home. Mohammad had relatives in Detroit, relatives who would help him come to the States and help him on the road to earning a living. Leaving Nadia behind with their four young children and Nadia's mother, he came to Detroit, working first as a jewelry peddlar.

War followed Nadia to Jordan. Nineteen seventy was a terrifying time for her. She recalls that "the Jordanian soldiers, they would come to the houses of the Palestinians to search for men. They would do what they wanted to the women and then kill them."

She remembered carrying the flag to greet King Hussein. She remembered when he was a friend to the Palestinian people. She shakes her head. She does not understand why the Palestinians are always the unwanted people.

Mohammed made good money as a salesmen, and so she was able to join him in Detroit, where more children were born to them.

My children, they are wonderful. I thank God for them. I talk to them, and they talk to me. My husband says "you always talk so much to the children." I tell them everything. I must talk about what is in my heart. They know how I feel. They know I was forced to marry my husband. I tell them that they must choose who they marry. I will not choose for them.

My husband is good to me. He turns his check over to me, and I pay the bills and give him something. I drive. He does not tell me what to do. I was forced to marry him, and even today I remind him of this. I can't help it. I can't help what is in my heart.

Now that my father is dead, my mother is much freer. My youngest sister was twenty when she married, and she chose the man she wanted to marry. My mother didn't say anything. She thinks like me. You have to live with the man you marry. You should be free to choose him yourself.

But I thank God for my children and for being here. People are good here. It is like my home. If I can't be in Palestine, then I want to be here. Some people complain that it is not good here for Arab people, but I don't think like they do. I thank God I am here. I pray five times a day—I don't want to go to Hell. I don't go to the mosque. I don't have time, and I don't want to gossip with the women, so I pray in my home.

I am happy to be here. I am happy to have my children, but my life is sad. My father forced me to marry.

🌾 *The Hands of ʿAʾisha*

Hana's life had many episodes, and she knew that her life had not been ordinary. She wanted it recorded for posterity, for her grandchildren and great grandchildren. She began making tapes herself, hoping they would find a listener. The first tape begins:

When I was a child the families were very close knit units. The children had very little time to get into big mischief. There were always chores to take care of before and after school: wood to be either chopped or brought in and stacked neatly by the wood stove, chickens to be fed, the goat to be milked, then breakfast and off to school.

The tapes are full of such reminiscences, pleasant childhood memories, memories of an Arabic village life-style lived in the early part of this century in the Dakotas. The tapes conjure images of little ones kissing the hands of their Arabic guests, of children gathered around their mother, Hana's mother, recounting story after story from *The Thousand and One Nights*. Weekends were exciting: stories, magic tricks, and huge feasts that her mother had been preparing throughout the week. The table would be laden with stuffed grape leaves, kibbeh, hummus, olives, pickles, baklava, hallaveh, sugar coated almonds. Hana recounts these stories as though she had not just heard, but lived each one of them.

She remembered, too, that each birthday she received a gold coin to be added to a necklace: an insurance policy against disaster.

Listening to the recorded voice of Hana leaves the impression of an idyllic childhood made magical by the stories of Arab heroes and heroines, some of them her own ancestors.

But sitting in a room with Hana, seeing this small, elderly, but not frail, woman a different picture emerged. Her eye contact was too direct, her voice too strong and definite to leave any doubt that her life had not been an easy path.

Her father's family were minor landowners in Lebanon, but he followed in the footsteps of his father, smuggling tobacco until the Ottoman Turks placed a bounty on his head, driving him out of the country and to America. He lived briefly in Massachusetts, learned the ways of peddling in America from other Arab immigrants, and then set off for South America only to return again in 1878, this time to the Black Hills to find gold. But peddling seemed a safer and more lucrative way to make a living, so he made his way by selling goods to the miners.

In 1885 he decided it was time to take a wife, and so he returned to Lebanon and married a girl, 'A'isha from his village. But he had not returned to Lebanon to stay. In a few years he returned to the Black Hills, leaving his wife behind with one child and pregnant with twins. By the time she arrived on American soil to join her husband, the twins were dead from cholera, and her eldest son had contracted an eye disease. He was not allowed to travel on with her. Instead he went with his uncle to Argentina, where he remained until he came to the Dakotas years later with his own wife and children.

'A'isha found herself uprooted from her family and from the rich vineyards of Lebanon, living in the bareness of the Dakotas, in a log cabin that her husband had built on the free land he was homesteading. He was still a peddlar and was, therefore, gone from early spring through the fall.

Another boy was born, followed soon by another set of twins. But the boy was bitten by a rattlesnake and died. For 'A'isha, this was a joyless land where she was haunted by fear: of Indians, howling coyotes, and rattlesnakes.

Hana describes her mother as if she had seen her with her own eyes. "My mother became hysterical, she said. She screamed at my father to take her back home to Lebanon or at least to some place civilized."

They went to a nearby city.

And here the litany of the births and deaths of children continues. Hana was the last born, the only girl to survive.

I never really loved my mother, not until she was dead anyway.

'A'isha's life, it seems, had been too hard. And perhaps someone had to pay for it. It seems Hana was the one to do it.

The childhood stories turn sour here. There was the time that her mother screamed at her, "Why did you have to be the one to live, when your golden sisters died?"

Hana retorted with, "I didn't ask to be born, and I wouldn't have asked to have you for a mother if I had."

She clearly remembers the harsh discipline. She also remembers playing "runaway horse" with one of her brothers. The brothers "were all princes in my mother's eyes."

Hana was the horse and her brother stepped on the rein. Hana fell and the pain in her shoulder was agonizing. She somehow managed to get herself up the stairs, which were outside of the house, and climb into bed. She never called her mother to help her.

Hana's father was away but returned two days after the accident. Everyone walked the mile and half "to the penitentiary" where they always met him when he returned from one of his journeys.

"Where is Hana?" he asked. Her mother said she was home in bed but that she did not know what was the matter with her. He carried his daughter to a doctor to repair the broken collar bone that she had sustained. Then, he went home and horse whipped his wife.

Throughout her life, Hana saw her father as her friend, her protector.

Her descriptions of him were glorious. He was the best—in everything. He was the one the neighbors complained to about 'A'isha's neglect of her infant Hana. He was the one who finally made his wife fearful of ever hitting Hana again. So, a gulf existed between mother and daughter, a gulf made wider by each of them. Overtures of kindness by her mother were rebuked by Hana. "I wouldn't allow her to reach me."

It was her father who had ambitions for her. Proud of his daughter's obvious gifts and intelligence and following the example of his lawyer friend, he sent the sixteen-year-old Hana away to the Brigg's School for Girls.

Her mother had other plans for her.

At the school for only nine months, Hana was invited to a party where she met a thirty-nine-year-old man named Omar Shukri. Also present at the party was her father's brother's son, brought from Lebanon to America specifically to marry Hana. But he had become involved with an American girl and married her instead.

After meeting Omar, Hana was called upstairs by a female cousin. There she met people who began questioning her about this man. Did she like Omar? Did he seem like a good man? She did not wish to be rude and said that indeed she thought he seemed very nice. She was asked if some-one was pressuring her to say these things. No, she said, no one.

She returned downstairs where she was greeted by crowds of the women and cheering from the rest of the gathering.

Hana had just been married to Omar Shukri. Learning that his cousin had been tricked, Hana's paternal first cousin became furious, and the party broke up into a great fist fight. Hana was invited to stay with out-of-state relatives to avoid the marriage, but her mother prevailed. It was the fear of bringing shame on the heads of her family that made Hana decide to be the wife of this man, Shukri, though when she arrived at his house, she ran in the door and locked him out.

For five years, while living in Detroit, she attempted to make a decent marriage with this man but finally decided she could not. Primary custody of their daughter was given to Omar, because, the judge wondered, how could Hana, with no job skills, ever hope to support the girl?

She never asked for help. This is a continual theme that runs through her life. "I wouldn't call my mother, no matter how bad the pain." Later she wouldn't ask her brothers for help, no matter how hungry she was.

She worked as a waitress, a maid, a hat check girl, anything to stay alive during the Great Depression, a time when dead bodies were commonly found in the alley outside her boarding house. Her one good friend was her landlady, a woman of Polish background who liked to gamble. In the basement of the boarding house gangsters were free to congregate. It was here that Hana met Alex, who went under the a pseudonym to protect his family from disgrace. Refusing his help also, she struggled through the Depression on her own until finally consenting to marry him. It was more of a friendship than a marriage, though. As she says, "there was a serious accident during the honeymoon, and Alex lost his manhood." He also suffered from TB and lingered for twelve years in a hospital in Kentucky until his death while his wife lived impoverished in Detroit with the one person she let help her, her landlady, Martha.

Besides the boarding house, Martha also owned a bar where Hana helped out in order to earn her room and board and a few dollars. But Hana was determined to work her way out of her poverty, especially since it was the cause of her losing any custody of her daughter. She applied for a managerial position in a local business. She had managerial experience, she told them. (In the later years of her father's life he had set up a business with his sons and brothers. She had visited the business and observed. Based on this, she believed that her lie wasn't complete).

It was here that Hana could demonstrate her talents. She learned quickly and could finally anticipate a bright future. But her mother, 'A'isha, intervened. She broke her hip for a second time and did what she had done the first time—ordered her daughter to come home to take care of her. Hana obeyed, patiently caring for her mother in spite of the fact that 'A'isha was living with her youngest son who had a wife who could have cared for her as well as Hana. Threatened with demotion by her company, Hana finally returned to Detroit but not without her mother's accusing her of ingratitude and neglect. As it was, Hana had remained too long and was demoted. It was during this time that her daughter, who now lived with her, developed severe blood poisoning. The priceless gold coins of the childhood birthdays were sold for $1000 to pay the medical bills.

Later there came a new job with an export company. Here, the photos came out. "This is me with Nasser. Here I am with the Prince of Saudi Arabia." She looks glamorous, beautiful. Like a person who takes dining with princes for granted.

Another marriage followed. "He was a charming playboy. He never grew up. He drank, was irresponsible. All his money went to night life." But she said this without reproach. She claimed she liked him. She blamed herself for never having had a good marriage. She blamed her total independence.

And there was no hatred for, or resentment of, her mother. It was at the time of her mother's death that Hana realized that she was actually fond of her. At her mother's bedside, Hana saw the woman who had worked so hard for the family. She pictured her kneading the meat for the kibbeh. She looked at her hands. They looked as smooth as a wooden carving, those hands that had kneaded the kibbeh.

🏶 *Abu Hassan*

Abu Hassan arrives home at five thirty every day, six days a week. He's tired, but he smiles warmly. Smiles form easily on his weathered, tired face. He likes to get along with people. He doesn't like trouble.

His daughter and wife are sitting in the small living room where the TV set goes constantly. His first act is to affectionately pinch his daughter on the cheek. She looks up at him admiringly, braced to leap up to bring him whatever he wants. On this day his two sons, students, are at work, one at a garage, the other at a grocery store. Whatever they earn will go into the "family pot." "What is mine belongs to my brother," the elder one said to me one day.

Because I am there, Abu Hassan does not rush off to shower immediately. Instead, he sits and has coffee with me; his hands, though washed, are stained with oil and grease, the signs of his trade as an automobile mechanic. He has held this same job for about two years. He receives an hourly wage, no insurance benefits, no vacation leave. When he was sick for a week he received no pay. Abu–Hassan sees no way out of this predicament. He knows little English and suffers from a chronic illness, both of which are impediments to finding better employment.

His wife worries all the time. "I am always nervous," she tells me on every visit. She is nervous about money. She is nervous about her family back in her home village in Lebanon, a village often bombed by the Israelis and a fighting ground for Hizb Allah and Amal. It was war and politics that drove them from Lebanon. One of their sons, angered by his treatment at the hands of Israeli soldiers, was becoming aligned with Amal. Abu Hassan, not willing to sacrifice a son for any militia, asked a relative to sponsor him in the United States.

The cousin who gave this initial assistance is Abu Hassan's only wealthy relative. Abu Hassan had hoped that this man would assist the family in purchasing a home, but has given only vague responses to their requests for assistance. All the other relations—of whom there are many— are in positions similar to Abu Hassan's. They are among Dearborn's working poor. There is never enough money to pay for the basics. For Abu Hassan there is the additional burden of suffering from a chronic illness, which requires regular doctor's visits and expensive medication. This is another source of stress for Abu Hassan's wife. She worries constantly about his health, preparing foods that she hopes will help his condition. She complains bitterly that he is never given a chance to rest. If it is not his boss making demands on him, it is his kinsmen.

On this occasion, Um Hassan is looking at the clock. She tells her husband to hurry and take his shower before his brother comes. He comes every evening during the week and spends most of Sunday at their home, usually with his wife and children. This evening she wants to leave before he arrives, so that Abu Hassan can take her shopping for a dress for her daughter. There is a wedding the following weekend, and the girl has nothing suitable to wear. Neither does Um Hassan, but she has given up on the idea of having a new dress for the time being. The last time she bought one, her sister–in–law admired it so ardently that she gave it to her.

As Abu Hassan is considered the senior member of the family in Dearborn; it is in his home that everyone congregates. This means that his nieces and nephews and cousins, along with his siblings, expect Abu Hassan's home to be open to them at all times; indeed, it is rare to find Um Hassan alone in the afternoon and almost impossible to find this house-hold free of extended family after Abu Hassan arrives home from work. Um Hassan does not hide her chagrin when discussing this steady flow of company. "Every weekend, I feed all these people. My daughter and I are tired from bringing them coffee and tea and fruit all day. My husband's niece and her husband leave, then his nephew comes. It goes on like this all day Sunday." Abu Hassan is more ambivalent about the situation. He shakes his head in agreement with his wife, yet adds, "What can you do? They are family."

Continuous afternoon and evening visits are not all they have had to endure over the past several months. Abu Hassan's sister's daughter arrived rather suddenly from Africa, expecting to remain for an indefinite period of time in her uncle's two bedroom home. She wanted to learn English and perhaps go to college here. Sleeping arrangements were adjusted so that Um Hassan, her daughter, and Abu Hassan's niece slept in one bedroom, and Abu Hassan and their two sons slept in the other. Abu Hassan finally responded to his wife's despondency over the situation by telling his niece that she could sleep in the living room. The situation was finally resolved when the young woman married the son of one of Abu Hassan's brothers. However, when Abu Hassan's sister came for an extended visit to celebrate the wedding, the unsatisfactory sleeping arrangements were resurrected.

It is plain to see that Abu Hassan would prefer to continue to feed and house his kinsmen, regardless of the expense, than to alienate them in any way. "He is too good," complains his wife. This is no doubt true, yet it also seems that Abu Hassan is deeply aware that in time these numerous brothers, cousins, and nephews will be expected to reciprocate his hospitality, though he himself might not be around to enjoy it.

🕎 Anisa

Anisa sits in her living room with her two teenage daughters, watching *Magnum P. I.* She wears a shapeless ankle length black dress, and her head is covered by a blue scarf that is allowed to slip back and expose some of her jet black hair. Her daughters' hair flows free and uncovered.

Anisa looks at the two girls and shakes her head.

It is so different for them growing up than it was for me. When they don't have school, they sleep until 11:00 A.M. and then sit and watch TV When I was young, I got up at six or six thirty and prepared breakfast. I was the only daughter, so I had to do all the work. When I was small I played outside with my friends. We played hopscotch, blind man's bluff, games like that. But when a girl becomes eleven or twelve she is not

allowed to play anymore. Then, I stayed inside and watched
TV which was only on in the evenings, not like here.

Anisa was born in Aden, southern Yemen.[1] For the first thirteen years
of her life Anisa's father was a distant presence. From thousands of miles
away in America he sent money to provide for the family. His restaurant
business must have been a prosperous one, since Anisa recalls moving
from a very small house to a rather large one, much larger than the one she
and her husband and four children now occupy.

For the thirteen years of her father's absence, Anisa, her mother, and
her two brothers lived with Anisa's maternal uncle. Anisa talks about her
childhood as if it were nothing remarkable. She states that she began
school at age seven and continued through high school.

In spite of the attempt of what was then the Peoples Democratic
Republic of Yemen to educate girls and women and to improve their
status, it was still a rare occurrence in Aden of the 1960s for a girl to go
beyond an elementary education. "Only about 3 percent of parents allowed their daughters to go to high school," Anisa says. "I went because
my mother wanted me to, because she had never had a chance."

Anisa's elder daughter curls her blue-jeaned legs under her as she sits
on the couch. She smiles and says, "It is easier to be a girl here in America
than back in Yemen." She recalls her one visit to Yemen when she was
four years old. She enjoys the memories of helping to feed her grandfather's
sheep and goats and of running and playing on the mountain near their
house, but she does not want to live in Yemen. Her preference for the
United States has to do with being a girl. "It is hard enough here," she
says. "My brothers both have jobs. They can go out. However, my sister
and I have to stay at home. It is much better to be a boy. Except for one
thing. The parents are stricter with boys. They don't hit girls like they do
boys."

"My boys used to help me around the house," said Anisa. "They
would clean floors, wash the dishes, everything. Now they say that that
work is just for girls." She shrugs her shoulders. There is nothing she can
do about it. "Both my sons want to become doctors," she says with pride.

"I want to be a doctor too," says the older girl. The younger girl,
Yasra, who is quieter, offers that she wishes to be a nurse.

Anisa claims that she approves of her daughters' ambitions. She herself is employed as a teacher's aid, assisting in English lessons for other

Arabic-speaking women. "Some Yemeni husbands don't want their wives to work. They don't want them to go out. My husband is not like that."

Anisa has been married to her husband, Mohammad, since she was eighteen years old. In 1974 a law was passed in south Yemen that required that a woman be at least sixteen years old at the time of marriage and that the groom must be at least eighteen years old, but not more than twenty years older than the bride. This law was passed to protect premenstrual girls from being married off to men their father's age and older. But, Anisa points out, fourteen-year-old girls like her daughter are still likely to be brides in Yemen.

Anisa relates that in south Yemen there is a great deal of variation in the freedom and rights that girls have. "In some families, girls and boys go out together before they are married."

"Alone?" asks her elder daughter in astonishment.

"Yes," says Anisa. She approves of this practice because she feels it is good to know a man before marrying him. She never dated anyone, including her husband. Mohammed was in America, working, when he wrote to Anisa's father requesting that he ask Anisa if she wished to marry him. Mohammed was a distant paternal cousin, so she remembered him from her childhood and consented to marry him. "I have been lucky," she says. "We have been married for nineteen years. We lived with my family for one month after we were married, then we came here. At first, I was excited about doing something new and different, but when I got here it was so difficult for me. I was so lonely. There was no one for me to talk to, nowhere for me to go. That was the worst part, being so lonely."

At five Mohammed comes in from work and immediately goes to another room to pray. Both Mohammed and Anisa pray five times a day, and they fast at Ramadan. Anisa is affiliated with the Mosque on Dix Avenue. She teaches Arabic there, but does not consider herself to be a very religious person.

"I cover myself, but not like some women." She indicates that her dress sleeves are a trifle short and that her scarf falls back on her head so that some of her hair shows. And she is not so concerned with what is and is not *haram* (forbidden) as are truly "religious" people.

A man comes into the living room and sits down, smiling. He is Mohammad's cousin who has returned to the United States for the first time since 1978. Anisa's daughters and her sons, who have just returned from work, debate the issue of how long this relative lived in the United States before his current stay. He is here to maintain his passport and to earn enough money to pay his expenses. Back in al–Nadra in north Yemen he has a wife, to whom he has been married since they were both fifteen. They have six daughters and one son.

Mohammad, Anisa, and their daughters are on their way to a Yemeni dance at Salina School. They believe that such events are important— important in keeping the Yemeni community in Dearborn together. It is through this club that the Yemenis of East Dearborn will improve their situation, Mohammad believes—just like the Jews and the Italians and the Polish did.

Mohammed firmly believes his children should learn Arabic. He has no wish for his children to lose their identity. He sees himself as a Yemeni as does Anisa. "I can never be anything else," says Anisa.

Her daughters insist that they would not marry anyone but a Yemeni. Now he will have to know English. "He will have to be like us—you know—a Yemeni-American!"

₪ Khalil

The Rammal family of al-Dwyer village in the Nabatiyyih district were known to be supporters of Bey Ahmad al-Assaad. One day the men from the various villages went to the bey to tell him that they wanted their sons to receive an education. They wanted his blessing, his support. Without it, they knew they had no hope of fulfilling their dreams. The bey told them that his own son, Kamel, was being educated. That was enough.

The story of the Rammal family is the story of the Shi'a of south Lebanon: poverty, oppression, and resistance with dignity. A religious minority within Islam, the Shi'a have their roots in oppression. The central theme, the pivotal scene of Shi'ism is the brutal death—the martyrdom—of Hussein, the grandson of the Prophet Mohammad. And he was not slain by outside enemies, but by those who claimed leadership in Islam.

The Shi'a of southern Lebanon saw themselves as oppressed, but dignified. Their sense of political helplessness was reinforced by a charismatic clergy; they were virtually unrepresented in the Lebanese government. They were considered too unimportant to bother with. So, their roads went unpaved, their villages went without proper schools and medical facilities, and when the Israelis, in their retaliatory raids against the Palestinians, also bombed Shi'ite villages, the government threw up its collective hands in helplessness, stating that "a weak Lebanon was a strong Lebanon." In other words, it was best not to tangle with the Israelis. But there was growing awareness among the Shi'ites that if south Lebanon had been filled with wealthy Druze, Maronites, and Sunnis, far more action would have been taken.

Many of south Lebanon's Shi'ites chose to flee from the despair that was their lives. A significant number migrated to Africa, others to the suburbs of Beirut.

The parents of Khalil Rammal were among those who chose Beirut. Attracted by the economic growth that centered around Beirut, the Rammals migrated to Chiah, a southern suburb of the great port city. Like the vast majority of people in Lebanon, the Rammals settled with others of their confessional group, and so Khalil was born near the Pine Forest where many other Shi'ites also lived. He gives his birth date as April 4, 1959, but he cannot be sure of this. Orderliness and record keeping have never been a trade mark of Lebanon. "Besides," states Khalil, "with so many children born, and so many dying, no one kept track."

Khalil was the first born of three surviving sons and one daughter, who was born later in the marriage. He was the first son born to an illiterate, poverty–stricken peasant woman hoping that her children would escape the kind of life she had lived. "I was her hope and she, my mother, was everything to me," Khalil says with great feeling.

"It was not enough for me just to be intelligent in school. I had to be the best. And so, I was always first in the class." By the time Khalil was ready for school they had moved to Burg al-Barginah, south of Chiah, where the Rammals enrolled their children in a private Shi'ite school. The rooms were small, tiny, in fact. A converted bathroom served as one of the classrooms, but this was like life at home where five people shared a two-room apartment, and the children could only play in the dirt in the cemetery.

As Khalil would leave the apartment each morning for school, his mother would bless him. "*Allah ma'ak.*" These words he still clearly remembers. They were not just empty words. He felt she was truly bringing God's blessings upon him, and they gave him the incentive to work. "Illiterate people are like donkeys," she told him, and so when he would come back home with evidence of being "first," the two of them would dance with joy.

Khalil's father, Ismael, worked at unloading boats at the Beirut port. "He was honest, hardworking. He didn't become rich smuggling goods like many of the other men did." From him Khalil learned patience, honesty, and discipline.

Khalil's parents made sure he went to the mosque and that he was trained as a Shi'ite, but there was nothing militaristic in this Shi'ism. This was a quiet Shi'ism, and Khalil still resists the notion of being identified with the bellicose Shi'ism of Iran.

Yet, it was an Iranian who helped changed the course of Khalil's life. Aside from his mother, it was the Imam Musa al–Sadr who was the most influential person in Khalil's life. He was the person most responsible for the transformation in self-image of the Shi'ite community of Lebanon. A *mulla*, trained in Iran, but with a world view that differed significantly from the *ullema* of his homeland, he assumed the role of spokesman for the poor and dispossessed of his new home.

As when he speaks of his mother, his fair-complected face lights up when he mentions the Imam Sadr. "He was a Ghandi type. He wanted peaceful reforms. He did not want war. He was the hope of all Lebanon. He was friendly with the Christians. he spoke in their churches. He was a friend to the poor, not just to the Shi'ites. The imam called the slums around Beirut the `Belt of Misery'" Khalil's voice is full of passion.

Khalil's youth ended quickly, and with it went a true private life. The Civil War broke out in 1975 when he was sixteen years of age. He did not fight. He did not carry a gun. He had never learned to hate the Christians or the Sunnis or the Druze. He and his family returned to al–Dwyer for two years to avoid the war. There was no schooling for Khalil during those two years, but he spent his time reading and following the news.

Not until the Syrians moved their forces into Lebanon did the family move back to the Beirut area. He still did not carry a gun. Instead he finished school and then began to write for newspapers and magazines. Khalil brushes all this aside. He would rather talk about the Imam Sadr: how he had formed a council early in the war for all factions to negotiate, how he fasted to end the fighting just as Ghandi had done.

But for all these attempts at peace-making, the *mulla* saw the need for the Shi'ites to have a militia of their own, a militia that calls itself Amal (Hope). To Khalil, it was the belief that fighting for the rights of other groups in Lebanon would never bring benefits to the Shi'ites that caused the militarization of his people.

Khalil fought the war with his pen. But it seems to have been done without great enthusiasm. One has the feeling that he would have preferred to have lived out his mother's dream for him in peace. As it was, he was fortunate. He came to America and worked for his master's degree, albeit without the state scholarship from Lebanon that would have been his had the Christians not had the monopoly on such perquisites in the early 1980s. And he has found a way to be useful to others through his work at ACCESS and on the boards of the Islamic Mosque of America and many benevolent associations. Still, there is a sad longing that one detects in Khalil. Lebanon had been his home, and it might have been a place in which he could have had a private life of his own.

Notes

INTRODUCTION

1. Consult, for instance, collections of essays and books from the 1980s and 1990s such as Earle H. Waugh, Baha Abu-Laban, and Regula B. Quereshi, eds. 1983; Baha Abu-Laban, 1980; Sameer Y. Abraham and Nabeel Abraham, 1983; Eric Hooglund, ed. 1984; 1985; Alixa Naff, 1985; Yvonne Yazbek Haddad and Adair T. Lummis, 1987; Eric Hooglund, ed. 1987; Baha Abu-Laban and Michael W. Suleiman, eds. 1989; Yvonne Yazbeck Haddad, 1991; Earle H. Waugh, Sharon McIrvin Abu-Laban, and Regula Burchardt Quershi, 1991.

   Earlier studies include those by Abdo Elkholy, 1966; Elaine C. Hagopian and Ann Paden eds. 1969; Barbara C. Aswad, ed. 1974; B. Abu-Laban and F. Zeady, eds. 1975; Ilyas Ba-Yunas, 1975.

2. See Edward Said 1981, Jack Shaheen 1984, Jan Terry 1985, and Michael Suleiman 1988.

3. Waldman (1991: 315) emphasizes this diversity, while noting the importance of traditions in Third World countries that they bring to their new land. She also cautions against the tendancy to equate modernism with secularization, and the tendancy to overgeneralize and oversimplify.

4. The strengthening of the family in the case of most Muslim groups as well as other groups such as the Japanese Americans is also due in part to their patrilineal organizing principle, which facilitates the pooling of resources.

ISLAMIC VALUES AMONG AMERICAN MUSLIMS

1. See, for example, Rabi'ah Hakeem, "Pointers on Choosing Marriage Partners" in *Islamic Horizons* 14 (November and December, 1985): 11–12.

2. Muhammad Abdul-Rauf (*Islamic View*, 103), observes that "a parent who allows his child to be of another faith is regarded to have rejected his own religion."

3. See, for example, Abdul-Khabir, "Prevalent Problems in Muslim Marriages" in *Al-Ittihad*, (July–December 1982): 19. This problem, of course, is not necessarily limited to marriages between Muslim men and non-Muslim women.

4. Yusuf al-Qaradawi, *The Lawful and the Prohibited in Islam* (Kuwait: IIFSO, 1984), 85. Cf. Gamal A. Badawi, *A Muslim Woman's Dress According to Qur'an and Sunnah* (Plainfield, N.Y.: Muslim Student Association Women's Committee, n.d.).

5. Negiba Megademeni, cited in "Muslim Women Developing a Theory of Islamic

Feminism," *Unitarian Universalist World* 16, no. 8 (August 15, 1985): 10. Cf. A. U. Alhaj Kaleem, "Emancipation of Women and Islam," *The Minaret* 8, no. 21 (November 1, 1981).

IMMIGRANT PALESTINIAN WOMEN EVALUATE THEIR LIVES

1. This comparison is barring the traumas both generations have faced from the loss of homes, villages, occupation, and exile.

2. This group of immigrant women in the United States is currently in the minority but growing rapidly. According to my subgroups, these women are among the autonomous immigrants and as the unmarried adult daughters of the chain and new, village immigrants. Chains are formed by emigrants who already have one or more relatives or friends who help them find housing and sometimes employment in the land of their destination. It is rare for women who immigrated to the United States already married to subsequently obtain a college education. While the chain and new, village immigrants are not normally college educated, daughters who remain single after high school usually are. Despite the fact that these women are attending college, as long as they are single they are very socially restricted. They look for the pay-off for their education after marriage.

TURKISH-AMERICAN PATTERNS OF INTERMARRIAGE

1. For a greatly expanded discussion of ex-military mixed couples' marriages and family life, see "Variations in Family Structure and Organization in the Turkish Community of Southeast Michigan and Adjacent Canada." 1984. Ph.D. diss.: Wayne State University, Detroit.

IRANIAN IMMIGRANT WOMEN AS ENTREPRENEURS IN LOS ANGELES

1. The names used in these case studies are pseudonyms.

PARENTS AND YOUTH

1. Integration is used here to indicate the ability to maintain the Islamic belief system at its central concept level, *tawhid*, and to objectify this belief system in the Western secular environment without compromising the Islamic principles or the Arabic heritage, living triple, but separate, lives (Islamic, Arabic, and Western), or withdrawing from the outside society.

2. The distinction between Islamic and Muslim is essential to understanding the variation in the individual's or the group's conceptualization and interpretation of Islamic principles. These principles can be interpreted and practiced within the particular Qur'anic context (Islamic) or within the particular socio-psychological context (Muslim).

3. To avoid further complexity, the word American will be used to indicate the association with Canadian and United States societies.

4. Islamicity may have different meanings to different individuals or groups. It is used here in the widest sense, in which an individual or a group may associate as his or her world view or ideological belief with reference to Islam as a way of life.

5. Strike and Posner explain what they mean by learning as a "rational activity," by distinguishing their view from the behaviorist's view of learning rather than excluding other factors in learning.

6. The model, developed by the author, consists of four parts. First, the central concepts (*tawhid*), accepting the Islamic world view that a human being is God's vice regent and that Allah is the only God (Qur'an 1:16). Second, the conditional concepts (*'ibadat*), the fulfillment of religious obligations, such as believing in the unseen, prayer, fasting, and so on (Qur'an 2:1–4). Third, the human interrelation concepts (*mu'amalat*), in which transactions are based on the belief that all humans are equal except in their conscientious constructive character (Qur'an 29:39). Finally, the outcomes (*a'mal*), a society that is free from harmful acts (Qur'an 2:5).

SEX AND THE SINGLE SHI'ITE

1. Pseudonyms have been used for the names of those interviewed.

2. In Salim's case, the mosque refers to the Islamic Center of America, the first of the Shi'ite mosques in the Detroit area and the one most heavily attended by the earlier, more assimilated Muslims and their descendants. However, those who favor *mut'a* are more likely to attend the other mosques which were founded by recent immigrants concerned with stricter interpretation of religious law. For further discussion regarding the distinctions among these mosques, see my doctoral dissertation, "Shi'i Islam in an American Community," 1991.

SOUTH ASIAN FAMILIES IN THE UNITED STATES

1. It should be realized that INS data are not complete. Despite deficiencies, this set of official information can reveal trends and topics for discussion and analysis.

2. Possible reasons may be the emigration of widows in this age group. Married women of this age cohort would generally have husbands who are still working and would not want to emigrate. Men above sixty may be widowers, since men have a longer life expectancy in India.

3. In a 1983 study of young people of Indian background in New York, 100 percent of the boys and 67 percent of the girls did not want arranged marriages, while 100 percent of the boys and 53 percent of the girls believed in dating (Nagarajan 1988). Though most of these young people would be Hindu, similar trends exist among young Muslims and reveal a clash of desires and values between generations.

4. According to religious rights, a marriage can be performed between two parties by taking an oath of acceptance (repeating "I do" three times) in the presence of a lawyer and two witnesses. The lawyer does not have to have a law degree, but should be a Muslim who understands Islamic marriage laws, he can explain the rights and duties to respective parties and, above all, can stand by and protect their interests in future disputes or problems. Thus a father can perform the wedding of his daughter. The witnesses should be adults who are well respected and trusted by the two families.

CHALLENGES TO THE ARAB-AMERICAN FAMILY AND ACCESS

1. In the l970s, the SEDCC successfully blocked the city's attempts to remove the residents and increase the city's tax base through rezoning the area from residential to heavy industry. The community brought a class action against the City which was found to be violation of approximately twenty-eight federal and state laws in acquiring the properties in the area. That period was one of intense struggle, and the community encountered attitudes of class and ethnic prejudice. Numerous members of the SEDCC were also active in ACCESS although there was also some competition between the two agencies for city funds (see Aswad 1974; Robinson 1984).

2. By 1993 ACCESS reported 60 percent of its total cliental reported less than $5,000 annual household income and 24 percent reported from $5,000–$10,000 (ACCESS 1993: 3).

3. Since the early survey, more cases of family crises and mental-health problems are being seen at the Center as people became accustomed to its procedures.

4. For a more extensive examination of this issue, see Aswad 1994.

ETHNICITY, MARRIAGE, AND ROLE CONFLICT

1. It has been observed repeatedly that migration proceeds along networks of kinsmen and friends who assist one another to migrate. This process is referred to as "chain migration."

2. Of course, the degree of conflict will be ameliorated to some extent if the individual is in a bilingual program at school, however, even in these cases linguistic competence, interaction with peers, and the influence of the media will make the role conflicts encountered significantly different from those experienced by parents.

3. Affect and sex are not necessarily coincident in the Middle East.

4. According to Islamic law and tradition marriage is not a divine ritual but a legal contract.

GROWING UP MUSLIM AND FEMALE IN AMERICA

1. Only in one case were we able to interview both parents. The fathers who were interviewed said that their wives were in Lebanon and South Yemen. Both parents of one subject were in Lebanon and so we spoke with her older sister, and one interview was canceled because the parents were away at the time of the interview.

FIVE IMMIGRANTS

1. Before 1990 Yemen was divided into the Yemen Arab Republic (north Yemen) and the Peoples Democratic Republic of Yemen (south Yemen). Today it is unified and called the Republic of Yemen.

Index

About the Authors

NILUFER AHMED, Ph.D., is an adjunct assistant professor of sociology at Providence College in Rhode Island. She has conducted studies on cross-cultural fertility and on women and class in Bangladesh.

BARBARA C. ASWAD, Ph.D., is a professor of anthropology at Wayne State University. She is editor of *Arabic Speaking Communities in American Cities* and has published articles on Arab and Turkish women in the Middle East and Arab American women. She is a past president of the Middle East Studies Association of North America.

NIMAT HAFEZ BARAZANGI has a Ph.D. in education. She is a visiting fellow at the Women's Studies Program at Cornell University. She specializes in curriculum and instruction, Islamic and Arabic studies, and adult continuing education. She has edited *Islamic Identity and the Struggle for Justice in the World Today*.

BARBARA BILGÉ, Ph.D., is a lecturer of anthropology at Eastern Michigan University. She is the author of articles on ethnicity and families, and on Turkish and other Muslim communities in the United States.

LOUISE CAINKAR has a Ph.D. in sociology. She is the director of the Chicago-based Palestine Human Rights Information Centre–International and author of *Palestine and South Africa* and a forthcoming book on Palestinian Women in the United States.

PENNY S. CASS is dean of the Indiana University–Kokomo, School of Nursing. Cass earned a doctoral degree in nursing from the University of

Michigan–Ann Arbor and specializes in maternal-child and HIV /AIDS issues. She has published in the areas of nursing education, the politics of nursing, and HIV and AIDS.

ARLENE DALLALFAR has a Ph.D. in sociology. She is currently a research associate at the Five College Women's Studies Research Center and teaches in the Department of Sociology at the University of Massachusetts, Amherst. She is completing a book on immigrant women, entrepreneurship, and the use of gender resources and social capital in ethnic economies.

CHARLENE JOYCE EISENLOHR has a Ph.D. in educational psychology and is a retired counselor at Ann Arbor Huron High School. She has conducted research on the self-esteem of female Arab adolescents in the American high-school setting.

NANCY ADADOW GRAY, M.S.W, A.C.S.W., is the director and a founding member of the Arab Community Center for Economic and Social Services (ACCESS), the first provider of bilingual/bicultural, Arabic/English family counseling, community mental-health, and substance abuse services in Dearborn, Michigan, which has one of the largest concentration of Arabs outside of their original countries.

YVONNE Y. HADDAD, Ph.D., is a professor of Islamic history at the University of Massachusetts, Amherst. She is an expert on Islam in America and author of numerous books and articles on Islam in America. She is author of *Muslims of America* and coauthor of *Islamic Values in the United States* and *Mission to America: Five Islamic Sectarian Movements in the United States*. She is a past president of the Middle East Studies Association of North America.

GLADIS KAUFMAN, Ph.D., is an associate professor of anthropology at the University of Wisconsin–Waukesha. She is the author of articles on South Asians in the United States and on various aspects of family and gender relations.

ANAHID KULWICKI, D.N.S., R.N., is an associate professor of nursing, Oakland University, Rochester, Michigan. She has conducted research on health care and attitudes among the Muslims in Dearborn.

SHAMIM NAIM, Ph.D., is an assistant professor of geography, University of Wisconsin, Waukesha. She is the author of articles on South Asians in the United States and South Asian geography, economics, and demography.

MARY C. SENGSTOCK, Ph.D., is a professor of sociology, Wayne State University. She is the author of *The Chaldean Americans: Changing Conceptions of Ethnic Identity* as well as numerous articles on the elderly.

JANE I. SMITH, Ph.D., is vice president and dean of academic affairs at the Iliff School of Theology in Denver, Colorado. She is an expert on Islam and coauthors of *Muslim Communities in America* and *Mission to America: Five Islamic Sectarian Movements in the United States* as well as numerous articles on women in Islam.

JON C. SWANSON, M.S.W., Ph.D., has published extensively on Middle Eastern migration. He is a clinical social worker at Southwest Detroit Community Mental Health Services in Detroit, Michigan.

LINDA S. WALBRIDGE has a Ph.D. in anthropology. She served as the assistant director of the Middle East Center, Columbia University and now teaches at Indiana University. She is the author of *Shi'i Islam in an American Community*, which is forthcoming from Wayne State University Press.